THE UNWRITTEN LAW

THE UNWRITTEN LAW

Criminal Justice in Victorian Kent

CAROLYN A. CONLEY

New York Oxford
OXFORD UNIVERSITY PRESS
1991

Oxford University Press

Oxford New York Toronto
Delhi Bombay Calcutta Madras Karachi
Petaling Jaya Singapore Hong Kong Tokyo
Nairobi Dar es Salaam Cape Town
Melbourne Auckland

and associated companies in
Berlin Ibadan

Published by Oxford University Press, Inc.,
200 Madison Avenue, New York, NY 10016

Library of Congress Cataloging-in-Publication Data
Conley, Carolyn, 1953–
The unwritten law : criminal justice in Victorian Kent
Carolyn A. Conley.
p. cm. Includes bibliographical references.
ISBN 0-19-506338-4
1. Criminal justice, Administration of—England—Kent—
History—19th century. I. Title.
HV9960.G72K463 1991
364.9422'3'09034—dc20 90-32733

1 3 5 7 9 8 6 4 2

Printed in the United States of America
on acid-free paper

To J. W. C.
who made this book possible
and necessary

Preface

This book is a social history of criminal justice in Kent, a county in southeastern England, between 1859 and 1880. In the past twenty years the study of crime and justice as an aspect of social history has been developed by a number of scholars. In addition to emphasizing the significance of the history of criminal justice in its own right, such studies also have broader applications. Although the criminal courts dealt with only a small proportion of the population, their decisions are an important indication of where and how limits were set for the society as a whole. One major argument of this work is that despite the trend towards regularization that David Philips has described in his seminal work, the findings and actions of the criminal justice system were still primarily determined by the values and priorities of the local community. Whether a particular action was defined and treated as a crime depended on a number of factors, among which the written law was often the least important. While the guarantees of due process made it highly unlikely that an innocent man would be convicted, the discretionary powers granted policemen, justices of the peace, trial judges, and juries made it possible for violations of the law to be considered non-criminal. The criminality of an offense was measured according to the age, gender, and social status of both the victim and the accused. Depending upon the circumstances, identical acts might be punished with a heavy sentence, considered a minor infraction, or totally ignored. Though socioeconomic class played a significant part in judicial decisions, explanations, when offered, were usually couched in terms of respectability and community.

The first chapter deals with the methods, both official and extralegal, that were used to police the community. It examines the crucial role of the justices of the peace, the powers and effectiveness of the newly established police force, and the extra-legal sanctions of rough music. Chapter 2 deals with violent crimes and the factors that determined which violent actions were criminal and which might be excused. The third chapter looks at the particular problems experienced by women who came before the judicial system only as victims or suspects. The fourth chapter deals with children, who were also at a distinct disadvantage before the courts. The last two chapters deal with the complex issues of respectability and class. Chapter 5 looks at those segments of society suspected of constituting a criminal class, and Chapter 6 examines the reactions of the courts and the public to the paradox of "respectable" lawbreakers.

Since this book first began as a dissertation project in the distant past, a great many people have offered support, advice, encouragement, and solace for which I am very grateful. While doing the original research in England I appreciated the collegiality of the Institute for Historical Research at the University of London, especially that of Robert Shoemaker, whose work on a similar project made me realize that there was hope for the criminal historian. My time in England would also have been infinitely less enjoyable were it not for the help and friendship offered by Peta Dessent Braddock, Pat Dessent, Janet Solomon, Marian and Paul Lewis, and Andrew and Sandra Ashbee, who provided guided tours of Kent.

Faculty and fellow graduate students at Duke University were enormously helpful. Thanks to Professors Richard Watson, Arthur Ferguson, William Chafe, Anne Scott, Charles Young, Ronald Witt, Jean Scott, and especially to Professor James Epstein, who took over the direction of the dissertation at a critical stage. Paul Krause, Marcy Lytle, Lance Grahn, Judith Miller, Karen Watson, Lorella Thomas, and Rene Echevarria also offered constructive criticism and support. I am especially grateful to Cynthia and David Hughey, whose friendship sustained me and my momentum even at the darkest moments.

Colleagues and students have also contributed. Professor David E. Harrell was particularly helpful in my introduction to the world of professional historians. The students in my seminar on crime and punishment offered invaluable assistance in deciphering what I wanted to say. I was also blessed with excellent graduate assistants,

James Baggett, Kay Blalock, Lewis Shannon, and Charles Hamilton. The office staff in the history department not only helped with the manuscript, they also prevented me from killing the word processor (an act whose criminality has yet to be determined). Thanks to Katharine Stark, Debbie Givens, and Gina Cole. James D. Rawls, who prepared the maps for this book, also offered constructive criticism of the manuscript and invaluable guidance on the computer.

My family has seen me through all the trials and tribulations of authorship with amazing patience. As my nephew explained, this book must be for all of us. I am especially grateful to J. Douglas Conley and Barbara Foster.

Finally, special thanks to William Kevin McCauley.

Birmingham
August 1990

C. A. C.

Contents

THE UNWRITTEN LAW

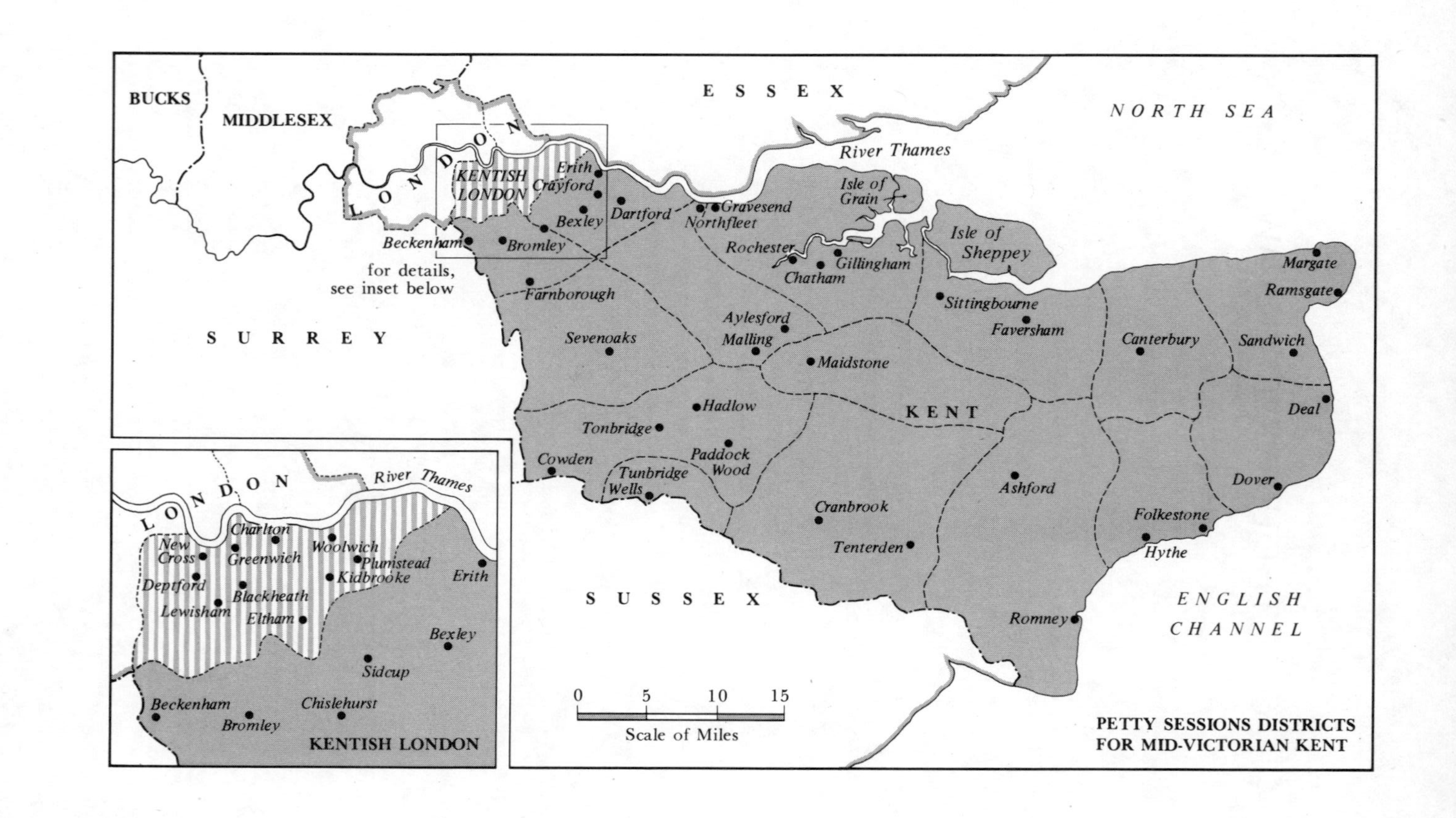

PETTY SESSIONS DISTRICTS FOR MID-VICTORIAN KENT

Introduction

During the nineteenth century the British government made several attempts to reform and "regularize" the criminal justice system.[1] But the reforms were often resisted as a threat to individual freedom and local autonomy. A major goal of this work will be to assess the degree to which the regularization of the criminal law actually determined the practices of local officials. Despite the new regulations and procedures, older, traditional patterns of judicial discretion and extra-legal community sanctions continued to be practiced with considerable support.

Theoretically a regularized system of criminal justice would provide sure and equal justice for all offenders without regard to circumstances or social status. But such regularization might threaten local autonomy, the traditions and customs of the community, and the social structure. In order to resolve the problems of regularized justice in a society dependent on clearly defined distinctions and expectations among persons, the men who ran the criminal justice system had to exercise considerable wisdom and discretion in defining both crime and justice. Their concept of the law had to include community standards and customs as well as the written statutes. They had to establish jurisdictional boundaries between local authorities and the central government, as well as between the government and the private citizen and his family. They also had to deal with the oxymorons of respectable law-breakers and law-abiding members of the "criminal" classes. The accommodation between the regularized system and recognition of social distinctions and time-honored customs was slow and not always successful.

Because of this necessary accommodation, evidence from the courts provides considerable insight into the society as a whole. Although only a small proportion of the population would ever have occasion to appear before the criminal courts, their cases defined limits. The verdicts of juries and the sentences given by judges provide the actual definitions of crime and criminality (which may or may not correspond to the written law). By indicating under what circumstances certain behaviors would not be tolerated and, conversely, under what circumstances identical behaviors might be condoned or encouraged, the courts reflect the fundamental values of the society regarding such issues as interpersonal violence, the protection of private property, the position of women and children, and the crucial Victorian concerns of respectability and class.

Respectability was the cardinal virtue for the Victorians, but for historians it is a very problematic term. Part of the power of the word stemmed from its lack of a precise definition; it could mean almost whatever the speaker wanted it to mean. But the ambiguity does not render the term meaningless. Though the definition varied enormously, the importance of "respectability" cannot be overestimated. As Trygve Tholfsen has written: "Of all the concepts essential to an understanding of class and culture in mid-Victorian cities, respectability is at once the most indispensable and the most ambiguous."[2]

G. M. Young likened respectability to Roman citizenship: "at once a select status and a universal motive . . . it could be indefinitely extended."[3] Though it was a status to which anyone could aspire, the requirements varied according to age, gender, and social and economic class. Some historians have suggested that "respectability" was a middle-class standard of behavior that the poor were required to adopt. "In reality, respectability was a social category posing as a moral category. The middle classes, in effect, were born respectable whereas working men had to achieve it through their own efforts."[4] Certainly in so far as the standards were uniform, they were those of the middle class. "Respectability was the name of that common level of behavior which all families ought to reach and on which they can meet without disgust."[5]

But the standards were not always uniform. The correspondence between middle-class standards and working-class respectability was close but not exact. Respectability was not simply imposed from above, it was also developed from within. In fact, independence was one of its most essential elements. Geoffrey Crossick has pointed out that "The double-edge to respectability provided its continuing satisfaction, being as much concerned with an individual's sense of self-respect as with any external recognition of his respectability."[6] Respectability was especially important for the working classes, as it distinguished them from the roughs who were part of the outlaw class. Even the very poor could be respectable. *The Maidstone and Kentish Journal* refers to "a respectable poor woman picking hops" and an editorial discusses the problems of "respectable vagrants."[7]

Maintaining respectable status required that one dress and behave as befitted the circumstances. Peter Bailey has argued that historians have erred in assuming consistency: "respectability was practiced in a more limited and situational sense than that of a lived ideal or a permanent code of values. . . . [R]espectability was assumed as a role (or cluster of roles) as much as it was espoused as an ideology."[8] This role-playing concept meshes with the emphasis on appearance. Crossick argues that "the idea of respectability was fundamentally Victorian in its concern for style and appearance above all else."[9] The first requirement was tidiness. "Cleanliness endowed a person, however poor, with respectability."[10] Beyond that, clothing had to be modest, in good repair, and appropriate to one's status.

Respectability depended on behavior as well as appearance. Most historians have agreed that the behavioral standards were largely negative. "There were many things that a respectable man might not do, and many of the tensions in Victorian social relations stemmed from disagreements as to what those prohibitions were."[11] Geoffrey Best suggests the following restrictions: "Respectable people did not get drunk or behave wildly; they maintained a certain propriety of speech and decorum of bearing; they dressed tidily and kept their houses clean and tidy, inside and out. That they were 'independent' and law-abiding goes without saying."[12]

But respectable citizens were not always sober and law-abiding, and people who broke the law did not automatically forfeit their respectability. Even during sentencing judges sometimes spoke in the present tense of the respectability of the person being sentenced. While it was clear that criminals were not respectable and respectable persons were not criminal, merely being convicted of violating the law did not render a person criminal or even non-respectable. The rules for respectable behavior varied according to perceived motive as well as whether the behavior was in public or private and whether the participants were accepted members of the local community.

Obviously class was also a factor in assessing criminality, but officials always insisted that justice was impartial. For the criminal justice system to maintain credibility and effectiveness, the majority of the public had to believe that the rich and poor were under the same laws. This is not to say that everyone either believed in or accepted the reality of equal justice. As E. P. Thompson has argued, the concept of impartial justice can be double-edged. "It became possible to define offenses as crimes against things, rather than injuries to men. This enabled the law to assume the posture of impartiality: it was neutral between every degree of men and defended only the inviolability of the ownership of things."[13] A justice system that defends the inviolability of ownership invariably works against those who own nothing. However, complaints that the law discriminated against the poor were invariably met with the argument that the law protected the property of the poor as well as that of the rich.

In order to examine the ways that the Victorian criminal justice system dealt with issues of class, respectability, gender, family, and local autonomy, I have focused on the workings of the justice system in the county of Kent between 1859 and 1880. In terms of both time span and geographical area this is an in-depth study of a small area.* As such it is subject to all the limitations inherent to local studies. However, whenever possible, events in Kent have been related to relevant material for other parts of England. Kent was a fairly representative southeastern county with a remarkably hetero-

*The dates for this study are the result of technical limitations. The criminal statistics were regularized in 1859, making comparisons over time possible. The ending date reflects the fact that until very recently, criminal records were sealed for one hundred years, and the bulk of the reseach for this project was done before the records for the 1880s were opened.

geneous population and a crime rate very similar to that of England as a whole, but there are elements of its history and social structure that are somewhat atypical.

Traditionally the men of Kent have been among the first in England to demand their rights as freeborn Englishmen, and the Kentish courts have often shown considerable sympathy for movements in defense of liberty. One of the most noteworthy characteristics of nineteenth-century Kent was the relative absence of serious class conflict. Michael Winstanley found that in rural Kent, "although perpetually conscious of their class, few laborers seem to have translated this into open hostility." As one man explained it, "There were certain people who were our superiors and we were supposed to adopt a courteous attitude to them. Nothing really terrible about it. We looked up to them and we expected them to be better than we were." Rather than seeking to emulate or displace their social superiors, workers sought respectability among their peers. "It was within their own class that laborers and their families strove to attain social acceptability and esteem."[14] The absence of overt class hostility made it easier for the justice system to continue to treat respectability as a legitimate consideration. It was not a question of wealth or education, but of meeting the standards appropriate to one's circumstances. That respectability rather than class was the determinant was important.

The peace of the Kentish countryside was at least in part the result of prosperity. As the garden of England, Kentish agriculture has been particularly successful and one historian of Kent has argued that "if there ever was a 'golden age' of village life, perhaps it was about 1860 or 1870."[15] In 1881 the Royal Commission on Agriculture heard the following glowing account of Kentish farming:

> Kent has a greater variety of produce, a larger amount of capital invested and yields a greater gross return per acre than any other country in the U.K. . . . [W]ithin easy reach of the metropolis with its enormous population and its insatiable demand for dairy and garden produce, for green forage crops, hay and straw; with natural beauties which attract to it a large resident population of wealthy consumers; with several popular seaside resorts; with a variety of soil adapted for the growth of many products which

> cannot be successfully cultivated in many other counties, the farmer is not dependent upon two or three commodities which everybody else can grow.[16]

Of course the actual circumstances were not quite as idyllic as painted. While some areas of Kent were among the wealthiest and most fertile in England, others were considerably less blessed. Only 10 percent of the soil grew hops and fruit, the most profitable crops. The farmers of east Kent grew mostly wheat and did not fare as well. Throughout the late nineteenth century, both population and wealth in Kent were shifting from the southeast to the northwest, and what may have been a golden age for some was the end of an era for others. The number of acres in east Kent planted in wheat fell from 244,000 in 1867 to 201,000 in 1887.[17] During the late 1870s east Kent's agricultural laborers struck when farmers attempted to lower wages to compensate for a fall in wheat prices. But even the strike of agricultural laborers was amazingly peaceful in Kent, reflecting the long-standing tradition of reasoned response to protest.

In addition to its exceptionally fertile soil, Kentish agriculture was also marked by the relative absence of great landholders. According to the *Domesday Book of Kent*, completed in 1873, there were 34,683 landowners in extra-metropolitan Kent and only 3 of them owned more than 10,000 acres.[18] Kentish elections had been "comparatively democratic even before the Reform Act."[19] Between 1832 and 1867 Kent had fifteen M.P.s, two each for east and west Kent, two each from the boroughs of Canterbury, Greenwich, Maidstone, Rochester, Dover, and Sandwich, and one each for Chatham and Hythe. In 1860 Kent had 17,635 voters out of an adult male population outside the parliamentary boroughs of 130,776. After 1867 there were nine M.P.s from east Kent, eight from mid-Kent and four from west Kent.[20] While it would be easy to overstate the harmony of the Kentish countryside, Kent did have a tradition that allowed a relatively large percentage of the population to have a substantial voice in the community.

Though agriculture was a primary source of wealth, Kent was not predominantly a rural county. In 1861 Kent's population was 38.4 percent rural, while the figure for England and Wales as a whole was 44 percent. Kent included twenty-seven towns within its borders, including parts of metropolitan London. Kentish London included a very mixed population from the urban slums in parts of Deptford to the wealthy suburbs of Kidbrooke and Blackheath. Most of the employment was through the government; hence the area was urban but not subject to some of the harsher effects of private industrial capital. Geoffrey Crossick found a pattern of class divisions without class conflict in Kentish London. "The most important influence of all was the absence of any continuing sense of class hostility." The working-class of Kentish London accepted an ideology of "respectability and independence, of justice and progress. . . . The issue was not the poor against the rich, or employees against employer." Crossick argues that like their counterparts in rural Kent, the workers of Kentish London recognized the distribution of wealth as a simple fact of life. "The evidence of business and industrial wealth may not have been relished by those who did not share it, but it had been earned in a legitimate fashion."[21]

Greenwich, Deptford and Woolwich, the three major towns of Kentish London, had maintained themselves as distinct communities, and within those communities there were clear social distinctions. "The very fact that you lived at New Cross meant you were someone better than the people who lived in Deptford. . . . And if you went a little bit further along to Lewisham, or Bromley, you were, oh! really somebody socially, you know."[22] Deptford was in a period of economic decline in the second half of the nineteenth century as the middle class left the area and the population became poorer and less stable. The area around Woolwich that included Plumstead and Charlton had grown at mid-century as the arsenal at Woolwich had been expanded during the Crimean War, and Plumstead provided housing for the artisans and supervisors who worked at the arsenal. Greenwich was the wealthiest of the three towns on the river, with Blackheath to the south contributing a number of civic leaders. "Blackheath, more than any other part of the area, was an important place for wealthy London businessmen and merchants to live."[23] The development of the railroad meant that the towns to the south of metropolitan Kent, Beckenham, Bromley, Chislehurst, Orpington, Sevenoaks, Bexley, and Sidcup, grew in the last half of the nineteenth century as they became bedroom communities for London.[24]

The Thames-side area east of Woolwich also grew "partly due to the railway link with London and partly due to industrial development." The population of Erith doubled between 1861 and 1871. Crayford, Dartford, Stone, Swanscombe, and Northfleet enjoyed similar growth. Unlike the areas in the southwest, which were primarily residential suburbs for people employed in London, the Thames-side was developing industry as well. Paper works at Crayford and Dartford, cement works at Northfleet, and ironworks at Erith were all important new sources of employment.[25] The edge of this area of development was the town of Gravesend, a traditional port and market town twenty-four miles east of London. Gravesend was the boundary of the port of London, where arriving vessels were required to take on custom officials.[26]

While London increasingly absorbed areas of northwest Kent, there were older towns in extra-metropolitan Kent with distinct images and traditions. Kent's oldest and perhaps most famous city was the cathedral town of Canterbury. "Canterbury was invariably referred to as a respectable dignified city by people from elsewhere."[27] While Canterbury claimed a certain dignity as the site of innumerable historic landmarks and as the administrative center of east Kent, it also had its less savory areas where brawls between the local working-class men and the soldiers stationed at the militia barracks were common.

Kent's other cathedral city also had its problems. Rochester was the home of an ancient castle and a very proud tradition, but the roughness of the neighboring towns in the Medway, Chatham and Gillingham, often overshadowed the niceties of Rochester. The dockyards at Chatham were the largest industrial works in extra-metropolitan Kent and in 1860 Chatham was the largest town in extra-metropolitan Kent. A large portion of the population was military. The Medway district included two forts, two navy ships, and three separate military barracks as well as the Military Engineering School. "An old saying described Chatham as a place where 'every third house is a beer house and every third man is a soldier.'"[28] Chatham was also the site of a convict prison.

South of the Medway district were the hop-growing areas. The area around Maidstone was particularly fertile, but hops were also grown in the area between Paddock Wood and Ashford and, on a more modest scale, between Faversham and Canterbury. Maidstone was the county seat and the center of the area that is still "per acre, the wealthiest part of agricultural England."[29] Another prosperous market town—albeit with a slightly unsavory image—was Ashford, which had enjoyed enormous growth as the crossing points of Kent's main railway lines. Tonbridge, Tenterden and Cranbrook were also market towns, though the latter two did not enjoy the largesse of the railroad.

The 1861 census reports that there were no manufacturing towns in Kent, but the relative lack of heavy industry was in some ways compensated for by the tourist trade. The railroads had provided a boost to the tourist industry as Kent's seaside resorts grew increasingly popular. Margate and Ramsgate, in the Isle of Thanet, had been rivals for the more select tourists since 1800, while Folkestone expanded rapidly after 1850. The hot springs of Tunbridge Wells had been fashionable since the seventeenth century and continued to flourish. The census also names Dover as a "watering place," though Dover's major claim to attention was as the main point of departure to the continent. Dover was also one of the Cinque Ports, the five coastal towns that had provided the coastal defense of England since medieval times and had enjoyed special privileges as a result. While Dover continued to flourish, the other members of the group in Kent—Sandwich, Romney, and Hythe—were all in relative decline as new modes of transport and defense passed them by. Sandwich and Hythe were developing as resorts, however, and the same transition from seaport to tourist center was being experienced by Deal. For centuries Deal had been a naval dockyard, but because of its lack of a sheltered harbor it was displaced by more suitable sites.[30]

In addition to the resident population and the tourists, Kent also housed a large number of soldiers and sailors. Kent's 133 public residential institutions included 16 military installations. Ten percent of adult males in Kent were military men as opposed to only 2 percent of all adult males in England and Wales. In addition to the barracks at Canterbury, Chatham, and Gillingham, soldiers were stationed at Woolwich, Maidstone, Deal, Dover, Folkstone, and Gravesend. Dover was the usual port of exit and entry for troops leaving and returning from service abroad. As such, it attracted a large population of liquor salesmen and prostitutes.[31]

Kent's population, which grew from 733,887 in 1860 to 977,706 in 1880, represented a broad range of occupations, backgrounds and traditions. While the findings of this study are based on the evidence from Kent and are therefore by definition peculiar to Kent, it is reasonable to argue that they may cautiously be extended to England as a whole.

The records used for this study include the Parliamentary Papers, the Home Office Criminal Registers, and the records from the Kent assizes and the Kent sessions of the Central Criminal Court. The annual reports of judicial and criminal statistics published in the Parliamentary Papers include the number and types of crimes reported, the age, nationality, and occupation of those committed to prison, and the outcome of hearings and trials. There are numerous but not insurmountable problems with the official statistics: reporting procedures vary from year to year and spot-checks indicate occasional mathematical errors, but by examining trends rather than actual figures, and comparing different records to check for obvious errors, one can form a reasonable estimate of the number and types of crimes being reported and the disposition of cases.[32]

The Parliamentary Papers give numbers only. For information about individuals the first source is the Criminal Registers from the Home Office, which include the name, offense, and verdict in every case brought before a grand jury at quarter sessions, assize, or Central Criminal Court. The Public Record Office also has the indictments, jury lists, minute books, and some depositions for cases heard at the Kent assize. The minutes of the Central Criminal Court are published.

In order to analyze the judicial and criminal records found in the Public Record Office one must first understand the procedures involved in prosecution. Even with a full-time police force and the theory of regularized justice, the system allowed a wide variety of outcomes. The major decision-makers were the justices of the peace, also known as magistrates. Stipendiary magistrates who heard cases in Kentish London were paid professionals with a minimum of seven years' experience as lawyers. The magistrates who sat in courts outside the metropolitan area were the traditional justices of the peace—local amateurs with no restrictions on training and experience. The powers of the magistrate immediately after arrest were considerable. He heard minor cases summarily (without a jury) at petty sessions and was empowered to sentence offenders to prison terms of up to six months depending on the offense.[33] In more serious cases the J.P. had three choices: he could commit the accused for trial, discharge him for lack of evidence, or hold him in prison on remand for up to eight days while the investigation continued. The most serious cases were bound over for jury trial.

J.P.s also presided at quarter sessions, jury trials for persons accused of all but the most serious offenses. The quarter sessions for Kent County were held at Maidstone and Canterbury. The equivalents of the quarter sessions for Kentish London were heard at the Central Criminal Court in London's Old Bailey, with stipendiary magistrates presiding.[34] In addition to the county quarter sessions, fifteen Kentish towns were authorized to hold separate borough quarter sessions.[35] While they were full jury trials, quarter sessions could not hear cases of treason, murder, perjury, arson, bigamy, abduction, concealment of birth, or any felony that could be punished with a life sentence for a first offense. With few exceptions, even these most serious offenses could only get beyond the jurisdiction of the J.P. if the magistrate at the initial hearing decided to commit the accused for trial. Technically a bill for some offenses could be presented to the grand jury without a prior hearing by the magistrates, but since the magistrates also sat as the grand jury at all jury trials it was virtually impossible for a case to go before a petty jury without the consent of magistrates.[36]

The most serious offenses were heard at the assize, a circuit court held in Maidstone two to four times a year. The judges at the assize were the professional judges who regularly sat on the high courts of Exchequer, Queen's Bench, and Common Pleas. These judges also heard cases at the Central Criminal Court in London, which served as the equivalent of the assize for London as well as a neutral ground for cases that were particularly controversial.

Two juries were involved in trials at quarter sessions and assizes. The grand jurors chosen from among the county magistrates first heard the depositions of the accused, the victim, and any pertinent witnesses in closed session. If the grand jury felt there was sufficient evidence to gain a conviction they formally indicted the accused, after which the evidence was brought before a petty jury in open court.

Although the official records for jury trials are complete, the records in summary jurisdiction cases are not. For these I have relied mainly on the local newspapers. The *Maidstone and Kentish Journal*, the local Conservative newspaper, was the major source; it usually listed the prisoners, sentences, and any information the editors considered relevant or interesting for each court session. In addition to giving fairly complete listings, the *Journal* was also available for the entire period and had the largest circulation of the extra-metropolitan Kentish newspapers. I also used other local newspapers, as well as *The Times.* While the newspapers reflect editorial bias and are not comprehensive, they do provide a great deal of information about the workings of the courts and general attitudes.

Because of the nature of these records statistical analysis is difficult. The numbers presented here are based on all available evidence; because of the extreme variability of judicial responses no sampling techniques were employed. However, conclusions based on numbers alone should be taken with extreme caution. Because of the considerable powers of the magistrates as well as the complicated procedures involved in the criminal justice system, statistics, even accurate ones, may not tell the complete story. As will become evident, regularized justice could still produce very irregular results.

1

Community Law: J.P.s, Police, and Rough Music

> The Law is the true embodiment
>   Of everything that's excellent,
> It has no kind of fault or flaw
>   And I, my lords, embody the Law.
>
> W. S. Gilbert, *Iolanthe*

One of the distinguishing features of the English criminal justice system is the extent to which the definition and treatment of crime depend on the active participation of amateurs, both as jurors and as J.P.s. Bruce Lenman and Geoffrey Parker have described the displacement of community law by state law as a "judicial revolution." Under community law based on Germanic traditions, a crime was an offense between men. Justice obligated offenders to compensate their victims. The community supported the victim in his demand for restitution, and ostracized offenders who failed to meet their obligations or who had committed acts so heinous that compensation was impossible. While crime and the appropriate compensation might be defined institutionally, the role of the government was limited to that of arbiter. State law, based on the Roman system, emphasized punitive justice. A crime was an offense against the law to be punished by the state.[1] State law came to England with the Norman Conquest if not before, but the jury system and the considerable powers of the J.P.s have preserved the element of community input. No matter what the state might say, a particular action was a crime only if a jury pronounced it one. As *The Times* explained, "The law was an abstraction, in reality it meant the verdict of a jury, upon which depended its practical enforcement."[2]

Further complicating matters was the fact that even as late as the nineteenth century England had no comprehensive criminal law code. To a great extent the laws had simply evolved. Because the Criminal Consolidation Statutes of 1861 and 1862 were an amalgamation rather than a coherent whole, they included glaring inconsistencies. In acknowledging the problem, one legal commentator concluded, "The answer to such cases is, that in the administration of the law, well-exercised discretion of the judges prevents any such inconsistency actually occurring."[3] The professional judges who heard cases at the assize were expected to use their discretion and influence to see that the true spirit of the law was carried out.

The twenty-nine justices who sat at the Kent assize between 1859 and 1880 had very similar backgrounds. All had trained at the Inns of Court, and thirteen were also graduates of Oxford or Cambridge. A few were sons of peers, but most came from professional families—sons of physicians, clergymen, or lawyers. Thirteen had served in Parliament before being appointed to the bench. But despite these similarities, they varied widely in their opinions. For example, the judges testifying before the Capital Punishment Commission in 1866 were split on such crucial issues as the efficacy of capital punishment, the proper procedures in cases of infanticide and suicide, and the validity of the insanity defense.

Whether and how much to direct a jury was a point on which the judges disagreed. Justice George Bramwell believed "the less the jury have to say the better," while his colleague Justice Samuel Martin felt that "juries almost always find a correct verdict, that they are as good a tribunal as can exist, and that they find an honest verdict on all occasions." Justice James Fitzjames Stephen agreed that "the law is carried out by juries, except in so far as it is opposed to justice."[4]

After receiving whatever directions the presiding judge chose to give, a jury was left to determine the fate of the accused on the basis of whatever definitions and standards its members chose to accept. By the County Juries Act of 1825, every male householder between twenty-one and sixty years of age with an assessed property value of £20 or more was qualified and liable for jury duty; in 1870 the property qualification was raised to £30. Convicted felons, peers,

M.P.s, judges, clergymen, Roman Catholic priests, ministers, lawyers, officers of the court, coroners, jailers, physicians, surgeons, apothecaries, military officers, Post Office workers, town officers, sheriffs, and constables were all exempt from petty juries. The average jury list for the Kent assize between 1859 and 1880 was 15 percent gentlemen, 12 percent farmers, 36 percent merchants, 30 percent skilled artisans, 5 percent clerks, and 2 percent laborers. While the social make-up of jury lists varied slightly from year to year, the variations had no discernable effect on the conviction rate, which remained at a fairly constant 74 percent. There was also no significant difference among the conviction rates at the assize, the quarter sessions, and the Central Criminal Court.

But even before a judge or jury could offer a definition or opinion, every case was first heard by a justice of the peace. J.P.s were appointed and dismissed by the Crown through the lord lieutenant. The only qualification for non-stipendiary magistrates was to own property of £1000 to sit in a borough court of £100 to sit in a county court.[5] Traditionally J.P.s came from the landed gentry, though the property qualification allowed the *nouveaux riches* to slip in as well. In 1859 a Rochester innkeeper was appointed J.P., to the utter horror of his future colleagues on the bench. "The body included a peer of the realm, three clergymen, three country gentlemen, two bankers, two gentlemen retired from the army, two from the civil service, and a merchant [who] naturally objected to being associated with anyone, however respectable, whose business vocations interfere with that independence which is essential to the free exercise of judicial function." The fact that farmers, bankers, clergymen, and retired army officers might also be somewhat prejudiced in cases involving agricultural laborers, forgery, church rates, and mutiny was not mentioned.[6]

Traditionally J.P.s had enjoyed enormous power. In her study of J.P.s in the period 1679–1760, Norma Landau found that "neither the central government, nor Parliament told them what to do, closely supervised their activity, or even insured that they acted at all. . . . They did what they did because they wanted to do it and thought they should do it."[7] Nineteenth-century magistrates were in some ways even more powerful than their predecessors. During the nineteenth century J.P.s were gaining increasing jurisdiction over property cases. The Criminal Justice Act in 1855 authorized two J.P.s to hear all cases of simply larceny in which the goods stolen were valued at less than 5s. or the accused pleaded guilty, as well as cases of attempted larceny. The maximum sentence if the goods were worth less than 5s. was three months. If the accused pleaded guilty to stealing goods worth more than that, the maximum sentence was six months. Cases heard under this legislation were still considered indictable offenses even though no jury was present for the trials. Once the accused consented to having his case heard summarily, no further proceedings were allowed.[8] The Summary Jurisdiction Act of 1879 extended the jurisdiction of J.P.s to embezzlement and cases involving the theft of goods valued at up to 40s.[9]

Since the magistrates also sat as the grand jury at assize, these untrained, unpaid J.P.s were making the vast majority of legal decisions. Though a trained lawyer served as a paid clerk of the court to advise the magistrates on legal matters, his counsel was not binding and was frequently ignored. But giving greater powers to the J.P.s made economic sense. The creation of the standing police force had greatly increased the number of arrests, and the cheapest and simplest way of dealing with the increase was to allow J.P.s to dispose of as many cases as possible. Since close to 90 percent of crimes were against property, extending summary jurisdiction in cases of theft greatly reduced the number of cases that required the expense of a jury trial. The assize judges favored leaving as much work as possible for the J.P.s. At the December assize in 1871, Justice Martin complained that "All of the cases were of an ordinary kind and he could not but think that an effort should be made in parliament to provide so as to save persons the trouble of coming here at this time of year." It could also be argued that local J.P.s were more knowledgeable about local concerns and more apt to have an accurate reading on the character of local suspects. In March 1865 Justice Bramwell explained that "the reason why he would not wish to try so many cases at the Assize, was that he thought the magistrates probably knew more about them—more about the habits of the people who lived in their districts."[10]

Certainly the breadth of his duties was likely to keep a J.P. well informed about life in his community. The duties and responsibilities described in the magistrate's handbook seem overwhelming: the J.P. received information and complaints for indictable and summary offenses, caused by either summons or warrant the parties charged to appear and answer, examined them, took bail, committed for trial in indictable cases, and convicted in summary ones. He also appointed parish officers, set parochial rates, tried offenders at general and quarter sessions, settled wage and rate disputes, and mediated between masters and servants, landlords and tenants, and members of building and friendly societies. In addition to their judicial functions J.P.s held civic posts. They were *ex officio* members of the Poor Law Guardians, land tax commission, sewer commission, road commission, highway board, board of prison inspectors, and board of conservators. After listing these duties the author of the manual duly notes that a magistrate could not act in cases where he had an interest.[11] Given the multitude of responsibilities, it was perhaps more noteworthy that magistrates usually managed to make fair and intelligent decisions than that they sometimes made prejudiced ones.

Though using J.P.s was cheaper and allowed greater local control, the gap between the requirements of the position and the qualifications of its holders could present serious problems. The most serious questions about magisterial competence were raised when magistrates chose to hear serious cases summarily rather than bind them over for trial. Since J.P.s were answerable to the Lord Chancellor rather than to the Home Office, the Home Secretary had little power to intervene. The hazards of the system were demonstrated by two cases heard in Maidstone during the autumn of 1868. In November, George Wright, a Maidstone laborer, cut his wife's throat. He was committed for trial and sentenced to fifteen years' penal servitude for attempted murder. A month later, James Alford Walter, also a Maidstone laborer, cut his wife's throat. His case was heard by different magistrates, who chose to hear the case summarily and sentenced Walter to four months. While the two injuries possibly may have differed in their severity, the discrepancy is nonetheless striking. As the editor of the *Maidstone and Kentish Journal* observed, "either Justice William Chanell [at the assize] was too severe, or the borough magistrates were too lenient."[12]

Another case of magisterial overreaching created a major scandal in 1872. George Braham, the landlord of the Market Hotel in Ashford, was accused of the attempted rape of a barmaid, Ellen Kingsland. Though they were not empowered to hear cases of attempted rape, the Ashford magistrates chose to hear the charges as an aggravated assault. The clerk of the court warned that the procedure was not legal, but petty sessions chairman Lieutenant Colonel Percy Grove was adamant. When the defense attorney presented extortion demands allegedly sent to Braham from Kingsland's family and friends, the prosecuting attorney withdrew from the case. Grove then announced that he would act as prosecutor as well as magistrate.

Grove as magistrate and prosecutor was very hard on the defense. When the defense presented witnesses who had heard Braham fire the girl shortly before the alleged assault, Grove dismissed the evidence as unacceptable. When a young man who had been standing less than ten feet from the scene of the alleged crime testified, Grove cross-examined him. The witness said that "several" people had been in the bar. When he later referred to the "many" people in the room, Grove accused him of contradicting himself, called him a liar, and ordered him out of the courtroom. After angrily dismissing the remaining defense witnesses, Grove found Braham guilty and sentenced him to two months' hard labor.

The proceedings were widely criticized and serious questions were raised. Two local newspapers called for Grove's resignation and reported that an examination of the barroom revealed that the attack could not have taken place as Kingsland claimed. At a public meeting held to protest the verdict, Braham's attorney announced that Kingsland had come to his office and admitted that she had made the whole thing up. The M.P. for east Kent appealed to the Home Office and Braham was released on the basis of his attorney's version of Kingsland's confession. Kingsland staunchly denied the attorney's statement; she claimed that she had been kidnapped by friends of Braham and offered thirty shillings a week for life if she would recant, but she had refused: "I declare that every word by me spoken and given in evidence before the Ashford Bench was in every respect perfectly true." The newspaper suggested that Kingsland be prosecuted for perjury, but Braham said he would follow the advice of his friends and let the matter drop. Grove, who wrote the newspaper explaining that he had been duped by Kingsland, continued to serve as a magistrate and J.P.s continued to hear sexual assault cases without a jury.[13]

Lawyers, newspapers, and M.P.s all warned of the potential hazards of the amateur judiciary. When magistrates refused to drop assault charges against a man the victim had identified as her rescuer, his attorney responded: "[I]f it pleases the court to find him guilty on such a charge as this and on such evidence, it will rest on them and will go the round of the country, and we shall have stipendiary magistrates with some common sense and reason." In 1870 the Bromley magistrates created a sensation when they sentenced a young carter to two months at hard labor for playing pitch-and-toss on Sunday. The young man had an excellent character, no prior arrests, and his employer spoke on his behalf. The usual penalty for the offense was a light fine. When the man's employer questioned the sentence the magistrates offered no explanation, but threatened to give the defendant six months' hard labor if they ever saw him again. The most succinct of a number of angry editorials appeared in the *Kentish Mercury*: "Apart from the disproportion between the offense and the punishment, the imprisonment will destroy the self-respect of the hitherto well-conducted carman, and will render the law and its ministers odious in the sight of the people." In 1875 when a carter was sentenced to three months in prison for defaulting on damages imposed for giving two weeks' notice in breach of a twelve-month contract, an M.P. complained that the case "reminded one of the high-handed proceedings of the magistrates of the last century and raised a question as to whether justice could be properly administered by an unpaid magistracy."[14]

The efficient administration of justice clearly required the active participation of the J.P.s. In theory their duty was to dispense justice without regard to persons, but for most J.P.s the very definition of justice depended on the persons involved. Nonetheless, nineteenth-century magistrates were understandably concerned about their public image. In 1877 Alfred Simmons, secretary of the Kent Agricultural Laborers Union and an elected member of the Poor Law Guardians, claimed that a Kentish magistrate had tried and convicted his own servant for absconding from service. The lord lieutenant and the quarter sessions chairman demanded that Simmons either identify the magistrate or retract his statement. Simmons retracted the statement.[15]

But while most J.P.s apparently did not hear cases in which they had a direct personal interest, they frequently represented class interest, especially in cases concerning servants. J.P.s, who were likely to have servants of their own, viewed theft by servants as a betrayal of trust. Under the Criminal Justice Act of 1855, servants who pleaded guilty to larceny from their employers could be sentenced by two J.P.s to a maximum of six months in prison. In at least one case J.P.s took a far more serious view of such offenses than did the general public. In 1859 two young servant girls in Ashford were arrested after their employer searched their trunks and found three dirty pocket handkerchiefs and three books. The girls, aged twelve and thirteen, explained that they had borrowed the books and been unable to return them because the library was locked. They had used the handkerchiefs for their employer's children. After their arrest the magistrates told them they must either plead guilty or remain in jail until the next quarter sessions, which would not be held for three months. They pleaded guilty, and though neither had ever been in trouble before, they were sentenced by the magistrates to two months' hard labor. "The greatest indignation prevailed throughout the borough at the unjust severity of the sentence. . . . [A]n immense meeting of all classes assembled at Town Hall." The meeting produced a petition to the Home Secretary to reverse the sentence, but as the sentence was legal the Home Secretary refused to intervene.[16]

The successful J.P. had to be sensitive to both state and community law. While his power was considerable and his jurisdiction increasing, as a local resident he could seldom afford to ignore public opinion. Though the decisions of magistrates were not always open to judicial appeal, unpopular decisions could be dealt with unofficially, sometimes immediately. In 1866 a wagoner at Tunbridge Wells sued his employer for back wages. The man had requested a day off from work in order to take out a summons on behalf of an orphan boy, but had been refused permission. On the advice of the county police superintendent the wagoner had taken the day off anyway. The police superintendent testified that he felt the summons was important enough to justify the time lost: "a poor man ought to have the same opportunity as anybody else to take out a summons." The magistrates denied the request for back wages and also fined the wagoner 10s. for absconding from service. "The decision evidently took the majority of those in court by surprise, and the amount of the costs was immediately subscribed by a number of gentlemen in court."[17]

Public sentiments about crime and punishment could be expressed in a number of ways. E. P. Thompson has observed that in the eighteenth century the norms and standards of daily life were largely enforced by extra-legal community "sanctions of force, ridicule, shame and intimidation."[18] Rough music, the ritualized public humiliation of persons deemed deviant, though never technically legal, had proved quite effective for centuries. Theoretically the presence of a professional police force after 1857 rendered extra-legal community sanctions unnecessary. Robert Storch found in his study of northern England that the police were actively hostile to these traditional behaviors. "Because stang-riding [a form of rough music] and similar customs represented survivals of old forms of popular justice or self-policing, because they symbolically short-circuited all modern agencies and bureaucracies of established authority, the police and magistrates were ruthless in their attempts to put them down."[19]

In Kent, however, the reaction of police and magistrates was considerably different. In cases where the victim of rough music was guilty of violating accepted norms, officials often turned a blind eye. Persons suspected of legally permissible but socially abhorrent behaviors such as adultery or incest were often subject to concerts of songs written especially for the occasion accompanied by tea trays, tin kettles, and drain pipes. Humiliation and minor vandalism were usually the only lasting ill effects. For example, when a man in Southborough, a small village just north of Tunbridge Wells, locked his wife out of the house after a quarrel, "his neighbors assembled, stones and brickbats were thrown through the windows and the door was burst open. The mob seized him by the heels and dragged him towards a pond with the intention of 'ducking' him." He had been summoned for assaulting his wife twice before and his neighbors had decided things had gone far enough. Though the police broke up the ducking, no arrests were made.[20]

In cases where the target of rough music brought charges, J.P.s usually announced that such conduct was disgraceful and could not be tolerated, and then dismissed the case for lack of evidence that anyone had been annoyed or disturbed. The arguments for and against rough music were well articulated in a case at Cranbrook in 1861. The defendants were charged with "unlawfully and riotously creating a disturbance in the public streets." They had staged a horn fair (another form of rough music) outside the home of a married man whom they suspected of committing adultery with his sister-in-law. The defense attorney argued "that an offense had been committed against public morals, and the musical soiree was got up as punishment to the offender." The prosecuting attorney replied that "this was no answer whatsoever to the charge, for however true such a report might be, the prisoners were not justified in joining such a tumultuous proceeding." Further, his client was not guilty of any immoral conduct and the implication of the horn fair had been most embarrassing. The magistrate dismissed the case on grounds of insufficient evidence, but noted that "these proceedings which were disreputable and disgraceful were of an illegal nature."[21] There the matter stood. However disgraceful and illegal rough music might be, it provided a fit punishment for those who offended public morals. J.P.s in Kent rarely punished demonstrations in favor of widely accepted standards of morality.

The legal definition of riot was broad enough to allow for these behaviors. A riot was "a tumultuous disturbance of the peace by three or more persons . . . which from its general appearance and accompanying circumstances is calculated to excite terror, alarm and consternation" (Riot Act of 1714). A gathering could be labeled a riot if the tumult was sufficient "to give firm and courageous persons reasonable grounds to apprehend a breach of the peace." If officials refused to acknowledge that any *reasonable* persons had been frightened, there was no riot, regardless of the size or behavior of the crowd.

In addition to humiliating persons suspected of sexual misconduct, the forms of rough music could be evoked against those who threatened the self-image or economic well-being of the community. In such cases local authorities not only allowed rough music, they sometimes actively participated. One such case occurred in Tunbridge Wells. In June 1864 William Webber, a seventy-year-old retired physician, wrote to the Secretary of State complaining that the sewage system in Tunbridge Wells was inadequate and that typhus and scarlet fever were epidemic in the area. Since Tunbridge Wells was a major summer resort and June was the beginning of tourist season, Webber's complaint created serious problems. By the time a public health inspector had arrived from London and pronounced the area perfectly healthy, tourists had already heard about Webber's letter and cancelled their reservations. By early July Tunbridge Wells was very hygienic and very empty. On July 4 a thousand local residents marched on Webber's home, burned him in effigy, and broke the windows of his house. The next night they returned with fireworks.

The police made three arrests: a fly proprietor, a billiard marker, and a laborer. At their hearing Webber angrily accused the police of doing nothing to stop the riot, and claimed that local tradesmen had provided free beer for the participants. Webber's household included his elderly wife, their invalid daughter, and another elderly couple, but police constables swore there was no evidence that anyone had been frightened or disturbed when bricks and lighted fireworks were thrown through the windows of Webber's house. The defense attorney summed up very neatly: "They all knew that in a country like England public safety must be preserved. One would not like to travel into matters that certainly would not influence their worships and to point to an existing cause and one which he might say had deprived many persons of their daily bread (loud applause in the court) but he was sure they would not take that into consideration." After promising not to discuss motives he went on to stress the wide support for the cause. "They would not be led away by their regard for public order to punish the unfortunate defendants, who happened to be there with many other persons holding a high position in the town." Finally, he argued, there had been no riot. "There was not a particle of evidence to show that a single person had been annoyed or disturbed." Despite the rousing cheers, the magistrates committed the defendants to trial, though, to Webber's dismay, they released them on bail.

Frustrated, Webber had an innkeeper summoned for providing beer for the mob and for orchestrating the assaults on his home. He also summoned two butchers, a grocer, a chemist, and a watchmaker, naming them all as co-conspirators. On the day of their hearing Webber asked for a delay, as he was afraid to leave his house because the crowd outside was still threatening. The magistrates denied his appeal for delay "as there is so much right feeling in the town that the law should take its course and that no violence would be done to anyone who appears here to give true evidence. Case dismissed (cheers)." The defendants then led a triumphant procession through the town accompanied by a brass band. After ordering Webber to pay court costs, the magistrates joined the procession.[22]

Justice Martin heard the case against the original defendants at the August assize. He released them, but added that the disturbance was "a scandalous affair and they must learn that persons were not to be insulted with impunity. He would also advise Mr. Webber not to write letters to the Secretary of State again." Webber also sued a group of local merchants and was awarded £20 damages, but after three years of futile efforts to collect, he gave up and left town, sending a final bitter, farewell letter to the same newspaper that had published his original letter to the Secretary of State.[23]

Webber had threatened the town's economy, but in 1859 similar tactics had been used against a man who threatened tradition in the interest of economy. Gravesend was the point of departure for most of the royal family's trips to Europe, and the local citizens took great pride in giving the royal travellers a proper send-off. Over one-third of the borough's annual tax revenues went towards these ceremonies. Nathaniel Edwards, a London law clerk assigned to the Gravesend branch of a major law firm, objected to the expenditure of £1100 per year on "the trappings of royal ceremony." In letters to the local press he urged his fellow rate-payers to join his campaign to stop this "misappropriation." He also wrote the queen to explain his position. When the Gravesend town council informed the queen of their plans to celebrate the next journey of Princess Alexandra, the future Princess of Wales, Her Majesty politely requested that no public funds be used for any ceremony. The local newspapers promptly reported the royal snub and named Edwards as the cause.[24]

The next day handbills appeared announcing that a "Rogue's March" would be held on Edwards' house. A week later the newspaper ran a vivid account of the proceedings:

> A little after 9:00 in the evening, the procession formed, consisting of a band of music, playing the "Rogue's March" followed by two persons attired as clergymen (with masks on) reading a mock burial service, then came the coffin, borne on the shoulders of four men in which sat the effigy of Mr. Edwards with a scroll of paper in his hand and an enormous pen behind his ear. The procession paraded the whole town increasing and multiplying considerably in its progress. On entering Hamer Street for the last time, the band played the Portuguese Hymn and when the procession reached Mr. Edwards' house (no. 29) they halted, and set fire

> to the effigy, which was so well got up that it continued slowly burning for twenty minutes when the head dropped off and the coffin was lowered to the ground. The scroll of paper (intended to represent the letter sent to the Queen) was burnt amid the cheers of the assembled multitude. This done, the crowd dispersed.

Edwards complained bitterly but no arrests were made. The newspaper argued that the absence of arrests was indicative of how well the crowd behaved. "Without entering into the merits or demerits of the case, we must say that the whole affair was conducted in a most orderly systematic manner." Though Edwards claimed people had thrown stones and fireworks at his house while the police did nothing, *The Gravesend and Dartford Reporter* claimed that there had been no malice involved. "There was no attempt on the part of the crowd to do any damage and if one or two windows were broken, it was the result of accident and not of design."[25]

Gravesend's other newspaper, the *Free Press*, reported that "five hundred people were present including the ragged, the ill- and well-dressed." Edwards also suspected that the local magistrates had aided the demonstrators.[26] Since no arrests were made, it is impossible to determine who sponsored and organized the procession, but the handbills and elaborate ritual certainly indicate substantial support. Obviously the police and magistrates could not have been unaware of a crowd of five hundred marching on a house, burning effigies and breaking windows, but apparently they felt no *reasonable* persons had been frightened. Edwards gave up and moved back to London.

Edwards and Webber had offended entire communities, and their tormentors included middle-class tradesmen and professionals as well as working people. In a case where the disturbance involved only workers the magistrates were less tolerant, but still sympathetic to local interests. In August 1866 the railroad brought French workers into Kent to hasten completion of a construction project in Cowden. Rumors spread that the French were being paid 4s. a day while the English earned 6s. a day. When some of the English workers were laid off, they attacked the French workers' settlement, drove the Frenchmen and their families out, and tore down their huts. Using bludgeons, they then drove the French to the railroad station. When the French used knives in self-defense the police finally intervened. The reactions of the local press were decidedly parochial. The *Tonbridge Telegraph* noted that "during the whole disturbance no private individual seems to have been insulted." The same article then listed thirty injuries to the French. At the quarter sessions the chairman expressed his outrage, not about the injuries suffered by the French but because "it was not to be tolerated for a single moment that powerful men like the prisoners, working together in large bodies, should take upon themselves to dictate to their employers whom they should or should not employ." The rioters were sentenced to twelve months each for their effrontery.[27]

J.P.s usually acted in the interest of the community, but they were also fully conscious of their duties to the propertied classes and the established order. Tolerance was extended only to those who represented majority views of morality. Rough music was meant to correct deviance; its use by dissenting minorities met with judicial and public disapproval. In 1863 a dissenting minister at Sandwich refused to pay the church rates. When his furniture was seized and sold at auction to compensate, members of his congregation burned the magistrate in effigy. The local newspaper reported the proceedings with disgust, complaining that the minister "preferred to gain a little notoriety by having a distraint put in rather than pay the legal demand in a manly way," but noted with satisfaction that the "stupid persons" who burned the effigy were fined 40s. each.[28] The "manly" thing was to conform; public disorder *against* prevailing norms was "stupid."

Though J.P.s made the bulk of the decisions in the criminal justice system, the front line against crime in the second half of the nineteenth century was the recently established standing police force. After 1857 every county in England was legally required to maintain a professional police force. In 1862 the introduction to the *Judicial and Criminal Statistics* in the Parliamentary Papers concluded: "The police is now considered to be maintained in a state of efficiency both as to numbers and discipline and to be equal to the duties required."[29]

Numbers are of course easier to verify than efficiency or discipline. In 1859 Kent was protected by several different police forces. Kentish London was patrolled by the R Division of the London Metropolitan Police (known as the Met). Headquartered at Greenwich, its 394 men were responsible for the Deptford dockyards and

Woolwich Arsenal as well as twenty-eight other parishes. The Kent County Police Force, established in 1857, manned thirteen station houses with one chief constable, twelve superintendents, and over two hundred men. Fourteen towns in extra-metropolitan Kent had their own borough police forces in addition to the county constabulary. The manpower of the borough police forces ranged from thirty-four in Rochester to one in Sandwich.[30]

Efficiency is harder to measure. *The Judicial and Criminal Statistics* indicate that during an average year, the police in Kent made arrests for about 70 percent of the indictable offenses reported to them. But these figures are of limited value because the police determined whether a reported offense was recorded as indictable. Efficiency was also hampered by the inevitable jurisdictional squabbles among the sixteen different forces operating in the county. The London Police had seniority, and with it a certain arrogance. The head of R Division assured a parliamentary select committee on police that farmers within his jurisdiction felt "themselves well off" despite higher taxes. "I should think there is not one-fifth the crime in the metropolitan district to what there is outside but I have no positive data." He believed envy was the major cause of tension between the Met and the Kent county force. "I know there is always a jealousy. Kent has adopted the superintending constable system which is a great failure."[31] In turn the Kent county force blamed the Met for chasing London's felons into the normally peaceful countryside.

The most serious clashes were between the county and borough forces. The borough police were scattered within the territory of the county constabulary and boundary lines were not clear. For example, when a murder was committed on a road leading out of Maidstone, both the Maidstone police and the county police claimed jurisdiction. In a heated exchange reported in the local press, the county police superintendent called the Maidstone superintendent a donkey and claimed his unwarranted interference had permitted the murderer to escape. The case was never solved.[32]

Despite the confusion, local control over the police took precedence. County and borough police forces were locally controlled, though subject to annual inspection by the central government. If the government's investigator reported that a local force was efficient, the national treasury provided a quarter of its annual operating expenses. All but three of the forces in Kent usually passed inspection. The smallest boroughs, Hythe, Tenterden, and Sandwich, failed regularly because of a lack of professionalism. Every year the inspector recommended that they be merged with the county force and every year borough officials rejected the suggestion.[33]

The desire for independence was based on economics as well as local pride. One of the major objections raised against the mandatory establishment of a professional police force was expense. In the small boroughs the constables often had other full-time jobs and policed on the side for very low wages. Merging with the county force would have meant increased taxes. As one resident of Hythe wrote: "I believe the inhabitants are entirely opposed to the introduction of the County Police in the borough and I hold it to be a cruel and iniquitous course to try and fix on this small town an additional charge of from £200 to £300 simply that we may see three or four lazy policemen parading our streets."[34] The Hythe borough police force seems to have been particularly inept. In May 1875 all three of the constables charged the superintendent with drunkenness on the job and tyrannical conduct. After hearing five hours of testimony, the local watch committee asked all of the constables to resign. Over the summer various citizen groups petitioned for their reinstatement and each of the constables was hired and fired again. Two constables who were brought in from out of town resigned in disgust within a month. In September the watch committee issued the following statement: "It is the duty of constables to carry out strictly and explicitly the orders of the superintendent. The latter is responsible if any of the orders are illegal or improper, but it is not for the constables to question them." The committee then announced that it would not hear any further charges against the superintendent. In October the local residents took matters into their own hands. A crowd of three hundred surrounded the police station demanding the resignation of the entire force. The local magistrates summoned thirteen of the demonstrators and fined them for "unlawfully loitering," adding that it "was rather cowardly and unEnglish for a crowd of three hundred persons to set upon three or four policemen." In November the watch committee finally decided to start afresh and fired the whole force.[35]

The problems in Hythe are significant, first because they clearly indicate that, far from being an oppressive presence, the police in Hythe at times were at the mercy—literally as well as figuratively—of the local populace. Further, one of the central complaints was that the police were a wasteful drain on the taxpayer. A man being paid for simply wandering about in a uniform struck many people as scandalous. Standish Meacham quotes one working-class detractor from London appalled at "the cheek to hold hand out for wages just f' walkin' about the streets."[36] The most striking example of such an attitude in Kent is from a homicide case heard at Central Criminal Court in 1868. A police constable who served with the Met division in Kentish London was charged with killing a man who provoked him by saying "he was only creeping about for a pension." The victim had struck his head on the pavement and died of head injuries after the constable, who was off-duty at the time, knocked him down. The accused was "given an excellent character" and sentenced to one week for manslaughter.[37] While the death was almost certainly unintentional, the incident does illustrate some uneasiness among both the police and the public about the sizable increase the introduction of the police made to the public payrolls. Police constables in Kent earned an average wage of 20s. a week, corresponding to the national norm; the amount varied among the various forces and according to seniority. Pensions also varied, but were important because in some boroughs the maximum age for a police constable was thirty-five, though the usual retirement age was fifty.[38]

Apparently most constables were reasonably conscientious in earning their pay. Over the period 1859–1880 only fifty-six constables in Kent were charged with neglect of duty, and most of them were guilty of minor offenses such as drinking, card playing, or sleeping on the job. A few policemen committed more serious offenses. Two Canterbury constables were convicted of inciting a laborer to steal so that they could fence the stolen goods, and a Met constable at Woolwich was convicted of stealing from a government warehouse.[39]

Two more embarrassing cases involved higher-ranking officers. In May 1861 the sergeant in charge of the payroll at the Rochester police station absconded with £30, a week's pay for the entire staff.

He was arrested two weeks later in a cottage on the Kentish coast. His faith in his fellow officers was apparently so slight that he did not feel it necessary to leave the county. He was sentenced to two years' hard labor. George English, the superintendent of the police at Ashford, was more cautious. He stole £360 from the house of a prisoner and promptly left for Australia. The county sent a man after him and he was arrested and returned for trial six months after the theft. Though it cost the police £300 to track him down, the chief of police argued that the money was well spent. "The conduct of the prisoner was most injurious to the police force of the county. In fact, they could not apprehend a prisoner without being taunted with his conduct." English was convicted of theft and fraud and sentenced to seven years' penal servitude.[40]

In addition to the economic concerns, there were philosophical objections to a professional police force. Until the mid-nineteenth century law enforcement in England had depended largely on local amateurs, with the army as the defense of last resort. As Norman Gash points out: "In England an efficient police was regarded even by the educated public as an un-British and tyrannical institution."[41] While the new police did not carry guns, their staves could be deadly and they were trained in swordsmanship. The high percentage of retired military men who joined the police further reinforced the image of an occupying army. In 1860 the Kent general sessions resisted a suggestion that the police be trained as a supplementary force for the local militia. "Should any disturbance arise among the lower orders of the community, the position of the police as an armed force would raise against them the hatred of the people, while in their present character they looked upon them as acting only under the law."[42] To further allay fears and suspicions authorities actively tried to recruit civilians and train them carefully. The chief recruiter from the Met felt that it took at least three years to train an efficient police officer and "that the intelligent part of the agricultural laboring community, after training, made the best policemen." The Kent County Constabulary tried to station married men with families in the rural districts in hopes that they would become part of the local community.[43]

Whether the public accepted the police as members of the community who were "acting only under the law" is, of course, a moot point. As David Jones has pointed out, a lack of violent conflict does not prove acceptance or trust,[44] but the figures for assaults on police do at least indicate the level of tolerance. They also indicate the enormous regional variations in attitudes towards the police. Barbara Weinberger, whose research centered on Warwickshire, argues that hostility toward the police was increasing during the 1870s and raises the question of why the police were unpopular in the nineteenth century. For England and Wales there was an increase of 3.5 percent in the number of assaults on police reported during the 1870s, but in Kent the number of assaults actually declined. If all history is local it may be that the history of relations between the police and the public are particularly so.[45]

Only one police officer in Kent was killed while on duty between 1859 and 1880 and only one civilian was killed by the police. Magistrates in extra-metropolitan Kent heard an average per year of 214 cases of assaulting the police (as compared with 781 common assaults among the general public), as well as 2 or 3 charges against the police. Policemen in Kent were more often charged with harassment than with outright brutality. Only two constables were indicted for assaults committed while on duty. In what appears to have been an act of vengeance, two policemen in Kentish London took off their identification badges and beat a man coming out of church so severely that his legs suffered permanent damage. The man's wife had earlier made a complaint about the police. One of the officers was sentenced to eighteen months' hard labor; the other was acquitted on grounds of insufficient proof of identity. The case drew little publicity and appears to have been an isolated incident.[46] Between 1859 and 1880, 170 persons were indicted by Kentish grand juries for assaults on the police. The conviction rate was 88 percent for assaults on police as compared with 79 percent for assaults generally. Sentences in these cases were comparable to those for assaults generally, but there was a marked variation between the sentences given by the assize judges and those given by the magistrates at quarter sessions. Sentences were less than six months in 70 percent of the cases at quarter sessions but in only 18 percent of cases heard at the assize and Central Criminal Court.

While the disparity in sentences between the quarter sessions and the assize reflects in part the fact that the most serious cases were heard at the assize, it is also evidence that the magistrates who sat at quarter sessions were especially likely to sympathize with local citizens against the still-new police forces. Even when suspects were convicted, magistrates sometimes reprimanded the arresting constable for being overzealous. In one case, for example, four navvies were sentenced to six months each for beating a constable, but the magistrate added that he thought the policeman had drawn his staff too quickly. Other charges were dismissed altogether when the magistrate felt the police had exceeded their duty. In 1871 a man successfully brought charges against Constable John Bushell for assault. Bushell told the J.P. that he had gone to a pub and found it full of "convicted thieves and strangers." In order "to satisfy himself that all was right," Bushell had hidden behind a bush and jumped out at the first man to leave the pub. When the man resisted being searched, Bushell, "fearing a general onslaught, used his staff in self-defense." The magistrates ruled for the victim and fined Bushell 40s.[47] The assize judges also suspected the police of occasionally exceeding their duty. In 1870 Justice Henry Keating said in his charge to the grand jury, "I am sorry to say that I have met with many cases where the police have gone rather out of their way in their cross-examination. They do not go for the purpose of obtaining information but rather they had gone for the very purpose to arrest." A year later Justice A. J. E. Cockburn dismissed a charge of assault on the police, adding that he felt "the police had victims enough."[48]

The surveillance and prevention powers of the police were a source of friction. Constables could arrest anyone they felt was loitering or behaving in a disorderly manner, as well as anyone who refused to give his name and address or whom they suspected might be about to commit a felony, misdemeanor, or breach of the peace.[49] Inexperienced constables sometimes looked askance at anyone who was out-of-doors and stationary. In one case a policeman in Rochester found a man sitting on a doorstep and ordered him to move along. As it was his own doorstep the man refused, whereupon the constable arrested him for drunkenness. At the hearing several witnesses testified that the man had been sober, so the policeman changed the charge to using abusive language and creating a disturbance. Though he had used no profanity, the man had yelled at the policeman as he was led away. The Rochester magistrates, who found the case highly amusing, assured the constable that they would certainly use profanity if the police tried to drag them off their own front steps. The case was dismissed, but the man received no compensation for his night in jail.[50]

Peaceful coexistence depended on a clear understanding of local customs as well as the law. Officers who interfered with traditions and routine often faced serious resistance. The most serious such confrontation came in Dartford in 1863. Guy Fawkes Day celebrations were particularly popular in Kent. Since anti-Catholic sentiments were strong, parades that mocked the Pope were higly satisfying emotionally; some saw it as a patriotic exercise. But to others the celebration had become an intolerable nuisance. In October 1863 the mayor and aldermen of Dartford decided to post bills warning that no celebration was to take place and that anyone participating in unauthorized festivities would be prosecuted. According to the local press, the mayor's decision did not reflect public opinion. The Guy Fawkes celebration was an honored tradition. "For many years, the people of Dartford have been accustomed to see a huge bonfire blazing on the night of Guy Fawkes Day, this fire being surrounded by hundreds looking on, shouting and gesticulating their admiration. In this annual tradition all classes took part, there can be no doubt that the majority relished the excitement." Determined to enforce their new policy the Dartford officials requested extra police. On the afternoon of November 5, the captain of the county forces arrived with one hundred constables. The police sealed off the High Street and marched four abreast up and down the street from seven in the evening until midnight, effectively preventing any celebration.[51]

Though the citizenry remained quiet on the night of the fifth, the next night they held a celebration of major proportions. In addition to fireworks, tar barrels, and bonfires, the delayed festivities included throwing stones at the police. New bills had been posted offering a 10s. reward for a policeman's head. The police reinforcements were gone and the ten constables who regularly served in Dartford were helpless. One policeman was cut in the face and several others were "very roughly handled." No arrests were made that night, but the next day eight persons were summoned on charges of "riotous assembly and assaulting the police and leading a noisy and tumultuous crowd of one thousand persons." The police testified that the accused men had led the disturbance and had been "insolent and abusive" towards the police. All of the defendants were skilled artisans whose employers volunteered to provide bail, but the magistrates refused, insisting that the accused remain in jail until the January quarter sessions. Local citizens formed a defense committee and hired a lawyer to appeal the decision. On December 5 a judge at the Court of Common Pleas overruled the magistrates. The men were released on bail of £50 each with £25 sureties—evidently the Guy Fawkes celebrations had some prosperous enthusiasts. After the men were released the defense committee met them at the railroad station with banners flying.[52]

Gathorn Hardy heard the case at the west Kent quarter sessions in January. Since the men had been indicted for riot, the prosecution had to prove that their actions had been "calculated to inspire terror." The defense argued that there had been no riot,

> as not a single witness had been called, unconnected with the police, to show that any of the inhabitants were placed in terror. The truth was but for the unnecessary interference of the police, everything would have passed off quickly, and nothing of this charge would ever have been heard. Why should the town of Dartford be selected from every other town in the county or kingdom, in an attempt to put down a commemoration by which the people of England for over two centuries had kept in remembrance of the failure of Guy Fawkes?

Hardy ignored the question and advised the jury that the law forbade such assemblies. The men were convicted of riot and sentenced to three weeks, and three of them received an additional three months for assaulting the police.[53]

The incident raises a number of questions. The motives for the original decision by the mayor and aldermen are unclear, as they apparently enjoyed little public support. The efforts of the defense committee indicate there was wealth as well as enthusiasm on the side of the celebrants. Though the police took much of the blame, if the Kent County Constabulary had been concerned about Guy Fawkes Day generally, they would not have dispatched well over a third of the entire force to one town. Whatever the motives for ending the celebration, town officials took a more subtle approach in 1864. The men who had formed the defense committee received appointments, for which it was a criminal offense to refuse, as special constables for the preservation of order. The newly named officers were also warned that if they failed to keep the peace on November 5, local taxes would be substantially increased to hire additional professional police. The new tactic worked and Guy Fawkes Day celebrations in Dartford were effectively suppressed.[54]

But the suppression in Dartford was a stark contrast to official views elsewhere in Kent. At Tunbridge Wells community leaders helped organize a huge bonfire along with fireworks and elaborate costumes. At Maidstone officials noted with regret that "there appeared less inclination on the part of the public to observe the day as hitherto." In most towns authorities either actively participated in or benevolently approved of the proceedings. The only arrests were for physically dangerous offenses such as throwing fireworks or setting fires in dangerous places.[55]

The role of the police at Dartford seems to have been largely imposed from above; nevertheless, as the instruments of suppression they bore the brunt of the reaction. In other cases individual policemen encountered resistance when they interfered with custom. The Irish residents of Kentish London regularly gathered on the Deptford High Street. Seasoned policemen and magistrates usually ignored them, but occasionally young constables tried to move them along. In one such case a rookie policeman told the Irish they must move along "because respectable people could not pass." When the Irish resisted, the constable called in reinforcements and struck one of the Irishmen. The crowd turned violent and began throwing stones. Four Irishmen were arrested for assaulting police officers. At the trial the police admitted that the spot was a regular gathering place for the Irish and that there had been no disturbance until the constable ordered the men to move. In their defense the Irish complained that the constables were "strange buggers." Though the defendants were convicted and sentenced to two years each, the testimony indicates that the local police and the Irish had reached a certain detente and that the incident stemmed from the actions of an inexperienced constable who did not understand the local customs.[56]

Because the police had to be aware of and respect the traditions and customs of the community, local control of the police was crucial. Kentish magistrates had led the battle against the establishment of a national police force during the 1830s and 1840s and had been instrumental in retaining as much control as possible for local authorities.[57] During the 1870s the threat to local autonomy was the major objection raised in Kent to the Contagious Diseases Acts, which empowered a national police force to arrest women suspected of prostitution and transmitting venereal disease. Local groups complained that: "The officers under the Acts were not our own police whom, as a body, we honor and respect, but men who were sent down from London and it was not part of our English constitution that we were to be governed by the War authorities in times of peace."[58]

Given the value placed on local autonomy it is not surprising that the most serious violence between the police and the public in Kent involved an imported police force. The national election in 1868 was the first held after the Reform Bill of 1867 had doubled the size of the electorate. Although the election riot has a long and glorious history in British politics, the large number of new voters probably enhanced official fears of disorder as well as incumbents' fears of the electorate. Bromley, a town on the outskirts of Kentish London, had long been controlled by the Conservative party. In 1868 the Liberals mounted a strong challenge to their control. The campaign in Bromley was a lively one, with both parties sponsoring elaborate demonstrations, but there had been no violence or vandalism and the police had not been called in at any point. Despite the peaceful campaign, on election day the local police were excused from duty and a two-hundred-man division from the Metropolitan Police Force arrived to keep order. The Liberals accused local Tory J.P.'s of requesting the force, but neither the local police nor the magistrates admitted inviting them.

On election day the officer in command of the imported division ordered his men to keep the streets clear. Anyone found on the street wearing the colors of the Liberal party was liable to arrest. During the day several respectable local tradesmen were arrested in front of their shops for resisting the police. Things came to a head when the police captain ordered his men to charge the length of the main street to make sure it was clear. During the charge a seventy-eight-year-old man, William Walter, was trampled to death.

When twenty Bromley residents were tried at petty sessions for assaulting the police, every local witness testified that all the assaulting had been done by the police. One man, a grocer, requested permission to speak on behalf of a dozen other local tradesmen who had been beaten. The magistrates refused to hear any testimony against the police and ordered witnesses to leave the courtroom when they began to testify about police assaults, saying simply, "The Bench was bound to believe the evidence of the police." Tensions were high. When the local magistrates arrived at a public concert the evening after the petty sessions they were booed and hissed. Denied legal redress, citizens wrote angry letters to the press, pointing out that there had not been an election disturbance in Bromley in over forty years and other than the actions of the police there had been no disturbance this year. "Not a pane of glass was broken, or any damage done to property."[59]

Several local citizens and newspaper reporters attended the coroner's inquest into the death of William Walter. A number of witnesses swore that Walter had been standing by himself with thirty feet of space on either side when a group of policemen went out of their way to knock him down. A local solicitor requested permission to produce "respectable witnesses to prove that there was the most brutal organized violence used towards peaceable, unoffending people. Gross violence was exercised by the police apparently brought down for the very purpose of beating the people and creating a disturbance." The coroner refused to hear the witnesses and warned the solicitor, "You had better not say such things; because the police are a body whose duty it is to keep the peace, and when soldiers or police were brought into a town, they came to keep the peace and not to break it."

After refusing to hear the evidence against the police, the coroner ordered the solicitor and all of his would-be witnesses to leave the courtroom. The police inspector who had commanded the division then testified that the Bromley residents had behaved very badly and thrown things at the police "who might, perhaps, have been provoked to behave a little roughly." He acknowledged hearing complaints, but the police "had not come down there to be laughed at and he did not want to be told his duty." He admitted ordering his men to keep the streets clear of Liberal supporters: "The police were acting under my order and what orders I gave them I considered to be necessary at the spur of the moment." The clerk of the Bromley magistrates then testified that after seeing the disturbances in the street he had asked the officer in charge to restrain his men. He was told, he said, "that Metropolitan Police Officers could not take any notice of any statement he might make." The superintendent of the imported division was the last witness. His only explanation of the arrival of the London forces was that they had come down "by official orders from Sir Richard Mayne himself." Mayne, the commissioner of the Metropolitan Police, had died between the incident and the inquest. The superintendent refused to give any further information about their presence and showed no remorse. "I did hear of several complaints of the misconduct of the police. Oh, yes, lots of complaints, they always complain."

The coroner's jury ruled that Walter had died of misadventure. In desperation, a group of gentlemen and tradesmen sent a memorial to the Home Office requesting an inquiry. Their most serious objection was to the importation of an alien police force, which they likened to an invasion: "our small and peaceable town was occupied by a large police force." If there was a legitimate threat of disorder, they argued, the proper course was to deputize local citizens as special constables. Bringing in outsiders was "an insult, implying as it does, our inability to maintain due order in our own borders." Local autonomy was critical; whatever the circumstances the local community was responsible for its own territory. The London division had no right to be there and no right to behave as they had. "Beside the primary objection to the course adopted, we allege that the conduct of the imported police was overbearing, violent and partial." The police had acted as agents of the Tories. "They appeared to regard persons wearing the colors of the Liberal party as dangerous and disorderly and acted toward them accordingly. Several individuals wholly innocent of any offense were injured by their violence."[60]

At this point the incident seems to vanish. The newspapers, which had been printing every word, do not mention it again, and no record seems to exist in the Home Office. In his study of election riots between 1865 and 1885, Donald Richter found no "recorded fatalities." Using parliamentary investigations and reports, Richter concludes that "the great majority of electoral disturbances occurred in small towns, and it was there that the absence of any effective policing was most conspicuous."[61] Clearly the Bromley incident does not fit this model—the evidence is that the overwhelming presence of the police provoked the violence. It is possible that the Bromley incident was an isolated one, though *The*

Times reports two other deaths as a result of election violence involving the police in 1868.[62]

The Bromley incident raises a number of intriguing albeit disturbing questions about the reliability of official records, the power of the police, and local autonomy. Since no criminal charges were brought in Walter's death and coroner's records are not made public, the only evidence is the reports in the local press. While the editors could certainly have exaggerated the callousness of the police as well as the extent of the brutality, they could scarcely have invented Walter's death. Even though the verdict was misadventure, Walter's death is clearly related to election violence, as were the two mentioned in *The Times*. Either official investigations were woefully incomplete, which is unlikely given the incredible detail surrounding most of the activities of Victorian bureaucrats, or the deaths were deliberately omitted from the records.

The Bromley incident is important evidence of the factors involved in the general relations between the police and the public in Kent. The most strenuous objections were to the presence of an alien force. A professional police force was tolerable to the people of Kent because the police themselves were local residents subject to local control. Imported police, regardless of their mission, were an insult to the community. The local police were responsible for enforcing and respecting the customs of the community as well as the laws of the state. The best guarantee that the police would honor both sets of rules was their required residency in the community.

Whatever the statute books said, the law in Kent was largely defined by the local J.P.s and the police, whose effectiveness and power depended in large part on the acquiescence of the local community. In return for the cooperation of the public, the J.P.s were expected to respect local custom and to preserve the rights and dignities of respectable locals. This is not to say that the J.P.s violated the written laws; the legal system and the powers of the magistrates were flexible enough to preserve local customs and priorities. Even the professional judges on the assize circuit acknowledged the importance of local knowledge in making judgments. The discretionary powers of the magistrates made it possible for technically illegal incidents of rough music and even more serious crimes to be dismissed for lack of evidence. The leeway given magistrates also meant that technically legal sentences could be publicly perceived as unjust. When the decisions of Kentish magistrates failed to meet community expectations, the public response was usually swift and vocal. The strong responses generated by actions perceived as unjust are an indication that the Kentish J.P.s were usually conscientious and reasonably competent in administering both state and community law.

Whether this level of accommodation between national laws and local traditions was unique to Kentish magistrates is a moot point. In his essay describing the regularization of law enforcement in the nineteenth century, Philips names the change from unpaid magistrates to stipendiary ones as one of the most important steps in institutionalizing the system.[63] The actual transition was a slow process. As late as 1883 stipendiary magistrates were only found in London and in other cities with populations of over 25,000.[64] Despite the rapid urbanization of the nineteenth century, this would still leave at least half the population of England under the jurisdiction of the amateur J.P.s. Further, in her research on the London police courts Jennifer Davis found a marked continuity between the role played by eighteenth-century J.P.s and that of London magistrates in the second half of the nineteenth century.[65] Despite the reforms of the nineteenth century, the laws and the men who made and enforced them still recognized the need for judicial discretion. The discretionary powers of the magistrates allowed the courts to reflect and reinforce the priorities and values of the community they served. The degree of protection offered by the law was not an absolute but was determined by persons and circumstances.

The police in Kent were also bound by community as well as state law. They were consciously presented and maintained as members and servants of their locale. Serious disturbances between police and public in Kent almost invariably involved imported police who did not acknowledge local customs and were perceived as an invading force. In order to keep the respect and cooperation of the public as well as the assistance and support of the courts, the police had always to appear to be acting under the law as perceived by the local community as well as the state. Kentish magistrates generally made a point of supporting the police when they were in the right, but showing little sympathy when their actions seemed arbitrary or suspect. While there were notable exceptions, the courts understood that maintaining strict and visible control of the police was vital to maintaining the public's faith in the justice system.

Since local control of the police was built into the system, public attitudes towards the police varied. Even in a single village, the level of mutual respect and tolerance between the police and the people would not be constant. Things were relatively peaceful most of the time in Kent, but historians doing research in other English counties have found evidence of serious hostility between the police and the people. The only general conclusions about attitudes toward the police in mid-Victorian England must be speculative and extremely cautious. It does seem safe to hazard the hypothesis that relations were better when the individual policemen on duty were known by the public and vice versa. Moreover, the degree of hostility between the police and the public also was influenced by the degree of serious class conflict in the community. Obviously, the more polarized a community, the more likely the police were to be perceived as agents of the ruling class. Ideally the tradition of community law meant that the police were the servants and protectors of all classes, but this ideal was never achieved completely in Kent or anywhere else. However, the courts and police in Kent did a better-than-average job of presenting themselves as adherents of this ideal. Although Kentish judicial authorities were sworn to uphold the laws of England, one of their most important requirements was to respect the laws, both written and unwritten, of the local community.

2

Violence: Fair Fights and Brutal Cowardice

> Whatever may be its intrinsic value human life should be highly prized by the law, and popular feelings should be directed the same way. But do not let us put it at one rate for one purpose and at another for another purpose. Life is daily sacrificed in this country for purposes of profit. Hundreds of lives are lost yearly in mining, in shipping and otherwise. I am aware that in such cases the life is taken by misfortune, it is not intended to take it. In one sense it is not but in another it is. If the facts show that on the average in such and such a work so many lives are lost; those who make that work purposely do an act the consequence of which is the loss of so many lives. Now it seems strange that life should be plentifully taken for purpose of profit but should not be touched for the purpose of saving a life.[1]
>
> Justice George Bramwell

As Justice Bramwell pointed out in his testimony before the Capital Punishment Commission of 1866, the value of human life was relative. Depending on the circumstances, an act of physical violence might be appalling, criminal, unfortunate, excusable, legal, or even laudatory. Judicial attitudes towards interpersonal violence depended on a number of factors: the motive, the relationship and relative status of the victim and assailant, the weapon used, and whether the incident occurred in public or private.

The criminal justice system itself used violence, though the number of crimes punishable by death had decreased markedly during the mid-nineteenth century. Even in cases of murder, the question of whether capital punishment was an effective deterrent was becoming moot. The Capital Punishment Commission heard a variety of opinions. Justice Bramwell pointed out that there was no reliable way to measure deterrence: "It should always be borne in mind that we have no statistics of the number of people who are prevented from committing crimes by the threat of Capital Punishment." Justice Martin concluded, "I cannot doubt that taking away life must create a deterrent effect." But Justice George Denman argued that the existence of capital punishment "led to the acquittal of a great many men," as jurors could not bring themselves to convict in capital cases. He also argued that the deterrent argument was invalid because murderers were "persons overcome by overwhelming passions which they will glut at all hazards."[2]

Between 1832 and 1862 Parliament abolished the death penalty for all offenses other than murder and treason. The theory behind the abolition of capital punishment was that by pronouncing fewer death sentences but acting on a higher percentage of them, the deterrent effect would be increased. Regularity and certainty would make for an effective system. In fact the change was designed to bring the law in accordance with practice. Murder and treason were the only offenses most judges and juries were willing to consider worthy of the death penalty. The procedure followed the usual pattern in that Parliament was legislating after the fact. Justice Bramwell told the Capital Punishment Commission that changes in the behavior of judges and juries always preceded changes in the law. As an example he cited evidence that executions for horse theft had stopped fifty years before capital punishment was legally abolished for such cases.[3] While the ratio of capital convictions to executions changed dramatically between 1832 and 1880, the change in the number of executions was considerably smaller (Table 2-1).

The reform of the penal code was far from complete, however, and the ambiguity of the law left ample room for judicial discretion and disagreement. One area of ambiguity was the distinction between murder, which was a capital offense, and manslaughter, which was not. Parliament discussed legislation defining the two offenses in 1857, 1859, 1860, 1861, 1866, 1871, 1872, and 1875. The consensus was that murder was reduced to manslaughter if the assailant had not intended to kill or the assault had been an imme-

Table 2-1. Average Numbers of Death Sentences Given and Executions Carried Out Per Annum

Period	Death sentences	Executions	Percentage of death sentences carried out
1832–1841	464	22	5
1842–1851	62	11	17
1852–1861	54	10	18
1862–1880	26	14	54

Source: Parliamentary Papers, 1865, vol. 52, *Judicial and Criminal Statistics for 1864*, p. 447. Figures for 1862–1880 are based on my own computations using the *Judicial and Criminal Statistics*.

diate response to a strong provocation. But the definitions of such crucial terms as "intent," "provocation," and "immediate" were left to judges and juries. The judges disagreed. Justice Bramwell believed that verbal provocation could be more incendiary than a physical attack. He also felt that "immediate" should include the preceding twenty-four hours. Justice Martin argued that killing was murder if, and only if, there had been a conscious deliberate intent to kill; provocation was irrelevant. Justice William Brett, on the other hand, did not feel that intent to kill was necessary: "If he did intend to do serious harm and death ensued he was guilty of murder."[4]

Such differences were not merely academic. The presiding judge's interpretation of the distinction was literally a matter of life and death for the defendant. Lord Chief Justice John Coleridge disliked manslaughter verdicts. In 1876 he presided over a case in which a wagoner was accused of killing his girlfriend. The man claimed they had both been drunk and she had died "by falling about on the other side of the bridge." The man denied any malicious intent:

> The poor woman must have met her death by my means, but I never had the slightest intention of killing her. I was rough with her and made her stand on her own feet and we fell backwards several times. There must have been some rough treatment but there were no blows.

The foreman of the jury asked Coleridge if they might consider a verdict of manslaughter. Coleridge replied that as the defendant had denied killing her, the jury must either convict him of murder or acquit him altogether. The defendant was convicted and hanged.[5]

A year later in a similar case, Justice Brett's directions brought about a very different result. A man was accused of killing his wife. The defendant had told a bartender that he thought it would be a good thing if his wife died, and the next day she was found dead with her husband's handprints around her throat. The defendant's mother testified that she had seen and heard her son abusing his wife. Justice Brett refused to give the jury any instructions regarding the possible verdicts, but after they returned a verdict of manslaughter he expressed regrets. During the sentencing he told the prisoner: "It seems to me that it is only the natural hesitation which we all have to avoid, except under most extreme pressure, the necessity of condemning people to death which has saved you on this occasion from a verdict of willful murder."[6]

Kent, especially Maidstone, had a reputation for being squeamish about the death penalty. The editor of the *Maidstone and Kentish Journal* claimed that "juries in Maidstone have been known to declare that they would never return a verdict which would render a man liable to be hanged." Justice Denman made a similar observation to the Capital Punishment Commission.[7] The reputation was undeserved. Twenty-two persons were hanged in Kent between 1859 and 1880, 7 percent of all those executed in England. As Kent was home to only 3 percent of England's total population, the county was apparently executing even more than its share.

Kentish juries were clearly willing to deliver guilty verdicts in capital cases and Kentish residents were willing and even eager to watch the executions. In April 1859 a crowd of four thousand, mostly women and children, turned out for the execution of a nineteen-year-old man. In 1863 six thousand came to watch a murderer hang. Such large audiences were by no means unique to Kent; public executions had been standard in England for centuries. Justice Martin argued that the public nature of executions was what made them deterrents: "It must be a terror to them that in the event of their committing murder they will be punishable by death and by public execution."[8]

During the 1860s, however, questions were raised about the desirability of such public spectacles. One witness warned the Capital Punishment Commission that public executions brutalized the observers so that they "turn away from horror of crime to interest in criminals." But a more revealing comment may have been Justice Bramwell's reply that the issue of public execution was "an extremely embarrassing question."[9] Capital punishment for murderers might be acceptable, but there was something about the way crowds relished the procedure that was not quite salutary.

In 1867 when a huge crowd gathered in Maidstone to watch the first double execution in thirty years, they were disappointed to find the scaffold surrounded by a thick black curtain. The same newspaper that in 1863 had complimented the crowd at an execution ("No accidents whatever, either to person or pocket occurred on this melancholy occasion") now commented: "The crowd numbered at least four or five thousand, we regret to say that there were a large number of women, some of them respectably dressed and a number of children."[10] Concern for decorum brought public executions to an abrupt end. In 1868 Home Secretary Gathorn Hardy, a former Kentish magistrate, ordered the modification of all English prison grounds so that future executions would be private. The issue was not whether the state should kill convicts but whether the public should be allowed to watch. Victorian officials preferred to keep violence, both legal and illegal, behind closed doors.

Executions were not the only form of state violence. Flogging was permissible under the Vagrancy Act. Also, after a panic over a perceived increase in armed robberies in 1862, Parliament granted judges the right to include flogging as a punishment in such cases.[11] In at least twelve cases in Kent between 1862 and 1880, judges ordered floggings of up to thirty strokes in addition to sentences of penal servitude. In 1875 when the Home Office surveyed magistrates, recorders, and sheriffs for their views on the use of flogging in assault cases, all of the Kentish magistrates urged that the use of flogging be increased, arguing that it was the most efficacious method of punishment. Several added that they believed magistrates should have the power to order birching as the standard punishment for all male criminals under the age of sixteen regardless of the offense.[12] Physical punishment was firmly established as a proper judicial response.

The right to chastise was not limited to judicial authorities. Fathers and schoolmasters were also legally empowered to chastise children and students. In addition to these legal forms of physical violence, there was also some support for the right to respond to any insult with physical force. As one local rector assured the magistrates when he was charged with assault: "[A] person was perfectly justified in administering chastisement when he was insulted in the street." Using force to settle a dispute or avenge an insult could still draw admiration, and not just from the lower classes. Though dueling had long been outlawed, some highly respectable persons still responded to insults with injuries. In 1859 a surgeon in Greenwich hit the town clerk with his walking stick in response to the insult of having his rates bill sent without an envelope. After explaining to the magistrates that he had been compelled to strike the man in response to his "ungentlemanly conduct," the surgeon was released on a £40 recognizance. In Erith a solicitor brought charges against the local vicar, who stabbed him with an umbrella and kicked him in the stomach. When the case was heard in 1864, the vicar explained that the quarrel dated back to 1856. The vicar was fined £5. In other cases an army officer assaulted a J.P. for taking his boots off in the presence of a lady, and two Dover aldermen squared off on the steps of the city hall. None of these actions were legal and magistrates pointed this out, but they do indicate the persistence of a belief in the right to respond physically when verbally provoked. In another interesting case a jury recommended mercy on account of extreme provocation for a laborer who killed a co-worker for calling him a "master's man."[13]

In addition to repaying an insult, violence could also be recreational. According to one commentator, "amicable contest" was a valid defense for assault.[14] In some neighborhoods, particularly in Kentish London, brawls sparked by drunkenness and rough language were common. In one case Justice William Wightman warned a jury not to give too much weight to the evidence of threats made by two men accused of manslaughter in a brawl. "We must recollect amongst men of the class of life to which the accused belong violent language is too commonly employed. It is not a very safe indication that the person using it harbors either any murderous intent or any serious malignity in his mind."[15]

A good fight might even draw admiration from a judge. In 1873 Justice Brett sentenced four soldiers who had beaten a man to death in a pub brawl to just four days in prison. "Although they had been guilty of an offense against the laws," Brett told them, "they would return to their regiments without a stigma on their character, as it had been a fair stand-up fight and the knife had not been used." The code and symbols of street-fighting were shared by both sexes. A woman appearing in Central Criminal Court charged with gouging out another woman's eye showed no remorse: "Now I am satisfied. I have got my revenge. You went in the middle of the road and said you would fight me. You threw your bonnet and shawl up. All right, we had a fair fight and you got the worst of it." The charge of felonious assault was dropped; it had been a "fair fight." A man who had been hospitalized after a stabbing explained to the judge at Central Criminal Court that the event had not changed his life: "I often get drunk on Saturday nights. I have been convicted of assaults five times—one was last Thursday—I have been charged twice since the prisoner has been in custody—I commenced when I came out of the hospital." His assailant was acquitted.[16]

Authorities showed little interest in deterring such violence. When a man who had sustained a head wound in a pub brawl asked a policeman for help, the constable refused. "He wanted me to take him to a doctor to get his head dressed—I said it was not my duty if he went into that locality and got his head broke he must put up with the consequences."[17] The lack of concern over injuries and even deaths resulting from pub or street brawls is evident in the sentencing patterns. Sentences were less than eighteen months in 91 percent of the assault convictions stemming from brawls. Even in the sixty-three cases in which persons died as a result of brawls, 86 percent of those convicted were sentenced to less than eighteen months.

Neither judges nor juries seemed to perceive brawling as a serious offense, even when the results were fatal, though exception might be taken when weapons were used. As Justice Wightman told a soldier convicted of stabbing: "It was not to be endured that soldiers should be allowed to draw their bayonets upon unarmed citizens during a quarrel instead of using the weapon with which nature had provided mankind—the fists."[18] But even though convictions were more likely and sentences slightly higher in stabbing cases, the sentences were still less than eighteen months 85 percent of the time (Table 2-2).

Table 2-2. Sentences for Assaults*

Sentence	All assaults		Brawls		Stabbing assaults		Robberies with violence		All homicides†		Deaths in brawls	
	Number	Percent	Number	Percent	Number	Percent	Number	Percent	Number	Percent	Number	Percent
Convicted	773	79	70	77	68	94	187	74	110	58	36	57
6 months or less	349	45	40	57	29	42	36	19	46	42	24	57
7–18 months	276	36	24	34	30	44	74	39	17	15	7	19
2–5 years	90	11	6	8	6	9	46	24	11	10	5	14
More than 5 years	58	7	0	0	3	4	31	16	36	34	0	0
Total charges	973		91		72		251		189		63	

*Percentages are of those convicted, not including pardons and findings of insanity.

†Excluding infanticide and accidents.

The idea that violence was acceptable but the use of unnatural weapons was not was even reflected in the behavior of muggers. Of the 251 robberies with violence brought before grand juries in Kent between 1859 and 1880, only 2 involved the use of a gun. When robbers did carry weapons, a threat usually sufficed. Only one robber actually stabbed his prey. The twelve robbery victims who were seriously injured had all been beaten and kicked. Although few muggers left records of their philosophies of violence, they seem to have used only as much force as necessary. Leon Radzinowicz quotes an eighteenth-century European tourist who was amazed at the mild manners of English criminals. "These robbers ill-treat only those who try to defend themselves. . . . [H]ighwaymen are quite polite and generous, begging to be excused for being forced to rob, and leaving passengers the wherewithal to continue their journey."[19] In his study of crime in the Black Country during the mid-nineteenth century, David Philips also found that robberies were often violent but rarely lethal. "Although violence was freely used, murderous weapons were seldom employed. . . . [T]he danger was of being beaten up, perhaps severely, but not of being knifed or shot."[20]

While violence as recreation or in response to a challenge might be condoned as manly, violence in property crimes was equated with cowardice. When a gang of teenagers attacked and robbed an elderly couple walking home from the market, beating the man and raping the woman, people were outraged. Such unprovoked brutality was rare, and the reaction on the part of the public was stunned disbelief. The editor of the *Kentish Express* wrote: "It is grievous to find that, amidst all our religious effort and high civilization, men should be found capable of such wicked, gross and cowardly brutality." The victims, an eighty-three-year-old farmer and his sixty-five-year-old housekeeper, had treated the youths to a drink before starting home. The gang had followed the couple into a field and beaten them so severely that neither of them fully recovered from the injuries. Justice Brett sentenced the men to fifteen years "to show all men that however old and helpless people may physically be, in this country they are not to be the subjects of brutal violence by men who are young and strong."[21]

Protecting the weak and innocent was ostensibly a major function of the criminal justice system. Consequently decisions in cases of robbery with violence or assault depended on more than just the amount of violence involved. While attacks on the innocent (that is, sober) respectable citizens who had done nothing to provoke an attack were punished severely, persons who were vulnerable because intoxicated received little sympathy. Most muggings occurred outside pubs, and the line between robberies with violence and drunken brawls was often blurred. Given these distinctions the sentences varied widely (Table 2-2). The heaviest sentences were reserved for cases in which victims perceived to be innocent had been seriously injured.

Extent of injury and the character of the victim were not the only considerations in assault cases. The social status of the accused as indicated by occupation or gender might also affect the decisions of both judge and jury. In Kent, soldiers and women were given heavier sentences than men. Middle-class men were least likely to be convicted, and only one middle-class male was sentenced to more than six months.

The consideration of differences between persons was even more clearly a factor in the treatment of homicide cases. Preserving the social hierarchy was a high priority for the Kentish judicial system. The impact of class considerations is clearest in a case heard in 1878. During an agricultural laborer's strike, the battered corpse of Arthur Gillow, the son of a local J.P. and gentleman farmer, was found near a recently purchased plowing machine. The case was important enough to be reported in detail in *The Times*, which lamented that "a very painful feeling has been created in the whole of East Kent by the murder of Mr. Arthur Gillow."[22]

Shortly after the crime was discovered, Richard Gillow, the victim's brother, advised the police to arrest Stephen Gambrill, the Gillows' wagoner. Gambrill's wages had been cut after the purchase of the plowing machine. Richard Gillow also claimed that the footprints at the scene of the crime were those of Gambrill. When the police arrested Gambrill, they found that he was covered with bruises, which they assumed were the result of his struggle with Gillow. The grand jury indicted Gambrill for murder.[23]

Gambrill's trial was well publicized and his defense attorney did his best. It took several days to empanel a jury, as the defense challenged every farmer on the jury list. At Gambrill's trial, the defense attorney argued that his client had been vandalizing the plowing machine when Gillow attacked him, and the bruises on Gambrill's body were evidence of self-defense. The prosecution countered by pointing out that Gillow's head had been bashed in and his throat cut, clear evidence of murderous intent. Two surgeons testified, one for each side. One swore that Gambrill had been covered with bruises at the time of his arrest and that the wound to Gillow's throat could have been made an hour after he had been knocked unconscious. The surgeon testifying for the prosecution said that he did not remember finding any marks of violence on Gambrill's body. Gambrill's cellmate testified that he had heard Gambrill confess to the crime.

The authorities viewed this crime as particularly heinous. In all the depositions the police refer to it as an "outrage," a designation not given any other homicide. More significant was the direction the presiding Lord Justice Henry Cotton gave the jury:

> It was their duty, not to consider the prisoner alone, but to consider the interests of society and protect society against the crime of murder. No doubt, it was for the prosecution to make out the case against the prisoner, but only to this extent, that the jury must be satisfied as reasonable men and without reference to such doubts as were utterly unsubstantial and unreal. . . . If he inflicted wounds calculated to cause death that implied malice. . . . It was not necessary that there be any evidence of malice or intention to kill previously to the act, for if the prisoner intended to inflict grievous injuries and they caused death, he would be guilty of murder.

After a twenty minute deliberation, the jury returned a verdict of murder. After Gambrill was sentenced to death, the local press ran stories reporting that Gambrill felt enormous remorse for killing his kind and generous master, while the sheriff of Kent received letters from landed proprietors all over England who wanted to serve as Gambrill's executioner.[24] Though Gambrill was guilty of homicide, the verdict and the reaction to it had far more to do with class considerations than the letter of the law.

But the social status of a homicide victim could sometimes work in favor of the accused. Even consideration as a homicide victim required a certain minimum status in the community. When a corpse was discovered near the beach at Ramsgate in 1859, the coroner and magistrates agreed that since the man was a stranger and quite possibly a foreign sailor it was not fair to use local tax money to pay for an investigation. Even though the man had died of stab wounds to the back, the coroner announced that it was an obvious case of suicide, and the body was buried without further inquest. The proceedings did cause some consternation, and a question was raised in the House of Commons. The undersecretary of the Home Office explained that the central government had no power to compel local authorities in such matters. The M.P. for east Kent added that if the coroner had felt it was important, the magistrates would have approved funds for further investigation.[25] The case was closed. A dead foreigner was of limited interest.

Gender might also lessen concern. In three separate cases, women of the streets were found raped and strangled. The first case in 1864 was the murder of Bridget Goodsall, a middle-aged woman who, according to the police, had "since the death of her husband, led a rather dissipated life." The police arrested two local laborers who gave contradictory statements. One of the men admitted raping her. The police surgeon said that the physical evidence showed she had suffocated while one man held her down for the other to rape her. The blood and hair of the victim were found on the clothes of the accused. At the July assize, after hearing the evidence of ten witnesses, Justice James Willes directed the grand jury not to indict as he felt there was insufficient evidence that the men had killed her. The fact that one of the men had confessed to rape was ignored, as was the medical testimony regarding the cause of death. The case was closed.[26]

In a similar case in June 1867 a "traveling woman" was found dead. Henry Roots, a local laborer, had been seen with the woman. When he was brought before the magistrate he had scratches on his face. He was discharged, but two days later a woman came forward saying she had seen Roots struggling with the victim. At the trial Roots's attorney questioned the reliability of the witness, who admitted that she had hesitated to come forward because she had been "deceiving her husband" when she witnessed the crime. After a fifteen-minute deliberation the jury acquitted Roots.[27]

In a third case in 1869 a woman's semi-nude body was found by the side of a road. Alfred Lawrence, a laborer, had been seen leaving a pub with the woman, and after the murder was found covered with mud and gravel, his clothes bloodied and his hands and face scratched. His footprints were found near the body. Lawrence confessed that he had raped her but denied killing her. In his charge to the grand jury Justice John Mellor announced that no murder had taken place. Lawrence was released.[28]

In each of these cases the victims were women of the streets, separated from their husbands, and of the very lowest social class. The victims were insignificant on at least two scales: they were not respectable members of the Kentish community and they were female. In cases involving adult victims the sex of the victim could have a decided impact on sentencing. In homicides other than accidents or brawls, a sentence of death was given in 55 percent of cases where the victim was an adult male, as opposed to only 24 percent of cases where the victim was an adult female. Forty-eight percent of persons convicted of killing women served less than five years.

The social status of the accused was also important. Any defendant had the benefit of the doubt in theory, but the class of the accused could help determine how much doubt was appropriate. Authorities assumed that murderers were always from the lowest classes. Justice Martin told the Capital Punishment Commission that only the lower classes could give useful information on the efficacy of the death penalty as "it is a very rare occurrence that any individual of the higher or middle classes is tried for murder."[29] Of the twenty-six persons convicted of murder in Kent between 1859 and 1880, twenty-two were either laborers or soldiers. The assumption was that respectable people did not commit murder. In the two cases in which middle-class persons were accused, the courts and the public worked to preserve this assumption.

In 1871 Edmund Pook, the son of a wealthy printer from Greenwich, was accused of murdering his father's housemaid, who had been found with her head smashed in with a hammer. When last seen alive she had told friends that she was going to meet Edmund Pook. An autopsy revealed that the victim was two months' pregnant. The evidence against Pook was impressive although circumstantial. Blood stains and hair matching the victim's were found on Pook's trousers. A clerk in a hardware store swore that he had sold Pook a hammer the day before the murder. A whistle that belonged to Pook, a bloodstained smock, and a hammer stained with blood were found at the scene of the crime. Several witnesses had seen Pook running from the murder site looking hot and excited.

Pook was indicted and tried at Central Criminal Court. His defense attorney presented love letters that Pook had written to two young ladies, and argued that with such respectable intimacies available, Pook would never have become involved with a domestic servant. Edmund's mother swore that he had been at home with her the entire evening. Chief Justice William Bovill directed the jury to acquit, and after a twenty-minute deliberation they did so. A newspaper editorial published immediately after the trial reveals a certain uneasiness: "The evidence against the prisoner was entirely circumstantial. . . . If the evidence on the part of the prisoner was true, an alibi was thoroughly established but apart from this the case for the prosecution was altogether of such a nature that no other verdict could have been delivered."[30]

The other case involving non-working-class suspects had all the drama of a gothic novel, and its outcome clearly reflected assumptions about what sort of people could be murderers. In 1877 Louis Staunton, a twenty-five-year-old artist, his brother Patrick, also an artist, Patrick's wife Elizabeth, and Alice Rhodes, Louis's lover, were all charged with the murder of Louis's wife. Harriet Staunton, the victim, was the niece of Lord Rivers and heiress to a considerable fortune. When Harriet had first announced her plans to marry Louis Staunton, her mother had gone to court in an attempt to have Harriet declared mentally incompetent. When the attempt failed, Harriet married Louis and her new husband forbade any further contact between Harriet and her family. Eighteen months after the wedding Harriet was dead. The doctor who examined her corpse said that she was five-and-one-half feet tall and weighed seventy-four pounds. A servant testified that the Stauntons had kept Harriet locked in a room on the top floor of the house and then waited for her to starve to death. Though the Stauntons lived in a small village in Kent, none of the neighbors even knew Harriet existed. Alice Rhodes had presented herself as Louis's wife.

The changes in public opinion during the process of arrest and trial in this case are fascinating. When Harriet died in April, her body was described as being filthy and emaciated. Her alleged killers were jeered by angry crowds on their way to the courthouse. At the July assize in Kent, Justice Stephen advised the grand jury that if the accused "had all conspired together to cause the death of the deceased they were undoubtedly amenable to a charge of willful murder." The four were duly indicted, but the trial was moved to Central Criminal Court because of fears for the safety of the defendants.[31]

At the trial in September, Louis Staunton, Alice Rhodes, and Patrick Staunton all swore that Harriet had been well fed and happy, and that her death had been a great shock. But Patrick's wife chose to break ranks. Her attorney argued that her husband had compelled her to commit the crime. When the judge ruled that coercion was not a valid defense in this case, the attorney begged the court to consider that "she had no means of doing that, the willful neglect of which was charged against her." Louis and Patrick had been determined to starve Harriet, and there was no way Elizabeth could have stopped them. The prosecution then presented letters from Louis to Alice discussing how wonderful their life would be once Harriet was out of the way. All four defendants were convicted and sentenced to death.

During the trial, however, the image of the people involved had changed. Harriet's mother had come across as a conniving witch; Louis Staunton as a handsome young artist tortured by an unhappy marriage; Alice Rhodes, who gave birth to Louis's child right before the trial, as a very pretty young mother who wept piteously because her child had been taken from her. After the death sentences were pronounced, protest meetings were held in several Kentish towns, and the Home Office received petitions for mercy. Such attractive, respectable-looking people simply could not have systematically starved a rich young woman. The Maidstone paper argued that the indictments had been brought merely to show disapproval; no one had expected a conviction. The jury had returned the wrong verdict. At worst the accused had been careless, nothing more. On November 3 the Home Secretary commuted the sentences. The Stauntons were sentenced to life in prison and Alice Rhodes was given a free pardon.[32]

Even though the judge and the jury in the Staunton case were convinced that the defendants were guilty, the verdict was unacceptable because it violated the fundamental belief that murderers were a breed apart. Nice, attractive people simply could not be murderers. As Justice Fitzroy Kelly told the Capital Punishment Commission:

> We are not dealing with people in the class of life of those who are assembled in this room, nor even with the middle classes, nor with any educated or intelligent classes, nor people with whom human motives will operate in an ordinary way; but we are dealing with a class of people of whom personally we know very little. We must consider the character and habits, the nature in general, of those classes of persons among whom such crimes are committed.[33]

It was, and is, more comforting to believe that murderers are monsters, beings who neither think nor behave as the rest of us do.

While the murderous stranger who attacks innocent victims without provocation is probably the most frightening criminal, he is also, fortunately, among the rarest. Only one homicide in Kent actually involved such a monster. In 1863 an eighteen-year-old laborer murdered a nine-year-old boy by slashing his throat, strangling him, and stomping his face. The killer confessed, and explained that he had wanted to be hanged and had simply decided to murder the next person he saw. After his trial he even wrote the victim's mother explaining, "I did not take his life for any ill-feeling towards him, it would have been anyone's fate who fell into my hands at that time." The local press was fascinated by this embodiment of the ideal murderer and ran his life story for the edification of its readers. The young man became a celebrity in the weeks between his trial and execution. Ironically, the paper noted that the motive for his crime had been "a yearning to die on the scaffold from a love of notoriety."[34] He got his wish. His crime was sensational enough to be fascinating and unusual enough to be horrifying but not immediately threatening.

All other homicides in which arrests were made involved people who knew one another. In 88 percent of the cases, homicide victims were either neighbors, relatives, or co-workers of their assailants. Though not formally recognized in law, the relationship between the victim and the accused was crucial both in deciding whether to call a homicide a manslaughter or a murder, and in determining sentences. One hundred percent of those accused of killing an employer or superior officer were executed. In six of these cases there had been no immediate provocation and a deadly weapon had been used, hence showing intent to kill; but the same factors were present in some other cases in which no death sentence was issued. On the other hand, domestic homicides were rarely treated as murders. Only 13 percent of those accused of killing their child or stepchild (excluding infanticide) and only 23 percent of those accused of killing a spouse were executed.

It is also worth noting that while soldiers were accused of only seventeen homicides, five of the persons executed for murder were soldiers. The fact that such a high percentage of homicides by soldiers were treated as murders reflects not only the fact that soldiers often killed superiors, but also that they were seen as a threat to the peace of the community. This is partly because soldiers were more likely to have arms, but the testimony in these cases also reveals a particularly ugly side to military life. Soldiers committed a disproportionate amount of all crime. The Victorian army had recruiting problems, and soldiers were often very young and totally unprepared for the rigors of military life. Alan Skelley has argued that "most offenses [by soldiers] were a reaction to the sudden harshness of military discipline, the strangeness of army life and the lack of anything to do in spare time but drink."[35] Each of the soldiers convicted of murder claimed to have committed the murder either to escape the army through the death penalty or to revenge ill-treatment by a superior officer. One nineteen-year-old calmly explained that he had shot his commanding officer because he had been "a tyrant, a rogue and a thief in his heart." The victim had docked the soldier a day's pay for insubordination. The soldier explained at his trial that during inspection the day after the docking he "took a fine sight of him and aimed for the middle of his back." His training must have been good; he killed the officer with one shot.[36]

While the relative social status of the accused and the victim was extremely important in distinguishing between murder and manslaughter, the method of death also had a significant effect on sentencing. Though weapons were not necessary—51 percent of homicides involved no weapon other than the fist—the use of one could prove intent. Sixty-three percent of those executed for murder had used knives. Eighty-two percent of those accused of homicides involving knives were convicted, and 77 percent of those convicted were punished by death. By contrast only 25 percent of those accused in shooting deaths were convicted. The three men who were executed for shooting deaths had each confessed with considerable pride. All the other shooting deaths were ruled accidental.

Using a knife was considered heinous, but attitudes toward guns were considerably less rigid. Guns were cheap and readily available. In 1864 Thomas Horton had committed suicide after trying to shoot his fiancée. The gunshop clerk told the coroner's inquest that when he sold Horton the two revolvers on the night of the crime, Horton had been so drunk he walked into a post. No one questioned the clerk about the wisdom of selling guns to a man who was obviously intoxicated. At a trial in 1865 a man testified that he had heard gunshots but "took no notice as boys are in the habit of firing off guns."[37] Firing a gun on a public highway was a misdemeanor punishable by a 5s. fine, but the only restriction on gun purchase or ownership was a 10s. license required after 1870. Olive Anderson found that Gladstone's government claimed the purpose of the license requirement was "to check lawless habits. . . . [T]he issues which counted most in debate, were poaching, the protection of birds from schoolboys and checking Irish violence in Britain."[38] But Kentish magistrates who heard cases of persons owning guns without licenses often took the opportunity to explain that it was purely a matter of revenue and that they would ask the Inland Revenue to waive any penalty.

In 1880 the editor of the *Maidstone and Kentish Journal* advocated better control of "the indiscriminate sale of pistols and revolvers," but he also admitted that "as a rule, thieves carry weapons for purposes of intimidation without any intention of putting them to serious use." Despite their availability only two robberies in Kent between 1859 and 1880 involved the use of firearms. The editor warned of other hazards: "We hear of their accidental discharge occasioning the death of many persons each year; and some unhappy men employ them as means of self-destruction." Guns caused accidents and suicides, the editor concluded, and "rarely, if ever do we hear of their possession proving of any use whatever."[39] About one death a year in Kent was the result of a shooting accident. Most often a child had discovered the gun and shot a playmate. The owners were usually censured for leaving a loaded gun lying about, but there is little evidence of concern about the potential hazards of the availability of firearms. Anderson found that in the Parliamentary debate over gun-licensing "reducing accidents was little mentioned, and reducing suicide not at all."[40]

In Victorian Kent guns were not the weapon of choice in homicides but were used more frequently in suicides—a crime the justice system found particularly difficult. Technically suicide was illegal, and persons who attempted it were liable to imprisonment. Those who aided and abetted a suicide were guilty of murder. In 1861 George Inkpen, a twenty-year-old hammerman described by *The Times* as a "simple-looking youth with a mild expression of countenance," was tried for murder at Central Criminal Court. He and his twenty-four-year-old girlfriend had tied themselves together and jumped into the Thames in a suicide pact. She had drowned but he had been rescued. At his trial Inkpen explained that she had suggested suicide, saying, "[I]t was no use of living." They had used bootlaces to tie themselves together and had been separated after hitting the water. He had tried to rescue her but failed, adding that they had both been "bad drunk." The jury foreman asked Justice John Bernard Byles, "If they believed the account given by the defendant was a true one, the offense amounted to wilful murder?" Byles replied, "Certainly it would." The jury returned a verdict of guilty with a strong recommendation for mercy, assuring the judge that they believed there had been "no spite, anger, malice, or deliberate intention to take the woman's life." Justice Byles donned the black cap, traditionally worn during sentencing in capital cases. After sentencing Inkpen to death, he added that it was a most painful case, that he agreed that there had been no malice, and that he would also urge that the Home Office commute the sentence. The report in *The Times* added that "there is no probability of the capital sentence being carried into effect." Within a month the Home Secretary had commuted the sentence to one year.[41]

The fact that Byles felt compelled to convict and sentence Inkpen for murder despite his belief that Inkpen had no malice or murderous intent is indicative of the considerable ambiguity surrounding the crime of suicide. It was against the law and had been since the thirteenth century, but the criminality of the act was not clear. Originally it had been a part of religious dogma that suicides were inspired by Satan. The law allowed the government to confiscate the property of suicides—a popular provision with the Tudors and Stuarts. But in the eighteenth century coroner's juries began to grow more lenient. By reducing the valuation of goods or declaring that the suicide had been *non compos mentis*, they protected the inheritance of his family. The verdict of *felo de se* that led to confiscation was less and less frequent after 1760. Michael MacDonald found that juries were most likely to return a verdict of *non compos mentis* when suicides "were prosperous and responsible persons of good reputation whose survivors could be greatly injured if their property was seized." Those who were likely to be ruled criminal suicides were "marginal members of the community in which they died: strangers, criminals, people in disgrace, servants, apprentices, abject paupers."[42]

In mid-nineteenth-century Kent the *felo de se* ruling was reserved for those who had committed serious crimes before their death. Even non-respectable suicides were given pauper funerals. When a man being held in Chatham police station hanged himself, the coroner ruled him insane. The coroner did add, however, that he "did not see why any blame should be attached to the police. If these men determined to commit an act like the deceased had done, the utmost vigilance would not prevent it." Between 1859 and 1880 coroner's juries in Kent ruled on 1,519 cases of suicide; only 19 were ruled criminal acts of *felo de se.* In all other cases the jury found that the victim had been "temporarily of unsound mind." The exceptions usually came when the deceased had attempted to murder someone else before killing himself. In 1864 a young man cut his fiancée's throat and then killed himself. The coroner's jury voted nine to four that there was no evidence of insanity, and found the deceased guilty of *felo de se.* The full penalties were invoked with all their superstitious overtones: "In consequence of the verdict the body having been placed in a coffin was that same night between eleven and twelve o'clock conveyed to St. Gregory's cemetery by four policemen and there buried." The police ordered a dissenting clergyman who arrived and asked permission to perform a brief service for the deceased to leave immediately.[43] The denial of Christian burial was the only means of vengeance left to earthly authorities.

Although coroner's juries might well feel sympathy for the survivors, and although it might reasonably be argued that there was nothing to be gained by attempting to punish the deceased, the leniency shown to successful suicides made the treatment of attempted suicides considerably more problematic. In Kent between 1859 and 1880, 371 persons were brought before the magistrates for attempting to commit suicide. Fifty-one were brought before the grand jury for indictment and thirty-seven were convicted. There was considerable confusion even among judges as to why attempted suicide was considered criminal. In August 1867 Justice Martin told a grand jury that in cases of suicide "the intention of the law is more that the prisoner should be kept in confinement and be properly looked after than that he should be punished." But a year later Magistrate Brook Bridges told a quarter sessions grand jury that "the taking away of life under any circumstances was murder in the eyes of the law, and if the jury were convinced that the prisoner had attempted to take away his own life, it was, in the eyes of the law, as serious as if he had attempted to take the life of any other person." The contradiction becomes even more confusing when one considers the sentences in each case. Martin sentenced his prisoner to six months; Bridges released his defendant on a £20 recognizance.[44]

Though 54 percent of those convicted of attempted suicide were released on recognizance after promising not to try it again, some judges believed a prison sentence of up to six months, during which the prisoner received counsel from the chaplain, could be beneficial. A few also felt prison would be a deterrent. In 1866 James Espinasse, the recorder for Rochester, sentenced a man to three months' hard labor for attempting suicide under the town hall. Espinasse explained that he was trying to stem an epidemic: "When we take up the daily papers we cannot fail to notice the enormous extent to which the crime of suicide extends. We read of love-sick scullions, sentimental housemaids and even forward school-boys attempting to destroy their life from some very foolish cause or another."[45]

Although the causes are rarely explained in the records, at first glance the evidence regarding the sex and age of defendants in Kent indicates that attempts were rarely made by schoolboys, though at least one of the accused was a housemaid. The most noteworthy thing about those brought before grand juries on charges of attempted suicide was that 35 percent of them were women, a much higher proportion than for any other crime except infanticide. Also, all the men and women who appeared before the grand jury for attempted suicide were over eighteen, making this the only offense for which no juveniles were indicted. But these figures tell more about who might be held criminally culpable in a suicide attempt than who might attempt. Anderson found that suicide among the young was a very real possibility.[46]

A number of highly respectable persons committed suicide, and their actions made the criminality of suicide even harder to establish. The daughter of the mayor of Hythe left the following note before taking her own life: "I have tried so hard to do my duty, but I cannot, but God will save me for Jesus's sake." In another case a local curate preached a sermon on suicide, citing the actions of the early Christian martyrs, and then went home and cut his own throat. The most jarring suicide was probably that of Justice Willes, the youngest man ever appointed to the Court of Common Pleas. After twenty-one years on the bench, Willes shot himself to escape severe ill-health.[47]

While it was clearly preferable that respectable suicides be deemed temporarily insane rather than criminal, only two persons who attempted suicide and failed were committed as lunatics. The editor of the *Maidstone and Kentish Journal* pointed out the irony of the practice: "It is rather peculiar that in these days a man who succeeds in committing suicide is usually pronounced a lunatic, while those who fail in the attempt are treated as criminals."[48] Although attempts were more likely to be labeled criminal, in fact both attempts and success were more often pitied than censured. A "crime" that injured only the perpetrator, could not be punished if successful, and was often committed by respectable persons, fit neither the procedures nor the prejudices of the judicial system. It was much easier simply to blame such action on sudden, completely uncharacteristic bursts of insanity.

Insanity was the best explanation for suicides, but it was not universally accepted as a defense for other crimes. Justice Bramwell assured the Capital Punishment Committee that "[m]any a man who declares himself to be under an uncontrollable impulse, finds that impulse controllable when a policeman is at hand. The duty of a man was to prevent himself from being governed by such feelings." Bramwell told a jury that a verdict of insanity required that "it should be made out affirmatively that the person accused at the time the offense was committed was not only not aware of the nature and quality of the act he was committing, but also that he was not aware that he was doing wrong." The law presumed that even a certified lunatic was lucid, unless the defense could prove that at the time of the crime he had been under a delusion which, had it been true, would have justified the act. Even under these circumstances there were those who objected. "It would appear to be a very strange course to commute a sentence of death in order that a lunatic life might be prolonged when it would not be done in order that a sane life might be prolonged."[49]

Nine persons accused of murder in Kent were acquitted on grounds of insanity, but at least four of the persons hanged for murder had also been treated for mental illness. Attitudes toward the insane varied from sympathy to revulsion to fear, determined in part by the perceived danger to the public. The four who hanged were all soldiers, while seven of the nine who were declared insane had killed their own children. One of the other two was a former mental patient who killed a co-worker with an axe. The ninth, John Atkins, had stabbed his wife in 1861. At his trial neighbors, local police, and a physician all swore that Atkins suffered from the paranoid delusion that his wife was unfaithful. He was committed to and spent the rest of his life in an asylum. Interest in the Atkins case was renewed in 1873 when his son Thomas was arrested for the murder of a policeman. Thomas's physician argued that insanity ran in the Atkins family and that Thomas was not responsible for his actions. The prosecution argued that John's insanity had been a sham and that Thomas was also in his right mind. Thomas was convicted and sentenced to twenty years for manslaughter, though he was later transferred from prison to an asylum.[50]

A verdict of insanity was more likely to be returned if the accused had killed a relative, for the same reason that persons accused of domestic homicides generally received lighter sentences: violence in the home was less threatening than violence in the streets. Similarly, since soldiers were an outside force let loose within the community, they were too dangerous to grant immunity even (or perhaps especially) if they were clearly insane. As with other homicides, public opinion could be swayed by the image of the accused and the victim. In 1879 when a former asylum inmate was shot by his wife's lover, the initial reaction from the public was antagonistic. The woman was hissed at by crowds outside the courtroom. After she wrote an article for the local paper explaining how the accused had helped her through the ordeal of marriage to a lunatic, reactions changed. The jury found the accused guilty of manslaughter and recommended mercy. Judge Cockburn sentenced him to only six months on account of his good character.[51]

Violence had a legitimate place in Victorian society, and few people would have favored its complete eradication. The criminal justice system, if not the law itself, was geared to regulating interpersonal violence, not abolishing it. Criminality in interpersonal violence hinged more on motive and victim than on degree of injury. While judges varied in their definitions of "insanity," "provocation," and "intent," the limits on violence were established with considerable clarity. Occasional bursts of violence among equals in a pub or among relatives in private were understandable; public assaults on inoffensive, respectable persons and any violence directed towards social superiors were not. In Victorian Kent the judicial system was concerned with allowing respectable people to walk the streets safely. To a large extent they succeeded.

3

Women: Victims and Suspects

> The law imperatively requires that there should be corroborative evidence on material points. Because otherwise no man would be safe. Is he or any other man on the unsupported testimony of a woman to have his character wholly and entirely taken away?[1]
>
> Defense summation at the trial of the Earl of Norbury for indecent assault

The Victorian criminal justice system was run exclusively by men. All judges, jurors, police, and legislators were men. Women were only involved as victims, witnesses, or suspects. Inevitably those crimes committed or experienced almost exclusively by women were treated differently than those not gender-related. Even when men and women committed or experienced the same crimes, judicial responses were not always the same.

The legal status of women, particularly married women, was a moot point. According to the eighteenth-century legal commentator Sir William Blackstone, married women were legal non-entities: "By marriage, the husband and wife were one person in law: that is the very being or legal existence of the woman is suspended during the marriage, or at least is incorporated and consolidated into that of the husband." Blackstone attributed this loss of separate identity to the noblest of motives. The woman is under the "wing, protection, and cover" of her husband. "Even the disabilities, which the wife lies under, are for the most part intended for her protection and benefit. So great a favorite is the female sex of the laws of England."[2]

This appraisal has been quoted by a great many people for a great many reasons, but it is not a completely accurate account of the legal position of married women in the mid-nineteenth century. Blackstone was mainly concerned about property law. Although the fact that woman's property legally belonged to her husband says a great deal about attitudes toward women, its effect in criminal cases was usually minimal.[3]

Blackstone and his nineteenth-century successors also implied that since they were under the legal control of their husbands, married women were not responsible for their own criminal acts. "The general rule is, that all persons are responsible for their acts done in violation of the law; but to this rule there are exceptions in favor of infants, insane persons, married women and irresponsible agents."[4] In 1869 Frances Power Cobbe wrote a feminist tract: "Criminals, Idiots, Women and Minors: Is the Classification Sound?" Some historians have assumed that the classification was rigidly applied in the courtroom,[5] but even the law commentators carefully limited the provision. Women *might* be relieved of responsibility for thefts committed in the presence of their husbands *if* they could prove they had been coerced. Married women had no immunity in cases of murder, robbery or treason, and authorities were divided over the status of misdemeanors.[6]

In practice the coercion defense seems to have been useless in the mid-nineteenth century. Lawyers used it three times in Kent between 1859 and 1880, never successfully. In each case the judge ruled that coercion could never be assumed and had not been proven. Justice Colin Blackburn warned one grand jury, "The law supposes that everything is in the property of the husband and that the wife is under his control. But in point of fact, in the lower positions of life that possibly may not be the case at all."[7] Like Mr. Bumble in *Oliver Twist*, most judges and magistrates evidently believed that if the law really thought that wives were always obedient to their husbands, "the law is a ass—a idiot."[8]

Married women in Victorian Kent were held responsible for their own criminal actions and sometimes for those of their husbands as well. In January 1863 Jessie Cooper was indicted for bigamy. Her first husband had abused and abandoned her and then spread false rumors of his death to escape his creditors. Believing the reports, Jessie had remarried. When her first husband was arrested and convicted of embezzlement he suggested that the police arrest Jessie for bigamy. Her new husband swore that he thought she was a widow. She was found guilty of bigamy and sent to prison, though the jury did "express their sympathy towards the prisoner."[9]

The proportion of crimes committed by women, married or single, appears to have declined during the nineteenth century. Gatrell and Hadden have suggested there was a sharp decline in the number of crimes by women in the 1860s.[10] David Philips found in his study of crime in the Black Country between 1835 and 1860 that the ratio of male to female criminals was three to one.[11] In Kent between 1859 and 1880 women were charged with only 15 percent of indictable offenses, though there is no significant change in the ratio during the period. While comparisons between local studies are always risky and the judicial statistics are not always reliable, the argument that women were becoming less criminal does seem plausible. The evidence in Kent also generally corresponds to Philip's findings regarding the kinds of crimes women committed. Among indictable offenses women were most likely to commit non-violent property crimes, accounting for 15 percent of non-violent theft. They committed only 8 percent of indictable assaults, 17 percent of homicides (excluding infanticide), and only 5 percent of violent robberies.

Though women committed fewer violent crimes than men, they did not necessarily shrink from a fight. Philips found that "where women were involved in robberies or assaults, they do not seem to have been notably less violent than men."[12] The same appears to have been true in Kent. The Rochester correspondent for the *Maidstone and Kentish Journal* took great delight in reporting assaults by women: "There were no less than thirteen assault cases at this court, all of the most trivial nature, in which the 'ladies' figured most prominently as belligerent parties." Women fought men as well as each other. In one case in which a woman had accused a man of assaulting her, the defense attorney produced two "respectable witnesses" to establish that she "had been the aggressor by throwing mud over him, spitting in his face, and other little pleasantries which are not yet considered fashionable in St. James."[13] Since most assaults involved the use of fists women were presumably at a disadvantage, though a few overcame the problem. Three of the women who committed violent robberies bit their victims.

Another woman was convicted of manslaughter after a pubkeeper she had bitten died of blood-poisoning.

Some historians have suggested that women became less assertive during the nineteenth century as ideals of feminine delicacy became more widespread.[14] Evidence from Kent does not support this suggestion. The number of women being charged with assault did not change significantly between 1859 and 1880; indeed in the Central Criminal Court there were more women indicted for assault in the 1870s than in the 1860s. While newspaper reports are not completely reliable as a measure of frequency, in 1880 the Rochester correspondent was still reporting cases in which women were fined or imprisoned for assaulting their husbands, the police, or other men.

Though the ideal of feminine delicacy was not necessarily reaching the women involved in pub brawls, it did affect the attitudes of the upper- and middle-class men who ran the justice system. Violence between the sexes presented a number of problems for judicial authorities. Chivalry and fair play demanded that the weaker sex be protected from the stronger, but the same logic implied that women were inherently inferior and must be dealt with accordingly. In order to merit protection a woman had to be obedient, submissive, and incapable of defending herself. Chivalry was reserved for those women who both needed and deserved protection—a relatively select group. The right to protection was based on the assumption that women were weaker, softer, and generally very different from the strong men who protected them. Therefore protection was often reserved for middle-class women. While it was possible for a working woman to be respectable, some of the more delicate aspects of the feminine ideal were clearly beyond her. "As for women of the working classes, at least one nineteenth-century essayist implied that such creatures were merely biological females and hardly deserved being called women at all."[15]

The chivalrous ideal and its corollaries created an atmosphere in which the judicial response to the physical abuse of women was partially determined by the woman's capacity to defend herself. Justice Brett expressed his outrage when he heard a case in which a man had strangled his invalid wife. "Although she was your wife and the person before whom all others in the world you should have protected, and to whom, in her feebleness and weakness you ought to have been more indulgent than to anyone else, you brutally ill-used her." Beating the defenseless was unmanly. "It shows a kind of violence in a man which is nothing but gross and wicked cowardice and sickness and brutality."[16]

But for violence towards a woman to be wicked, the woman had to be defenseless. Judges usually found violence by women far more reprehensible than violence by men, even when it was a defensive reaction. Twice in the 1870s women who had been seduced, abused, and abandoned retaliated by blinding their seducers with sulfuric acid. In both cases the men freely admitted the relationship. "She used to work at our place until I seduced her after which I went to see her occasionally. I don't know how many children I have had by her." "I kept company with her and visited her on several occasions but was engaged to someone else." They also showed no remorse about physical abuse. "I remember her saying she had a fractured rib and she said I had fractured it—I know I hit her when she complained of a black eye—That is the only time I hit to disfigure." Both women were convicted but recommended to mercy on account of extreme provocation. In each case the sentence was five years. In contrast, a man who put out the eye of a woman who left him was sentenced to only four months after explaining that he "was regularly drove to do it from her aggravation."[17]

Since judges were far more likely to condone male violence in response to aggravation than they were to sanction female retaliation, the abused woman was trapped. If she fought back she could be convicted and would likely face a longer sentence than her abuser; if she took the man to court the judge might well decide that she had provoked the violence by not behaving in a properly submissive manner. Married women were particularly constrained. Even though it was legally possible to obtain a divorce, the process was complicated, expensive, and unreliable. As one judge explained, "It cannot be too widely known that this court has neither the power nor the inclination to deal with the mere unhappiness of ill-assorted unions."[18]

Even when a divorce was granted a woman could still find herself at the mercy of her ex-husband. An example of this is the case of Amelia Chittendon, a woman who obtained a divorce from her husband and then opened a dress shop with her own funds. Three times in 1871 she applied to the courts for protection from her ex-husband, who had threatened her life. Each time the court rejected her request. In October 1871 her ex-husband broke into her house and cut her throat. He was arrested and tried at the December assize. In his charge, Justice Martin told the grand jury that cases in which estranged husbands attacked their wives were "of the common and ordinary kind. It would probably turn out that these were not serious crimes." After the trial, however, Martin announced that the Chittendon case was serious because the motive had been revenge rather than jealousy. Martin explained that "the motive of jealousy is not so unworthy as that of revenge," and sentenced Chittendon to twenty years "to show that people will not be permitted to use such weapons, and to cut people's throats in such a manner."[19]

The distinction between the delicate, fragile woman and the strong, masculine man was essential to the Victorian definition of marriage. When a farmer's wife in Headcorn sued for divorce on the grounds of drunkenness and cruelty, Justice Willes denied her plea as she had not proved that her husband's behavior was a danger to life and limb. Willes also blamed the wife "for she knew his feelings on certain subjects and did not conform to them. . . . [S]he will do well to seek such remedies as may be found in the forces of natural and domestic ties, for it will now be her duty to return to her husband." Again, a woman merited protection only if she were submissive. The husband, according to Willes' worldview, was fulfilling his prescribed role. "If her husband was a bold, rough and somewhat reckless man given to sudden outbursts and using when under excitement strong and unbecoming language, he was at the same time neither implacable, nor vindictive and there was a special absence of any evidence to show a want of that manly spirit which was the sure safeguard of the weaker sex."[20]

That women needed a safeguard was acknowledged. Justice Gillery Pigott complained in 1873 that "women must be protected and the manner in which they were treated was often a scandal."[21] The problem was that women most often needed protection from the very men who were their guardians. Eighty-three percent of all adult female homicide victims were killed by either a spouse, a cohabiter, or a would-be lover. Most domestic manslaughter cases fit the same pattern: a man with a history of abusing his wife went too far, and instead of administering the usual beating he killed her.

Often the motive was that the women had been disobedient or had in some way failed to provide the respect and response the man demanded.

Domestic violence was a serious problem that Victorian judicial authorities treated with ambivalence. The legal position with regard to wife-beating was changing over time. In the eighteenth century Blackstone had explicitly upheld the husband's right to strike his wife with a rod no thicker than his thumb. "For, as the husband is to answer for her misbehavior, the law thought it reasonable to entrust him with the power of chastisement."[22] His nineteenth-century successors did not support this argument. Justice Stephen concluded that though a husband had the right to deprive his wife of her liberty, he did not have the right to strike her.[23] The law did provide some protection against domestic abuse. Under the 1854 Act for the Better Prevention of Aggravated Assaults Upon Women and Children, two magistrates could rule summarily in cases where women, or children under the age of fourteen, had suffered actual bodily harm as the result of an assault. The maximum sentence was six months or £20, as opposed to the three-month maximum sentence for most summary offenses. Unfortunately the records of cases tried under the act are of limited value. There is no distinction made between spouse abuse, child abuse, and assaults by strangers. In Kent the situation was confused even further since magistrates sometimes chose to hear indecent assault cases under this act. Given all these caveats, it is possible to show that the average numbers of cases heard under the act was sixty-three in the 1860s and forty-seven in the 1870s.[24]

But prevailing attitudes often undermined the legal sanctions against domestic abuse. Often the physical abuse of women, especially wives, was seen as chastisement. Though a husband had no legal right to strike his wife, many judges sympathized with men like the wife-beater who lamented, "Is my wife to insult me without remedy?", and the eighty-year-old man who explained that his eighty-year-old wife was such a problem that "beating her with a stick was the only way to manage her." One magistrate advised a beating victim to "abstain from irritating her husband." The chairman of the Tunbridge Wells petty sessions refused to pass sentence in wife-beating cases until he knew "whether she was a woman whose bad temper gave her husband no peace, or whether the fault was his."[25]

Magistrates were not the only officials who suspected women of bringing attacks on themselves. When Viscount Raynham proposed a bill authorizing corporal punishment for wife-beaters, one M.P. warned that working-class women were already taking advantage of the Act of 1854. "It was common among women addicted to vices to say to a husband 'you brute! If you hold up your hand to me I'll give you a sixer!' Some honourable members spoke on the subject as if there was no such thing as a bad woman. The honourable members had probably some experience of the venom of an angry woman's tongue." The undersecretary for the Home Office warned that women might even plot to be beaten: "It must be remembered that a mischievous and ill-tempered woman could very easily impose on a magistrate and by aggravating her husband until he struck her might contrive to bring him into police court, rid herself of his society, and disgrace him."[26]

The disgrace had more to do with the public knowledge of wife-beating than the violence itself. As a police inspector explained after arresting a man for beating his wife on a public highway, "men must not commit a breach of the peace even on their own wives." Relations between husbands and wives were to be kept strictly private. When a domestic dispute in Canterbury led to a full-scale brawl, the *East Kent Times* complained that "the lower classes take their domestic squabbles out in the street. A loose-tongued virago and her sable husband quarrel and the whole city is thrown into a state of excitement." But quarreling in public was not limited to the lowest classes. In May 1859 Samuel Newbury, listed in the court records as a gentleman, was tried at Central Criminal Court for stabbing his wife with a butcher knife after she threw a hairbrush at him. Their servants had broken up the fight after Newbury chased his wife out the front door of their Greenwich home. Newbury was acquitted, as the court ruled that there was equal blame on both sides.[27]

Both public officials and private citizens preferred not to involve themselves in domestic disputes. When attorneys were able to settle a domestic assault case out of court a judge praised them for "effecting an arrangement that has prevented an exposure that must have been painful to all persons interested." Twice in the 1870s migrant hoppers were accused of beating their wives to death on public highways. Though there had been numerous witnesses in each case no one had made any attempt to interfere. A witness admitted that he had heard the woman scream "you are killing me by inches," but he felt it was not his place to interfere. A police constable who had witnessed one of the beatings told the court that "I did not speak to them as the woman did not ask for my assistance or complain to me."[28]

The policeman's reluctance to intervene was understandable. There was considerable disagreement as to what circumstances justified police interference between husband and wife. The problems were highlighted in a case heard at Central Criminal Court in 1859. A man was chargd with manslaughter in the death of his wife. The prosecuting attorney admitted that the evidence regarding cause of death was insufficient, though "there could be no doubt that for some time past he had treated her very brutally." The victim's son and a neighbor both testified that "The police were applied to, but they refused to interfere because they had not seen any blow struck." The prosecutor argued that the woman would still be alive if the police had acted. Justice Bramwell summed up the problem: "It was not required for the police to see an assault actually committed to justify them in interfering . . . it was their duty to interfere to prevent the commission of an assault. At the same time there was a good deal to be said for the police for complaints were constantly and readily made when they were supposed to have interfered in such matter too hastily." Such complaints were sometimes acted upon. In 1871, a police constable was fined for "common assault" after he stopped a man beating his wife. Though the wife said the constable had been kind and considerate and the police superintendent spoke on the constable's behalf, the magistrate ruled the interference unwarranted. Neighbors and police only interfered when the attacks were perceived as excessive, clearly unjustified, or too public.[29]

The reluctance to interfere stemmed in part from the notion that a woman was the property of her husband or father and that the courts had no jurisdiction in their relationship. Women were not slaves, but some legal scholars did regard them as possessions. As late as 1890 Henry Stephen wrote that "the custody of a wife's person belongs to her husband."[30] While Stephen qualified his statement with legal niceties, many of his colleagues apparently sympathized with men like the wife-beater who told a Kentish magistrate that "she was his property and he should knock her about as he pleased." A respectable woman belonged to one man, going from her father's possession to that of her husband. This concept was made clear in a case heard at Central Criminal Court in 1859. A young man had secretly married his landlord's daughter, who continued to live in her parent's home. When her father learned of the marriage he had the husband charged with taking the girl from the possession of her father. Justice Martin heard the case and gave the following explanation to the jury: "The Court considered that it was impossible to say that the girl was in her father's possession though she was in his house, because she was in the lawful possession of her husband, and her father could never have possession of her in the same sense as he had before; possession did not mean having anything in your house or in your hand but having a legal right to it." The man was convicted and sentenced to twelve months in prison.[31]

Sexual possession was also crucial. Under the headline "ELOPEMENT AND CAPTURE OF A WIFE" a newspaper reported that a nineteen-year-old woman had left her husband for another man. She and her lover were arrested, he was charged with stealing the clothes she wore, which were the property of her husband, and she was returned to her husband's custody. Adultery could also justify violence. Justice Bramwell told the Capital Punishment Commission that "if a slight blow may justify such heat of blood that the killing is only manslaughter, surely if within twenty-four hours a man were to rush upon a person who had committed adultery with his wife, one would think that ought to be sufficient provocation."[32] One man who stabbed his wife and her lover was sentenced to only fourteen days.

The definition of women as possessions was closely connected with their financial dependence. As one middle-class bureaucrat explained, "dependence on the man for support is the spring of modest and pleasing deportment."[33] During the nineteenth century the idea that respectable men worked while their wives stayed at home gained prominence. Though some working-class wives clearly had to work outside the home in order for the family to survive, such an arrangement was considered highly undesirable. The idea that men faced the working world while women took care of the home had the endorsement of working class leaders. Henry Broadhurst, the head of the Trade Union Congress, said that one of the goals of the labour movement was to "bring about a condition where wives and daughters would be in their proper sphere at home, instead of being dragged into competition for a livelihood with the great and strong men of the world."[34]

The notion of separate spheres gave women sole responsibility for housekeeping.[35] Wives were expected to do all cooking and cleaning, and failure to meet these requirements could be offered as justification for a beating. Magistrates dismissed one case against a wife-beater, pointing out that "in extenuation the wife is lazy and neglects the home." Even when the husband was not the sole breadwinner, the wife still bore full responsibility for the home. One magistrate dismissed a wife-beating case because he was "disposed to believe that a good deal of fault rested upon the wife, who appeared to have left to go to work without making proper provisions for her husband at home."[36]

A certain level of domestic violence may have been expected. Even the victims of abuse often argued that abuse was a normal part of marriage. One woman told a judge: "My husband has been convicted of assaulting me once. The best of men may do that." Abused women often refused to testify against their assailants. Justice Brett complained that "the women who had been barbarously used, knocked to pieces almost would say nothing about it. Having been near death's door, they lied to shield the men who so grossly ill-used them." In one particularly brutal case a carpenter had chased his wife through the streets of Maidstone, beaten and stabbed her, and then attempted to set her on fire. He was indicted for attempted murder but his wife refused to help the prosecution, insisting that she remembered nothing. When the police surgeon said that was probably because she had been comatose she persisted, "I do not remember my husband knocking me about and do not think it likely he would." The jury convicted the husband of unlawful wounding, a minor offense. Justice Wightman called the verdict insufficient for such a cowardly and brutal crime and gave the maximum allowable sentence of eighteen months. But other judges often dismissed cases in which the victim refused to testify.[37]

Generally the judicial response to cases of domestic abuse was determined by the court's perception of the character of the accused and his victim. A man of "good character" could usually chastise an "immoral" or "irritating" wife or girlfriend with relative immunity. Character was not synonymous with class. For example, in December 1862 Major Murton, a wealthy farmer, was accused of beating his wife to death after one of the two prostitutes he had brought home for the evening complained about her presence. Despite four defense witnesses of highly respectable character, Murton was convicted and sentenced to three years. Justice Byles said during sentencing: "I know that it will be a severe punishment, for you have hitherto occupied a respectable position in life—you have filled the office of overseer, church-warden and surveyor." Murton was thunderstruck by the sentence: "But I provided handsomely for her!" The newspaper noted that "There did not appear to be any one in a very crowded court who felt the sentence was too severe."[38]

A year later, a man from the other end of the social spectrum was convicted of the beating death of the woman he lived with. James Palmer, a laborer, explained that his twenty-five-year-old lover had angered him by saying that she planned to earn her living in a tap room. Justice Pigott sentenced him to just three months in prison but felt compelled to explain the light sentence: "It was the minor offense of manslaughter. The blows were a mere chastisement. She was not his wife, or sister, or legitimately a member of his household, but human nature is human nature and he was provoked because she was drunk."[39] Pigott evidently believed that the master of a household had the right to chastise his women as he saw fit. One cannot help but wonder if Palmer might have been let off completely if he had been legally married to his victim.

The ideal was that all women should be dutiful wives, but according to the 1861 census 31 percent of the women in Kent over the age of twenty were not married. Most of these single women had to be strong and self-sufficient in order to survive. But self-sufficiency was not necessarily an admirable trait for a woman. A physician warned a Parliamentary committee that "All gregarious employment gives a slang appearance to the girls' appearance and habits. That which seems most to lower the moral or decent tone of the peasant girls is the sensation of independence of society which they acquire when they have remunerative labour in their hands."[40]

Many of the women who appeared before Kentish magistrates worked outside the home. In addition to earning their own living some were also guilty of drunkenness, infidelity, verbal abuse, or other indelicate behavior. Whether such women deserved protection was a moot point in male-dominated courts.

Women in groups were also perceived as potential trouble-makers. Female inferiority and dependence were best preserved in isolation. Wife-beaters often explained that they had been forced to beat their wives to keep them from associating with other women. One man blamed all his domestic problems on "women who were gin drinkers and who said to each other, 'You come to my house to have a cup of tea and I will go to yours and take tea.'" Another told a magistrate that he had blacked his wife's eye because she was "so thick with the woman next door."[41] Men often complained to the courts that beatings were the only way to keep their wives away from their mothers and sisters.

A woman who drank or was verbally abusive usually forfeited her right to protection. Similarly, a man who was sober and of good character could be excused for a violent outburst. One man was acquitted of his wife's death after his defense attorney pointed out that he was a veteran. This notion—that a good man had the right to beat a bad woman—was upheld by Justice Cockburn in 1879 when he sentenced a shoemaker who had beaten his wife to death to six months. The man had an excellent work record and the wife had been a drunkard who allegedly refused to give him money to pay the rent. After being criticized in the London press, Cockburn justified the light sentence, saying: "There can be little doubt that the wife wished to spend the money on drink, or that her refusal to let her husband have it was accompanied by foul and abusive language habitual to her. Exasperated he struck her, but no doubt under great irritation."[42]

That Cockburn felt obliged to defend the sentence reflects some change in attitudes. Sentences in domestic homicides did grow more severe during the late 1860s. At the assizes between 1859 and 1866 five men were convicted of beating their wives to death. The maximum sentence given was Murton's three years. Between 1866 and 1880 nine similar cases were heard in Kent and seven of the men were sentenced to more than five years' penal servitude. While the numbers were small, it is evident from the example of Justice

Pigott that the change involves something more than mere chance. In 1863 Pigott had given Palmer only three months; in 1873 he sentenced a man to twenty years' penal servitude for beating his wife to death as chastisement for drunkenness.[43]

Though the evidence of changing judicial attitudes is fragmentary, there was a significant change in legislation in 1878. The amendment to the Matrimonial Causes Act empowered magistrates to order separations in cases where husbands were convicted of aggravated assaults on their wives. The court could also order the husband to pay a set weekly amount to his estranged wife to cover support for herself and the children. Beginning in July 1878, J.P.s in Kent routinely issued such orders in cases of working-class spouse abuse. The acceptance and implementation of these provisions indicates that Kentish magistrates accepted the principle that a husband's financial responsibilities toward his wife did not give him the right to abuse her. Though the problem of domestic abuse was by no means solved, the legal protection of women from their spouses did at least seem to be improving.

Although domestic abuse usually involved a female victim, another serious crime was even more gender specific. Rape presented particular difficulties for the criminal justice system.[44] The history of rape laws reveals much ambiguity about the nature of the offense. In 1890 Henry Stephen pointed out that under Roman law "stealing away a woman from her parents or guardians and debauching her, was made equally penal whether she consented or not." The crime was one of theft, a young virgin being perceived as the property of her parents; consent was not an issue. The Saxons and Normans had treated rape as a crime of violence with consent a crucial consideration. Their laws had included special provisions to prevent malicious accusations. As Stephen indicated, while the English tradition acknowledged a woman's ability and right to consent, it also made the offense very difficult to prove. The modern definition of rape comes from a statute of Elizabeth I, which states that rape is "the carnal knowledge of a woman forcibly and against her will." Although several statutes after that altered the sentencing (for example, capital punishment for rape was abolished in 1841), the basic definition remained unchanged.[45]

This legal definition of rape left a great deal open to interpretation. Exactly how much resistance was necessary to establish that the act had been against the will of the woman was left to the discretion of the judge and jury. Since consent was the crucial consideration and third-party witnesses were rare, the verdict often depended on whether the court chose to believe the victim or the accused. Most judges and jurors still carefully heeded the warning of the seventeenth-century commentator Sir Matthew Hale that rape "is an accusation easy to be made and hard to be defended by the party accused; one wherein the court and jury may with ease be imposed upon, the heinousness of the offense many times transporting them with indignation, whereby they may be over hastily carried to the conviction of the accused on the testimony of false and malicious witnesses."[46] In fact judges and juries in Victorian Kent fought against such impositions manfully: the conviction rate in rape trials was only 41 percent—for felonies generally it was 74 percent.

But acquittal and conviction were not the only possibilities. Only 21 percent of the men accused of rape actually stood trial for that offense. Twenty-six percent of the charges of rape or attempted rape heard by Kentish magistrates were either dismissed or heard at petty sessions as minor offenses. In a few cases the reduced charges were appropriate, but more often the magistrates were clearly overstepping their authority. In 1859 the Ashford magistrates heard a case in which a sixteen-year-old transient orphan had been assaulted on a public road. A surgeon testified as to marks of violence and evidence that the victim had been a virgin before the attack. The accused, a wagoner, had scratch marks on his face, and witnesses had had to pull him off his victim. Nevertheless the magistrates found him guilty of common assault only and fined him 10s. In another case the magistrates dismissed a laborer accused of raping two teenage girls at knife-point. Despite the scratches on the man's face, the bench felt the man could not be held for trial as the victims were to blame for not helping each other more. Another justice of the peace said of an attack on a fifteen-year-old: "It was a serious charge, but a jury would probably not convict, therefore the prisoner is discharged."[47]

The grand jurors were also reluctant to indict for rape. Grand juries in Kent heard 321 cases of sexual assault on adult women between 1859 and 1880 (cases involving the sexual molestation of children will be considered in the next chapter). They brought no bills of indictment in 11 percent of the cases, indicted 31 percent of the defendants for rape, and returned an indictment for attempted rape, assault with intent to ravish, or indecent assault in the remaining 58 percent of cases (Table 3-1). While medical evidence was usually included in the depositions presented to the grand jury, the decision as to whether the charge should be rape or attempted rape was rarely influenced by whether the act had actually been completed. Rather, the lesser charges were used when "respectable" men were accused of rape and the evidence was too serious for the case to be dismissed altogether. In at least one case the reverse procedure was used. After sentencing a coachman to seven years' penal servitude for the rape of a gentleman's daughter, Justice Byles "was pleased to state that the young lady [the victim] would leave the court a virgin."[48] Whether her social status reinstated her virtue or merely rendered the charge more serious than the physical evidence indicated is unclear.

"Indecent assault" had an even vaguer legal definition than did rape. The law itself merely described the offense as "an indecent assault on a female person." Justice Brett explained to one jury: "I cannot lay down the law as to what is or is not an indecent assault beyond saying that it is what all right-minded men, men of sound and wholesome feelings would say was indecent."[49] Indecent assault cases could be heard at quarter sessions as well as the assize. The maximum sentence for indecent assault was two years, but 42 percent of those convicted served less than six months.

Table 3-1. Verdicts and Sentences for Sexual Assaults on Adult Females*

	Indecent assault		Attempted rape		Rape	
Sentence	Number	Percent	Number	Percent	Number	Percent
Convicted	78	83	59	67	41	41
6 months or less	33	42	12	20	0	0
7–18 months	41	53	34	58	0	0
2–5 years	4	5	12	20	6	15
More than 5 years	0	0	1	2	35	85
Total charges	94		88		99	

*Percentages are of those convicted.

Because of the seriousness of the offense, rape trials could only be heard at the assize. But the professional judges also had some qualms about rape cases. At the spring assize in 1878 Justice Henry Manistey of Queen's Bench dismissed all the rape cases on the assize calendar before any evidence was presented. At another session Lord Chief Justice Cockburn dismissed a case without a hearing because he believed it was incredible that the accused, a respectable married father of four, could possibly have raped a teenage domestic servant. In this case the magistrates had set bail at £300 because of the serious injuries suffered by the victim.[50]

Even in those cases in which the jury was actually allowed to hear the evidence the prosecution faced a very difficult task. Though the law itself did not mention physical injury, most judges and juries assumed that anything less than a violent struggle implied that the act had not been against the will of the woman. Justice Mellor advised one jury that a case "might turn out not to be a rape as there were no marks of violence upon the person of the prosecutrix." In another case a soldier was acquitted of rape because the victim had "evidently, to a certain extent, been consenting as her injuries were very slight." Any indication of carelessness on the part of the victim could destroy a case. A man accused of raping a woman in a hop field was acquitted "not because the jury thought no assault had been committed, but because she had acted foolishly in going with the prisoner through the gardens. But for this he would have been doubtless convicted."[51]

Given these assumptions, defense attorneys routinely tried to establish consent regardless of the circumstances. In 1872 a laborer was accused of raping a wealthy farmer's daughter in a public park at two o'clock in the afternoon. His defense attorney asked the victim, who still bore bruises from a savage beating: "Did you not smile up at the prisoner?" At the same session Alfred Ralph, a bricklayer with seven previous convictions of indecent assault and attempted rape, was indicted for raping a seventeen-year-old girl who had been returning from church. A surgeon testified that evidently she had been stunned by a blow to the back of the head and then raped. The defense produced a witness (Ralph's cousin) who swore that Ralph and the victim "looked happy together." Ralph was acquitted.[52]

Judges and juries also assumed consent if the victim and the defendant were even slightly acquainted. A young man accused of raping a young woman who had agreed to let him walk her home was acquitted at the judge's direction. He had apologized and she had shown too little resistance. In a similar case, a tailor's assistant raped a sixteen-year-old girl. After the assault, the man had gone to the girl's parents to apologize, telling them "he knew he had treated the girl very badly and would marry her at once." The victim's father had ordered him out of the house. After hearing the prisoner's deposition that "he had often romped with her in the kitchen and she never objected," the grand jury chose not to indict.[53]

Despite the difficulties prosecutors faced, rape was considered a serious offense. Men convicted of rape received higher sentences on average than those convicted of any other crime except murder. In Kent forty-one men were convicted of rape between 1859 and 1880, and all of them received sentences of at least five years' penal servitude. It is the circumstances in these cases that provide the practical definition of rape regardless of the statutes. Based on the evidence in these cases, rape was defined as a brutal act of violence usually committed in a public place on an apparently respectable woman who was previously unknown to her assailant and had done nothing even to acknowledge his presence. In at least 70 percent of the convictions, the assault occurred in public and the victim and the accused were total strangers. Thirty percent of the victims in these cases sustained permanent injuries, and 25 percent were victims of gang rapes.

Public assaults were more likely to result in convictions for two reasons. First, witnesses were more likely to be present. As Justice Chanell told a grand jury, "it was extremely important to see whether the parties charged and the prosecutrix had been surprised or at all discovered in the act, so as to see whether the woman might or might not have been the consenting party." Second, assaults in public were particularly disturbing. As one justice explained, "it was heinous that a married woman could not leave her home in broad daylight without being set upon." Maintaining public order was as important as protecting women. One magistrate told a man convicted of an indecent assault on a married working woman that he "had been guilty of very disgraceful conduct which would not be permitted on a Sunday." Most judges seemed to agree with the magistrate who remarked that "things had come to a pretty pass if respectable young women returning to their master's house were to be attacked with impunity."[54]

Once inside the master's house, however, the rules might change and judicial officials were considerably less concerned about the safety of young women. Young domestic servants were particularly likely to receive short shrift from the courts. Only one employer was convicted of raping his servant. Sixty-five percent of the employers accused of raping servants were indicted for indecent asault; half of those so indicted were acquitted, and all but two of those convicted were let off with a fine. The one exception was Thomas Parker, who had publicly boasted of twenty-five sexual assaults on a thirteen-year-old servant; he was sentenced to fifteen months. The other jail sentence for an indecent assault was given to a retired army captain who had raped a servant in a railway carriage. He was sentenced to three months and was "clearly stunned at the sentence."[55]

According to the rules of evidence, a rape victim's credibility could be judged from the circumstances: "If she presently discovered [made known] the offense and made search for the offender; if the party accused fled; these and the like are concurring circumstances which give greater probability to her evidence."[56] Obviously, if the rapist held a superior position, he was unlikely to flee. If the victim were very young and in his employ, she might well hesitate to come forward with the charge. In 30 percent of the cases in which domestics charged their employers with rape, the magistrates dismissed the charges, leaving the victims bereft of both reputation and employment. Employers could also take legal vengeance. In one case a young girl had her employer arrested after suffering repeated sexual assaults. The magistrates dismissed the charges against him and fined her for being absent from service without permission.[57]

Outraged women were expected to complain, yet any working woman was keenly aware of her position. One girl whose employer had come to her room and raped her in the middle of the night explained that she had been afraid to scream because she feared her mistress would blame her. When two sons of a gentleman were accused of raping a maidservant, the victim explained that she had been too ashamed to tell anyone other than the cook and her assailants' sister about the assault. The defense attorney asked whether it was "reasonable to suppose that a young woman could be forcibly violated in such circumstances? Why had she quietly served at breakfast the very man who she desired to make out had committed this unpardonable outrage upon her?" Both defendants claimed to have had sex with her dozens of times with her consent. The magistrates dismissed the case.[58]

Some employers felt that financial compensation could justify a sexual assault. A gentleman charged with the rape of a fourteen-year-old servant was shocked when her parents refused to take money to drop the charges. Her parents' faith in the system may have been shaken, however, when he was let off with a £5 fine. When the earl of Norbury was charged with the rape of a fourteen-year-old servant his attorney argued that "the girl has no cause for complaint for, assuming her statement to be true, that Lord Norbury had been with her, she had received compensation." Another employer, Thomas Screech, raped his seventeen-year-old servant and then bragged of his conquest to the neighborhood constable. In a medley of all the standard excuses, Screech's attorney argued that the girl's testimony was invalid because she was unsure of the date; that there had been no assault; and that the girl had consented and Screech had paid her. Both Lord Norbury and Screech were fined £1 for common assault.[59]

The verdicts and sentences in cases involving employers and servants illustrate the fundamental consideration in most rape trials—the perceived character of the victim versus the perceived character of the accused. Attorneys argued, often successfully, that a client's respectability rendered him incapable of committing a rape or an indecent assault. Frequently, even during sentencing, judges would refer to the respectability of the prisoner. Instead of the assault stripping the offender of his credibility, more often his respectable status was grounds for acquittal or a reduction in sentence. Only 34 percent of men who were described as respectable and accused of sexual assaults were convicted of any offense, and only one respectable man was convicted of rape. The figures for offenders who were not deemed respectable were 59 percent convicted of some offense and 22 percent convicted of rape.

Constables could almost always rely on their uniforms as proof of good character. At least seven policemen were charged with sexual assaults and every one was either acquitted or dismissed with a small fine. When Constable Benjamin Watson was accused of raping a seventeen-year-old girl, he was acquitted after the girl "confessed she had previously made a charge of the same nature against another man." Three years later Watson was again charged with an indecent assault. The magistrate, describing Watson as "a respectably dressed young man with an excellent character," refused to hear any evidence. Magistrates dismissed charges against a Maidstone policeman who admitted entering a woman's home at night and indecently assaulting her because "the complainant had not borne a particularly moral character, and it was further contended that nothing but a little harmless fun had passed between the two." When a borough constable in Dover was charged with rape, his attorney argued that his being a veteran of the Crimea "stamped him as a man utterly incapable of committing such an offense." Despite eyewitnesses to the assault, "respectable men" testified to the defendant's good character. He was fined 10s. for common assault. Another man charged with the rape of a twelve-year-old domestic servant was acquitted despite several witnesses. The man's brother-in-law testified that he had "never known anything against the prisoner and he had been a police constable for four years."[60]

Officers in the military were also given special consideration. In 1865, a Royal Marine lieutenant was charged with assaulting a fourteen-year-old girl at a fair. He had grabbed her, dragged her into some bushes and thrown her to the ground. Witnesses, hearing her screams, had rescued her and handed him over to the police. At the trial, the victim "underwent a stringent and lengthy cross-examination; her answers were given most clearly, and her evidence in no way shaken; although she wept bitterly and fainted away when outside the court." Her rescuers and the arresting officers all swore that the accused had offered them money not to testify. The defense attorney warned of "the danger of convicting upon such testimony. A conviction would lead to his client's loss of prospect for life. Although he did not deny that she had been molested to some extent, he urged that she had exaggerated what had occurred." After a few respectable witnesses testified to the defendant's good character, he was acquitted.[61]

It was not commission of a sexual assault but imprisonment for it that damaged a man's respectability. After a man was convicted of an attempted rape, the newspaper noted that "the penalty [two months] is a very heavy one and its consequences may be utterly ruinous to a career of hitherto unsullied respectability." In another case, a woman pleaded for leniency for the young man convicted of the attempted rape of her daughter because she feared a long sentence would destroy his prospects. Twice, married women who had required medical treatment after assaults refused to testify against their assailants as they did not wish to injure their characters. In a case in which a retired military hero was convicted of the attempted rape of a lady in a railway carriage, the sentencing judge explained, "I have to treat this case as a sudden outbreak of wickedness in a man who up to this time has borne a high character. In these circumstances, I wish to spare you the physical degradation, which would probably be to you a torture, which would prevent you retrieving your character." He fined the defendant £500 and sentenced him to twelve months without hard labor. Respectable men might be accused of committing sexual assaults. They might even be convicted. But their respectablity and character were not seriously undermined unless they served a sentence at hard labor with common criminals.[62]

An editorial published after two respectable men were convicted and fined for indecent assault reveals the firm conviction that charges against respectable men were not truly credible. "A police officer whose business is to protect the public and a gentleman who was able to bring forward the most respectable witnesses are not the persons we should be inclined to suspect of such acts." Still, the editor felt these extraordinary cases might serve as a warning. "It will probably have a salutary effect upon those detestable fellows who prowl about our streets apparently ready to take any mean advantage they may be able." The editor believed such types were readily identifiable. "Policemen should keep an eye upon the whole fraternity and bring to justice every man who dares in any way to molest women or children."[63]

Clearly respectable men would not belong to such a fraternity. The very word "rape" evoked the image of a delicate woman brutally assaulted by a subhuman beast. As one defense attorney argued, "[I]t seemed to him almost incredible that a man at all above the level of an animal should without speaking with a woman or having the slightest indication given him that his advances would be received should [*sic*] behave in such a manner." Even repeat offenders were not stigmatized as members of the fraternity. In 1877 a man charged with indecent assault was shown to have been convicted over twenty times for similar offenses. The maximum sentence for indecent assault was two years; he was fined £2 and released. When another laborer with several prior convictions, including a ten-year sentence for rape, was convicted of a sexual assault on a three-year-old child, he was sentenced to one month.[64]

Theoretically a woman's right to protection under the law was absolute. Legally, raping a prostitute was just as much a criminal offense as raping a lady. Stephen noted with some dismay that "the law of England holds it to be a felony to *force* even a harlot."[65] But law and practice were not synonymous. In 1864 Justice Charles Pollock took pains to explain to a grand jury that "whatever the occupation of a female, or in whatever way she may choose to earn her living, she is entitled to protection from brutal violence." The grand jury then duly indicted two soldiers for rape, but after the defense attorney pointed out that the victim had been a prostitute for fourteen years, the jury acquitted them. In 1876 the grand jury refused to return indictments in three cases involving assaults on prostitutes despite Justice John Huddleston's admonition that "these unhappy women commanded the protection of the law as much as the most virtuous."[66]

When a victim was a prostitute or a drunkard, the conviction rate dropped to 10 percent. Under the rules of evidence, the victim's character could be considered in assessing her credibility as a witness. The rules stated that "if she be of evil fame, this carries a strong presumption that her testimony is false or feigned."[67] One laborer indicted for the rape of a married woman was acquitted after the defense "elicited a number of facts that showed her character previous to marriage had been shamefully immoral." In another case magistrates dismissed charges after a police constable described a victim as "dissipated, drunken and forward." Even assize judges did not always believe in equal protection. When Justice Kelly learned that a rape victim had a record of thirty-three arrests for drunkenness, he stopped the trial despite a grand jury indictment and eye-witness testimony.[68]

The social status of the victim was always a consideration. In 1863 the Ashford newspaper reported that "great indignation has been produced by several brutal assaults on females." Three "respectable working women" had been attacked. "But in one instance very lamentable consequences have ensued. A lady was going to tea at the house of a friend when a fellow suddenly sprang out upon her and most shamefully assaulted her." The lady had been "in violent hysterics ever since."[69] The paper did not report the effect of the assaults on the working women; presumably they went back to work. Since the ideal image of a lady called for sexual ignorance, hysteria was the only possible response. Working women, however, were expected to cope with reality. Every case of sexual assault involving a victim identified as a lady went to trial, and 87 percent of cases resulted in a conviction. In jury trials where the victim was a domestic servant, the conviction rate dropped to 43 percent. In addition, magistrates dismissed the charges in 40 percent of the cases in which the victim was a working woman. However, despite the different expectations for ladies and working women, the judicial bias against women was still more compelling than considerations of social status. The laborer convicted of the four assaults in Ashford was sentenced to only six months.[70]

It was difficult for the males who ran the criminal justice system to fully comprehend the criminality of rape. In the years since Steven Marcus offered William Acton as a representative of "the official views of sexuality held by Victorian society," further research has indicated that many of Acton's contemporaries found his views bizarre and eccentric. But many Kentish judges and jurors seem to have agreed with Acton's assessment of male sexuality. "Virility seems necessary to give a man that consciousness of his dignity, of his character as lord and ruler, of his importance. . . . It is a power, a privilege of which the man is, and should be proud."[71] While it was the duty of a respectable man to refrain from abusing this power, sexual aggression was perceived as normal, healthy, and inevitable. Judges often viewed sexual assaults as little more than regrettable lapses of self-control. One young man of "good character" convicted of the attempted rape of a respectable elderly woman was sentenced to only six months as "it had only been a drunken impulse."[72]

A male under the age of fifteen could not be convicted of rape regardless of the circumstances. One Kentish youth was acquitted of the rape of an eleven-year-old girl after his father and sister swore he was only fourteen. When the victim's father went before the court with a birth certificate showing the accused was already fifteen, the magistrates refused to grant a charge of perjury and advised the father to forget the entire incident. Even when the accused was legally of age some judges reduced sentences for young assailants. When a seventeen-year-old boy was convicted of the attempted rape and strangulation of a fifteen-year-old girl, the judge sentenced him to only six weeks, explaining that the leniency was on account of youth. In another case a twenty-one-year-old man, convicted of a sexual assault on a seven-year-old girl, was sentenced to six months. Justice Mellor explained that he deserved leniency "on account of his youth and previous good character." At the same assize Mellor sentenced a sixteen-year-old boy with no prior convictions to seven years' penal servitude for setting fire to a stack of hay.[73]

These allowances for "normal" impulses and youthful exuberance meant that sexual assaults were rarely perceived as inherently criminal. The original Roman laws against rape had conceived it as a property crime against the male relatives of the victim. Although the English laws had never completely accepted the Roman concept, the presumption that women were the property of men was still important. Judges accepted the distinction between rape and adultery or promiscuity, but the loss of virginity or marital chastity reduced a woman's value regardless of the circumstances. Justice Henry Hawkins told a man convicted of raping a twelve-year-old that "he had ruined a poor little girl."[74] The concept of rape as the theft of virtue also altered perceptions as to who was the injured party. Men sometimes accepted monetary compensation from men who had assaulted their wives or daughters. One case was dropped after a man accepted a sovereign from a man accused of raping his sixty-year-old wife. Another man took 12s. to drop his wife's case. In both instances a surgeon had already sworn that there was medical evidence of rape and injury.[75] Though rape victims had the right to prosecute independently, judges routinely dismissed charges if the victim's male protector had accepted compensation.

The ideal male/female relationship was one in which the male was the strong protector and guardian of the weak and innocent female. To be worthy of protection by the courts a woman needed to be under the supervision of a man. Though most men probably believed that assaults on respectable women were wrong, the idea that unsupervised women were available was also widespread. In discussing a case in which a woman had been raped in a railway car, Justice Brett remarked, "It seems to suggest that a defenseless woman, if she is alone in a public conveyance with a man, may expect some outrage from him. It is not true. . . . There may be now and then a man who gives way to passion, but it is not characteristic of this country."[76] It may not have been characteristic, but "giving way to passion" was not necessarily criminal, either. The mental step was easily made from the position that all women should be under the protection and supervision of men to the view that those who were not under such control were fair game for tests of manhood or outbursts of youthful exuberance.[77]

Sexual assaults by normal men were called "drunken impulses" or "sudden outbreaks of wickedness" or "harmless fun" or "seduction." By this logic, if a woman had escaped supervision and provoked an assault or allowed herself to be seduced there was no victim and no crime. Women who brought rape charges were themselves suspect. In court records and newspapers the "prosecutrix" is usually depicted as careless at best, and often as deceitful, unnatural, and hopelessly corrupt as well. The alleged assault is often referred to as a seduction. As one *prosecuting* attorney explained to a jury, "He admitted that the defendant could not, for an attempted debauch, be convicted of an attempt to violate. . . . If it was seduction, it was not a criminal offense." Justice Brett then directed the jurors to remember that the issue in an attempted rape case was not whether the accused "intended to compass his object partly by force, partly by persuasion, and partly by exciting her passions, but whether he intended to use all the force of which he was master, and to use brutal violence to effect his object."[78]

If a victim had suffered serious and lasting physical injuries, conviction was more likely. This was partly because the injury proved lack of consent, but injury also had a psychological effect. The courts were most sympathetic to women when they had been rendered completely helpless. As Justice Kelly told a grand jury, "whatever might be the character of a woman, she was entitled to be protected against the violence of men." In addition, the criminality of rape was more comprehensible to an all-male jury when the physical violence was severe enough to constitute a felonious assault regardless of the sexual element. Two brick-makers who had beaten and raped two female field-workers were sentenced to twenty years each because their victims had required lengthy hospitalization. Lust could be excused; gratuitous violence could not.[79]

But if there were no serious injuries men saw no evidence of a crime so heinous as to be called rape. One defense attorney complained that the prosecution had unfairly "insinuated because he [the defendant] yielded to temptation and seduced a girl, he was guilty of committing a rape on her; but if they believed that statement, no man against whom a charge of that kind was brought would ever have the slightest chance." In this case a married man was accused of raping a sixteen-year-old servant. Neighbors had seen the girl running out into the street in terror. A surgeon testified that she had been raped and severely beaten. The defense attorney expressed his regrets for the seduction but argued that "in hundred of other cases of similar character the prisoners had been justly acquitted." While the defense attorney was probably right about the record for acquittals, in this case his adversary cleverly pre-empted the character argument. The prosecuting attorney pointed out that the victim was the respectable daughter of respectable working people and that "the girl's character was at stake as well as the prisoner's because if they came to the conclusion that her evidence was false it would stamp her for life as a bad character." The jury returned a guilty verdict and Justice Willes sentenced the man to ten years.[80] The prosecuting attorney had used the physical injury and the threat to the victim's character to create empathy in the jury. Since men could not be rape victims, he reminded them of losses they could understand from their own experience.

But this case was an exception. Most victims of sexual assaults were deemed to have lost their character as well as their chastity. The women were blamed for failing to protect themselves from "normal" male impulses. Stephen argued that the Romans supposed that women "never go astray, without the seduction and arts of the other sex. . . . But our English law does not entertain quite such sublime ideas of the honor of either sex as to lay the blame of a mutual fault on one of the transgressors exclusively."[81] In fact, if the act were consensual the blame lay most heavily on the woman. The most striking example of this is a case from Bromley: "Henry Wells, laborer and Emma Bishop were charged with committing an immoral offense in the cricketing field at Bromley. The case having been proved the female prisoner was committed for one month's hard labour, and the other prisoner was discharged."[82]

A woman who brought a charge of sexual assault was making a public issue of her loss of virtue. Such brazenness was highly suspect. As one defense attorney told a jury hearing a case of attempted rape: "Now, the complainant, upon her own confession—and she seemed to glory in the fact—was the wife of a returned convict, the mother of a prostitute, and one who spent her days in rioting and her nights in debauchery. The complainant was therefore just one of those women likely to prefer a charge of this kind."[83] Allowing brazen women to take advantage of men would only create more problems. As the attorney general warned the House of Commons in 1873, "The more we make a woman feel that she was to look after herself and not yield to inducements to go wrong, the better in his judgement would it be for the whole female sex. It was not the really virtuous who were ready to expose their shame."[84]

Rape victims were suspect on at least three counts: they were female, they had been at least temporarily outside the supervision of male guardians (it was unthinkable that their guardians might have been their assailants), and they were publicly announcing their loss of sexual innocence. Judges and jurors frequently concluded that no man should lose his respectability, let alone his freedom, for the mere seduction of such unworthy creatures.

4

Children

It is very hard to be punished so long as I have been and kept away from my children.[1]

Statement by a woman convicted
of killing her four-month-old son

Although women were at a disadvantage in Victorian society, children were even more vulnerable. The 1861 census states that "Among the unproductive classes are children; their playful acts and joys which they give their parents have no exchange value."[2] But for many poor families unproductive members were a luxury. Normally children under the age of ten were not employed, but there were no guarantees that anyone else would provide for them. The Victorian state had neither the inclination nor the funds to assume the responsibilities of parents. Ideally the Victorian family was a sanctuary into which the government should never intrude. The reluctance to interfere with the family was an important reflection of basic attitudes toward liberty, self-sufficiency, and the role of the law. As one philanthropist explained in 1874, "That unit, the family, is the unit upon which a constitutional government has been raised. . . . Whatever the laws have touched they have not invaded this sacred precinct."[3]

The degree to which the laws might interfere with parental rights and responsibilities was the central issue in a series of court cases heard during the 1870s. The Peculiar People, a religious sect in Kentish London, banned all medical treatment because they believed faith alone should suffice. The question of whether religious liberty gave them the legal right to deny medical aid to their children was first raised in 1872 when two children died of smallpox. Their father, John Hurry, was indicted for manslaughter. In his deposition he explained, "I called in no medical advice, it is contrary to my creed. I trust in the Lord for being solely able to save the life of my child." The significance of the issues involved was not lost on the attorneys. The prosecutor pointed out that:

> He would not dispute the sincerity of the religious opinions held by the defendant, but he argued that those opinions being contrary to the community, and the results being productive of great public injury, they ought to be discountenanced and condemned by the law. He added that the prosecution was brought by the parochial authorities and was brought in no vindictive feeling, but simply in the public interest.

The defense attorney likened the case to witchburnings and cited "religious tyranny and medical despotism" as its cause: "When to the other vices of this country a slavish fear of contagion was added, the glory of England would truly have departed." Hurry was convicted of "unlawfully neglecting to provide medical aid to his children whereby their lives were endangered." Hurry assured Justice Byles that while his sect had previously been unclear about the law on this subject, "now they knew it they will submit to it as they were the last people who would break the laws of their country." Hurry was released on a £50 recognizance.[4]

But the interpretation of the law depended on the presiding judge, and in 1874 Justice Pigott rendered a different interpretation. Another member of the sect was indicted for allowing his two-year-old son to die from pleurisy. Although a physician testified that the child had suffered a great deal and could have been saved with medical care, Pigott ruled that "there was no case to go to the jury of any crime. I am clearly of the opinion that no judge sitting in the Criminal Court would be justified in saying that a parent who exercised his best judgement, though a perverted one, in dealing with his child was guilty of criminal negligence." A year later Justice Blackburn heard a case in which the circumstances were virtually identical: a two-year-old child had died of pleurisy and the father, John Downes, had failed to provide medical aid. After noting that he was familiar with Pigott's decision in the earlier case, Justice Blackburn told the jury: "In my opinion the law casts a duty upon a father who has custody of a helpless infant to provide all that is reasonably believed necessary for the child including if it be ill the advice of persons reasonably believed to have medical skill and I shall ask the jury to find the prisoner guilty." The jury convicted Downes as directed and Blackburn sentenced him to four days. In September 1876 Downes appeared before the court again. This time his seventeen-month-old daughter had died of scarlet fever. Downes argued that he "had never heard it said that they were compelled by law to have a doctor." The clerk of the court who recalled the earlier case assured Justice William Field that the precedent had been clear. Field sentenced Downes to three months in prison.[5]

While Downes had certainly heard Blackburn's statement regarding the law, his position was still defensible. The judicial and medical experts disagreed. Pigott had based his ruling, at least in part, on the fact that there was no absolute proof that a physician could have saved the child. The lack of judicial consensus reflected more than just doubt about the efficacy of medical care, however. The more profound issue was whether the state had the right to compel a parent to act against his own beliefs in regard to his child. Pigott believed parental rights were inviolate so long as the beliefs were sincere and the intentions good. Blackburn believed that the law could and should compel parents to behave "reasonably."

The issues raised in the Peculiar People cases were given a wider hearing as a result of the controversy over smallpox vaccination. In 1853 Parliament had passed a law requiring all parents to have their children vaccinated within four months after birth. Such legislation was philosophical anathema to many Liberals who saw it as a violation of liberty and conscience. As a concession to opponents of compulsion, no funding was provided for enforcing the law. The legislation having been rendered meaningless, smallpox epidemics continued. In 1869 the Vaccination Act authorized funding of £20,000 for enforcement and made failure to comply punishable by a 20s. fine.[6]

The legislation was highly controversial. Its backers argued that public health took precedence over freedom of conscience and parental autonomy. While opponents saw it as a violation of liberty, they also feared vaccination as a threat to health. Thomas Brookwell, chairman of the Anti-Compulsory Vaccination League in Kent, had been fined for refusing to have his other children vaccinated after his eldest son suffered serious complications as a result of the vaccine. The first meeting of the Anti-Vaccination League in Kent was held in Dartford at the Working Man's Institute. At this and future meetings physicians and others lectured on the dangers and inefficacy of the vaccine. One speaker argued that the vaccine was part of a plot by doctors to keep diseases in the world so that they would become rich. Another claimed doctors favored the vaccine because it caused consumption. At a meeting at the Rochester Corn Exchange a memorial was ratified for presentation to the prime minister: "Vaccination is a dangerous and useless practice; it is a violation of civil and religious liberty and a bill should be introduced for repeal of these unjust and tyrannical Acts."[7]

In addition to medical qualms, the act was also considered objectionable because it overrode the principle of double jeopardy. A parent would be fined over and over until his child was vaccinated. Default in payment of the fine resulted in seizure of property or imprisonment. A person who violated this law could not fully repay his debt to society with anything less than full compliance. The frustrations experienced by the opponents of compulsory vaccination and the implacability of those who had the law on their side is apparent in the following account of a hearing at Rochester:

> Samuel Joseph West was again charged with neglecting to have his child vaccinated. The Defendant admitted the charge and produced a certificate which he stated proved that a child had died from vaccination. He therefore showed cause why he should not have his child vaccinated. The Clerk said that was no cause whatever in law.
>
> *West:* Why are not other people punished like me? Why is there one law for me and another law for other people?
>
> *Clerk:* You must not allow your temper to get the master of you. Do you deny that your child is unvaccinated?
>
> *West:* No and it never shall be so long as I breathe. If I steal a horse or kill a man I am only punished once; here I am punished several times over. (*to vaccination officer:*) This parliament will not be dissolved before you'll have to get another situation or go to the Union.
>
> *Chairman:* Hold your tongue or it will be the worse for you.
>
> *West:* Why don't you punish other people?

> *Chairman:* You are fined twenty shillings and eight shillings costs. Will you pay?
>
> *West:* No, I will not pay. I will rot in gaol before I'll have my child vaccinated.
>
> *Chairman:* Fourteen days.
>
> Defendant again broke out in a violent tirade against the law and was removed from court by order of the Bench.

West was not alone in his martyrdom. In 1878 C. W. Nye was welcomed back from his eighth prison term for failing to have his child vaccinated. A procession from the railway station concluded with a mass meeting at the Corn Exchange, where speakers asked that vaccination be made a penal offense.[8]

The Vaccination Act set highly significant precedents in that it gave the state the power to compel a parent to have a medical procedure performed on his child and gave the courts considerable power to punish non-compliance. The anti-vaccination forces may have had valid points regarding the law, but they were on shaky grounds medically. The vaccine worked, and no argument about individual liberty could win over a procedure that eventually would eliminate one of the world's most dreaded diseases. The individual's conscience, his scientific and religious principles, and his control over his own children were all superseded by the state's obligation to protect society as a whole. In this important early battle between social welfare and parental rights and liberties, social welfare won.[9]

While the state was willing to intervene on matters of public health, the responsibility for the welfare of individual children usually rested solely with their parents. In addition to upholding the ideal of the inviolate family, non-intervention reflected the more practical concern that rate-payers not have to support the children of idle reprobates. One of the leaders of a private charity made his beliefs clear in his opposition to a proposal to give free meals to school children: "It is better, in the interests of the community, to allow the sins of the parents to be visited on the children than to impair the principle of the solidarity of the family and run the risk of permanently demoralizing large members of the population by the offer of free meals to their children."[10]

Officials in Kent were on guard against the dangers of demoralization and unnecessary expense. In 1865 the master of the Rochester Workhouse refused to admit a four-year-old girl found wandering in the streets. A local magistrate reprimanded him, but the master staunchly insisted that until he had proof that the child was an orphan she was not the responsibility of the community. The Poor Law Guardians dealt with many suffering people but they tried to remain objective. As one member told his colleagues, it was important not to let "sympathies run away with judgement. We are acting as men of business."[11]

The law required that parents provide food, shelter, and clothing for their children, and they were liable to a three-year prison sentence if they did not. But to gain a conviction on a charge of parental neglect, the prosecution had to prove that the child's life had been endangered or its health permanently damaged, and that the parents had been financially capable of providing for it. Judges took these provisions seriously. In 1871 Justice Blackburn heard charges against a couple whose six-month-old son weighed only seven-and-a-half pounds. He directed the jury to acquit because the prosecution had not proven that the child's health had been permanently injured nor that the parents had sufficient means to feed it.[12] Parents were expected to apply to the Poor Law Guardians before allowing their children to starve, but only those deemed truly needy and deserving were accepted. Parents who left their children in the workhouse could be punished under the Vagrancy Act. In Kent during the 1860s an average of 71 persons per year were tried summarily for leaving their families chargeable to the parish; in the 1870s the average number of cases rose to 113 per year.

A poignant example of a parent caught in the contradictions of the system is the case of Mary Pevy. Pevy, a thirty-year-old unwed mother from Margate, gave birth to a daughter in the Dover Workhouse in 1877. After she and her daughter were released, Pevy took a job as a cook to support herself and the child. This required her to wean the child and leave her with neighbors. Pevy was arrested for abandoning the child and sentenced to three months in jail. While Pevy was in jail the child was kept at the workhouse, where her health improved markedly. Upon her release from prison Pevy begged the authorities to keep the child at the workhouse, as she had no job and no means of caring for it. Her request was denied. She then pawned her clothes to buy corn flour, bread, sugar, and milk to make gruel to feed the child. When that supply ran out she again applied to the workhouse and was again rejected.

Pevy said the child was ill, but the workhouse physician said there was no evidence of disease; it was merely starving. The child died the next day. When Pevy went to apply for a pauper's grave to bury her little girl, she was arrested for manslaughter.

The workhouse physician attributed the death to poor nutrition as a result of poverty. "Amongst the poor classes the mortality is much greater than amongst the richer class. I account for this by the fact that the poor cannot afford sufficient money to obtain milk, but substitute corn flour and other cheaper and improper food. I do not say that the child had been absolutely starved. I can't say whether the child had been insufficiently fed or deprived entirely of food." Pevy was acquitted but there was no change in the admissions policy of the workhouse.[13]

Of the fifteen people indicted for manslaughter as a result of neglecting a child, ten were women. Since only 17 percent of all persons charged with manslaughter were women, it is clear that the neglect of a child was particularly defined as the fault of the mother. This is interesting in light of the fact that the legal possession of and authority over a child rested entirely with the father. While mothers had no legal authority, fathers apparently bore little of the day-to-day responsibility for child care. When James Tassell, an attorney at Canterbury, was honored for his contributions to the community, he thanked his wife: "If Mrs. Tassell had not done her duty as a wife, and relieved him of all care with reference to his children and household, he should never have been able to do anything."[14] In his study of Victorian fathers in the professional classes, David Roberts concludes that "remoteness, physical and psychological, formed a prominent feature of many a nineteenth century father. . . . [F]or many, children were a bother: they misbehaved, they were noisy and they wasted valuable time."[15]

Though no middle- or upper-class father in Kent was accused of child abuse or neglect, it seems plausible that judges and jurors who felt they had neither the time nor the duty to tend to their own children might sympathize with working-class fathers who offered the same excuse. One defendant successfully argued that he had not noticed that his children were emaciated or that his daughter had been carrying her broken arm with her other hand: he had been at work all day. Another begged the court to excuse his wife's cruelty to the children because if she went to jail it would create problems for him. His statement combined a claim of non-involvement with the presumption that domestic violence was normal and inevitable:

> He had heard that his present wife was unkind to the children, he never saw her beat them severely. His wife was kind to them at first. After she had a child of her own, she was inclined to give them a bang now and then. What was he to do? If he knocked her down and killed her he would be tried for manslaughter; or if he gave her a black-eye he was liable to six months hard labor. "I admit she is of a very excitable temper. If I saw her ill-treat either of my children I would not be accountable for what I did. I hope that you will give me as little trouble as possible. If you punish her you punish the wrong party. You cannot injure her without injuring me. I was never present when she hit the child."[16]

Since fathers were not expected to be actively involved in child care, the courts often accepted neglect by widowers as regrettable but inevitable. When the ten-month-old daughter of a recently widowed plasterer starved to death, the coroner explained that the man had been drinking heavily since his wife's death and had completely ignored the child. The grand jury refused to indict him. In another case a seven-year-old boy was found wandering the streets covered with vermin. Charges against his father were dismissed after he explained that his wife was dead and he could not afford child care.[17]

The courts were reluctant to convict widowers of child neglect or abuse, but they were even less willing to allow the children to become wards of the court. A widower who had broken three of his daughter's bones and had threatened to kill all six of his children was fined and released with the children in his custody. In another case a widower charged with child abuse asked the court to place the child in another home. The magistrate replied that it was not the court's responsibility to provide for his child. When a five-year-old boy, emaciated and covered with bruises, was brought before the Plumstead magistrates the local Poor Law Guardians refused to prosecute the case. Since the child's father was employed and not a pauper, the child was no concern of the Guardians. The case was dismissed.[18]

Though fathers were rarely punished for the neglect of their children, children without legal fathers were at even greater risk. Of the forty-four Kentish homicide victims between the ages of forty-eight hours and twelve years, at least fourteen were illegitimate. Unless the mother had brought a successful paternity suit within one year of birth, the father of an illegitimate child bore no legal responsibility. In one case a couple that had lived together for eight years were accused of abusing their children. The woman was sentenced to six months, but the judge ordered charges against the father dismissed. Since the parents were not legally married the father, according to the judge, "was morally guilty but legally free."[19]

In addition to those who died of neglect, six children were beaten to death by their parents and fourteen others were beaten severely enough to justify indictments against their parents for assault. Beatings classified as assaults must have been extremely severe, for fathers had the legal right to chastise their children and the provision was broad enough to encompass fatal injuries. "Where a parent is moderately correcting his child and happens to occasion his death, it is only misadventure, for the act of correction was lawful; but if he exceeds the bounds of moderation either in the manner, the instrument, or the quantity of punishment, and death ensues, it is manslaughter at least."[20] Moderation is in the eye of the beholder, and magistrates tended to take a broad view of parental rights. A J.P. in Hadlow offered instructions to the mother of a nine-year-old boy who had scratched a fence. After being assured that the father had "knocked the boy down and severely punished him," the magistrate replied: "Tell your husband that flogging is the proper way to punish a boy and not to hit him on the head, because he could get himself into trouble if he injured him."[21]

Even using a weapon was not necessarily treated as a serious offense. A woman who killed her ten-year-old son when she threw a knife at him for being noisy was sentenced to fourteen days. The judge explained that "[s]he and others must know that neither parents nor anyone else can use with impunity such a dangerous weapon as was used in this case." In another case a woman was accused of beating her stepdaughters with a cat-o'-nine-tails and fire-tongs. The prosecutor duly noted that "a parent has a power to inflict a moderate punishment with a lawful weapon but tongs were unlawful."[22]

Since court records only include those cases in which someone felt legal limits had been breached, they are not a valid indication of how many parents actually used corporal punishment. Patricia Branca concluded, based on her study of manuals written for middle-class women, that "by the third-quarter of the century it was a fairly well-accepted principle of child care that physical chastisement was to be rarely employed and only when all else failed."[23] Though the right to chastise was recognised by the law, there were detractors. In 1859 a woman wrote the *Maidstone and Kentish Journal* to complain about having seen small boys beaten in the streets: "I trust your insertion of this will set authorities to rid us of such disgusting evils."[24]

But authorities were very slow to act against child abuse. In Harold Perkin's memorable phrase, the English in the nineteenth century "diminished cruelty to animals, criminals, lunatics and children (in that order)."[25] There are at least two plausible explanations for the chronology: the tradition of chastisement and the unshakable faith in the sacred bonds between parent and child. In 1871 Lord Shaftesbury, who had been a major influence behind much of the legislation against child labor, was asked about legislation to prevent parental abuse. He replied, "[T]he evils you state are enormous and indisputable, but they are of so private, internal and domestic a character as to be beyond the reach of legislation, and the subject, indeed, would not, I think be entertained in either House of Parliament."[26]

Though authorities were reluctant to interfere with the parental right to chastise, they usually responded when cases of gross and deliberate cruelty were brought before them. In 1879 the captain of the Kent County Constabulary took a severely beaten five-year-old boy into his home in addition to bringing charges against the boy's stepfather. The stepfather's attorney argued that the child "was a very bad boy, a spoilt child, and correction was necessary. The boy had killed three chickens and lost half a sovereign. He was obliged to correct him to let him see who was master." Unimpressed, the magistrates sentenced the defendant to two months' hard labor.[27] The most important element in this case was that the police captain took an intense personal interest. Unless an outside adult was aware of a problem and willing to take the necessary steps, child abuse cases were unlikely to come before the courts.

When an incident of abuse did become known, the public reaction was often harsher than that of the magistrates. In one case neighbors pressured authorities to prosecute Stephen Cavey, who had beaten his four-year-old stepdaughter, doused her with cold water, and forced her to stand outside all night. At the trial Cavey admitted he had forced her to eat her own excrement. When he entered the courthouse Cavey had to be surrounded by police officers to protect him from a lynch mob. The quarter sessions chairman told Cavey he "was sorry that anybody existed who would treat a child in that manner. I think you are a dirty brute." Having expressed his indignation he sentenced Cavey to six months, and in the next case sentenced a woman to twelve months for stealing clothes.[28]

Alert neighbors were often the surest protection abused children had. When a couple at Leeds were tried for beating their ten-year-old daughter to death, the local vicar wrote letters to the press pointing out that the parents were strangers in Leeds. The members of the community would have acted immediately had they known about the situation.[29] In almost every case abused children were found in locked houses. When neighbors had an opportunity to become aware of serious abuse, they acted, as seen in the following case from Gillingham, where three children were discovered starved, beaten, and covered with boils.

> Public indignation was speedily aroused on the facts becoming known and on Tuesday afternoon and evening crowds of women in a most excited state assembled in front of the house where the woman was concealed. A large number of tin-kettles were brought. An entrance was effected at length—women and boys entered the house in numbers with the intention of getting hold of the wretched woman. Her husband had taken flight and it was only the kindly interference of the grandmother which prevented her receiving from the hands of the crowd the treatment she richly deserved. On Wednesday the crowd again gathered howling and beating on kettles until about 2 A.M. An effigy was burned. Though the Board of Guardians had immediately issued a prosecution order, the tin-kettling and effigies continued until the woman appeared in court.[30]

The heated public reaction in such cases is particularly significant in light of the debate over historical attitudes toward children.[31] While the courts may have been reluctant to interfere, neighbors were not. Persons who did not love and care for their children were perceived as monstrous and unnatural. In 1863 neighbors of a Dover family reported that three children were being starved and beaten by their parents. After the children had been removed from the home and the mother sentenced to six months' hard labor, the magistrates praised the neighbors for their actions. "It presented only another instance showing the poor were more anxious to assist each other than people in a higher class were apt to imagine."[32]

Despite the magistrates' patronizing tone, child abuse was not limited to the poor, though they were perhaps more likely to be discovered and prosecuted. In 1866 a woman living in a fashionable suburb was charged with beating her stepdaughter with a rope and a poker. On the basis of evidence from the child's governess she was convicted and sentenced to three months. In another case, Adelaid Lomax, the wife of a wealthy retired journalist in Margate, was accused by a servant of abusing her seven-year-old daughter, who had been beaten and starved. At quarter sessions Lomax was sentenced to twelve months' hard labor. A third case was heard at Central Criminal Court in 1863. A downstairs maid testified that her mistress had submerged her four-year-old daughter in cold water and then thrown the child down the stairs. The child had died and the mother, Helen Englehart, was charged with manslaughter. At her trial the defense attorney argued that his client was only guilty of an error in judgement. The jury found her guilty of aggravated assault. Before sentencing her to eighteen months Justice Byles told her, "I know that you have been treated by the authorities with a humanity which you failed to show towards the infant whose death you unquestionably hastened." In cases in which middle-class women were charged with child abuse, the sentences were as heavy or heavier than those normally given to working-class parents. Nothing was less ladylike than abusing a child.[33]

Assaults and homicides involving children were the only crimes in which women were represented in proportion to their numbers in society as a whole. Sixty-one percent of the persons indicted for assaults on children were women, as were 51 percent of those indicted for killing children over forty-eight hours old. Women were expected to be responsible for children, but mothers did not enjoy the same right of chastisement as fathers. Furthermore the use of physical violence was always more acceptable from a man. The fact that women were most likely to kill children may also indicate that male dominance had been accepted and internalized. In twentieth-century studies of women who kill, researchers have found that 40 percent of the victims are husbands and only 21 percent children.[34] In Victorian Kent only one woman killed her husband, while 71 percent of the victims of female killers were children. Though women in Kent seldom attacked their husbands, the only two Kentish women executed for murder between 1832 and 1880 were convicted of murdering their children in retaliation for mistreatment by their husbands.

In 1866 Ann Lawrence was charged with slitting the throat of her four-year-old son and then attacking her husband with a bill hook. In her deposition she said that she and her husband had been happy, "but I have very recently found out that he has got another woman at Malling who has got two or three children by my man." Her husband told the court that she had confessed to him that she had killed the child to get him out of the way, but throughout her trial Ann Lawrence claimed that her husband had killed the child. She was convicted and sentenced to hang. Two weeks before the execution the prison chaplain reported that she had confessed to killing the child while "frenzy-mad" over her husband's infidelity.[35]

The other capital case involving a woman was that of Frances Kidder, who was convicted of drowning her eleven-year-old stepdaughter. Kidder had taken the child out at midnight and returned alone. Neighbors swore they had heard her threaten the child, and when the corpse was discovered it bore signs of a struggle. In her deposition Frances did not mention the child at all. Instead she kept repeating the phrase, "I have always kept myself respectable." Her defense attorney argued that she had actually tried to save the child, and further that "she had been harshly treated by her husband and that had made her reckless." On the day of her execution a crowd burned her husband in effigy, and jury members were quoted as saying that they believed the husband's mistreatment should have been grounds for mercy. The local J.P.s refused to hear charges against those who had burned the effigy.[36]

Killing a child to spite another adult was the motive in at least nine of the child homicides. One man even announced that he intended to have revenge on his lover by killing her five-month-old child. Another man confessed to killing a six-year-old boy because the child's mother had refused to go out with him. After a fight with his seventeen-year-old wife, Charles Brown threw their infant son across the room, crushing its skull. Perhaps the most chilling case of such misdirected anger in Kent was that of Alfred Holder. The twenty-five-year-old army cook calmly explained that he had cut his eleven-month-old son's throat because he wished to be hanged. "It is out of no spite to my wife; it is all through a sergeant of ours. He has tormented me for many months, and tried to injure me all that he could and get me out of my place, and more than that, he has spoken wicked things against my wife and I could not stand it. . . . [S]he could not support the child, so I thought I had better take the child's life than another's, as he had no soul to save."[37]

Of course such behavior unfortunately is not unique to Victorian Kent. Studies done in the 1960s found that the common factor among child homicides was "anger and rage directed toward a child who is an object upon which anger felt toward the murderer's parents, spouse or sibling has been discharged."[38] The motives and circumstances of child homicides in Kent were not markedly different from those of the late twentieth century; modern studies have found that single parents, stepparents, and "unstable emotional relationships" are usually factors in child homicides.[39] In Kent, of the forty-five homicide victims between the ages of forty-eight hours and twelve years, 67 percent were either stepchildren or illegitimate and all but six were killed by a parent or stepparent. In the Kidder case *The Times* reported that Kidder "who was not aware until after their marriage that her husband had a child by another woman seemed to have conceived a great dislike to it." Justice Bramwell explained that he had given the death sentence because the law "was the only protection stepchildren had." Bramwell was not alone in his suspicion of stepparents. When a Chatham magistrate suggested dropping abuse charges against a stepmother since the children had been placed in domestic service and were out of danger, the chairman replied, "Oh nonsense, this is not the only case where children are mistreated by stepmothers." Stepfathers were even more of a threat. In five separate cases in Kent stepfathers battered children to death.[40]

But while the circumstances were familiar, the numbers are not. Forty-three percent of homicide victims in Victorian Kent were under the age of twelve. In England and Wales in 1974, only 4 percent of homicide victims were children; in the United States during 1961–1974, only 3.4 percent. Even after disallowing cases in which an infant was killed by its mother within forty-eight hours after birth, children were still 23 percent of homicide victims in Victorian Kent. Jeremy Sharpe and others have suggested that a high percentage of domestic homicides may simply reflect a low homicide rate among outsiders. While the argument may be valid for earlier periods, it does not hold in this case. In addition to the much higher proportion of child victims, the overall homicide rate in Victorian Kent was nearly twice that of Great Britain in 1974.[41]

The value placed on a child's life as compared with that of an adult can be partially assessed by looking at sentencing patterns in homicide cases. Table 4-1 gives the sentences for all homicides for which the offender was convicted excluding brawls, accidents, and infanticides within forty-eight hours after birth. The discrepancy is obvious; while 55 percent of those convicted of killing adult males were hanged, 68 percent of those convicted of killing children served less than eighteen months.

That the court's estimate of the value of a life was related to age is even more evident in the treatment of the eighty cases in which the victim was less than forty-eight hours old. As Sir James Fitzjames Stephen assured the Capital Punishment Commission, "the crime is less serious than other kinds of murder. You cannot estimate the loss to the child itself, you know nothing about it at all. It creates no alarm to the public."[42] Though there was no explicit legal distinction between infanticide and any other form of homicide, the law did provide another category for such cases. A woman whose infant was found dead under suspicious circumstances could be prosecuted under a statute passed in 1803 that defined the lesser crime of "concealment of the birth of a child." The legislation had been passed as a response to the fact that juries refused to return manslaughter verdicts in such cases.[43]

Both the law and the procedures were lenient in such cases. A magistrate could not order a woman to undergo a physical examination to determine if she had recently given birth.[44] Further, once the charge had been reduced from manslaughter to concealment, the jury could only convict if there was proof that the woman had actively tried to conceal the corpse. No woman in Kent was convicted of killing her newborn infant between 1859 and 1880. Sixty-

Table 4-1. Sentences for Homicides by Age and Gender of Victim

	Victim					
	Men		Women		Children	
Sentence	Number	Percent	Number	Percent	Number	Percent
6 months or less	4	20	6	24	11	39
7–18 months	1	5	1	4	8	29
2–5 years	0	0	5	20	1	4
More than 5 years	4	20	7	28	2	7
Death	11	55	6	24	6	21
Total charges	20		25		28	

two percent of the women so charged were convicted of concealment of birth but received very light sentences; 86 percent of them were under six months. In the seven cases in which the sentence was more than six months, either the corpse had been severely mutilated or the mother had a prior conviction for the same offense. Only one woman received the maximum sentence of two years.

The Capital Punishment Commission of 1866 considered whether such leniency was appropriate and asked witnesses whether infanticide should be considered a separate offense. Justice Bramwell felt that to codify a distinction between infanticide and other types of homicide would set a dangerous precedent; moreover, a legal distinction was unnecessary: "The jury is always told, 'There is a possibility of the child not having been born alive despite the medical evidence, therefore you must acquit her.' Such direction is not reasonable but it is always given and the jury is always glad to acquit." Justice Willes said that if he thought a woman convicted of concealment of birth had actually killed her infant he sentenced her to eighteen months instead of the usual one or two. Justice Kelly probably touched on the central issue when he suggested a special category for cases "involving the murder in the lowest classes by women of their illegitimate children which unfortunately is a very frequent occurrence."[45]

Both the frequent occurrence of infanticide and the court's ambivalence towards it were a reflection of the larger problem in Victorian society of the proper attitude toward illegitimate children.

The concept of marriage as a *legal* requirement was a fairly recent development. A wedding, duly recorded in the parish register, did not become the sole binding form of marriage until Lord Hardwicke's Marriage Act in 1753, and the provisions of the act were not extended to nonconformist chapels until 1836. Jeffrey Weeks argues that "the new marriage laws had the effect of making the betrothal less binding and of sharply differentiating the married from the unmarried, hence making the difference between licit and illicit sex more important."[46]

Such a distinction would make bearing an illegitimate child considerably more shameful. Of course the stigma would be traumatic only for those who were concerned about respectability. That the ideal of premarital chastity was not universally accepted is clear from the fact that between 1840 and 1870 38 percent of the brides in Ashford were pregnant.[47] At petty sessions in 1863 "one female acknowledged that she had three illegitimate children and her sister had five. Their father said they were 'moral and well-conducted girls for Ashford' for which he was strongly censured by the Ashford magistrates." In order to establish paternity a woman had to bring the child's father to court within a year after the birth of the child and produce corroborating witnesses. For women with no aspirations for respectability the procedure was not impossible. In paternity cases, unlike cases of sexual assault, the character of the woman was not a consideration; prostitutes were able to win support cases. A woman in Mersham cheerfully acknowledged that she was receiving paternity payments from five men for six children. Another woman who admitted having seven sweethearts won child support from a young man in Woolwich.[48]

A man's social status would not protect him when the magistrates had to choose between the defendant's resources and those of the parish rate-payers. Doctors, tax collectors, solicitors, and even clergymen lost paternity suits. In 1866 a vicar at Sandwich was ordered to pay child support by the civil courts and was suspended from his clerical duties for three years by the ecclesiastical courts. Ten years later a choirmaster at Rodmersham was named in a paternity suit by his seventeen-year-old servant. He wrote the court asking for leniency as he "had suffered most terribly." The court ordered him to pay 5s. per week and said it was the worst case they had ever seen.[49]

The number of paternity suits being brought in Kent declined during the period from an average of 30 per year in the 1860s to 20 per year during the 1870s. It may be that the social stigma attached to unwed mothers increased. One indication of growing intolerance is the changing coverage given such cases by the Kentish press. Before 1861 the *Maidstone and Kentish Journal* discreetly referred to "affiliation cases" and did not print the names of any of those involved. In August 1861 the paper switched from the term "affiliation" to the considerably stronger "bastardy," and during the late 1860s and 1870s the paper did not hesitate to publish names and circumstances.

The social consequences of unwed motherhood were discussed during a court case in 1866. An attorney objected to allowing testimony from a witness who had an illegitimate child: "It affects her respectability and status in society." The judge replied that "She has as much right to be believed as anyone else. It may affect her respectability, but it does not weaken her credibility."[50] Bearing an illegitimate child would be most traumatic for women who strove for respectability, most notably domestic servants. For them the public humiliation involved in filing a paternity suit could be unbearable. In addition to the social stigma, the legal procedures also worked against them. As John Gillis points out, a respectable woman who was discreet in her affairs would not be able to produce corroborating witnesses for a paternity suit. In his study of infants left at a London foundling hospital, Gillis found that a large proportion of them were the children of "mature women in respectable domestic employment." He suggests that in most cases the parents had planned to marry but, in keeping with the ideology of self-reliance, had delayed the wedding until financial independence was achieved. If the woman became pregnant before marriage was economically feasible, "for men the shame of exposure outweighed the guilt of abandonment."[51]

In the cases Gillis studied the women could leave their babies with a charitable institution, but respectable domestic servants in Kent did not have that option. The fact that illegitimacy and respectability were mutually exclusive doubtless contributed to the rate of infanticide in Kent. Eighty-three percent of the women charged with concealment of birth were domestic servants, and 73 percent of them were twenty-one or older. Rather than being young innocents, they were mature working women who could not cope with unwed motherhood. Many simply chose to deny the reality of pregnancy. The cause of death was usually strangulation or loss of blood from improper severing of the umbilical cord, circumstances that indicate a failure to provide for the child rather than an active decision to kill it. After hiding the child or corpse in a water closet, suitcase, or bureau, most of the mothers returned to their work and tried to pretend that nothing had happened. As one woman told the police, "I was so frightened I did not know what to do." In another case, a forty-year-old cook told a fellow servant, "I think I am going to have a slight miscarriage." She then gave birth to a fully developed live infant and hid the child in a trunk while the other servant ran to tell their mistress. After the body of the infant (who apparently had died of suffocation) was found and the mother arrested, her only comment to the police was, "I was very ill."[52] An illegitimate child was a problem a respectable domestic servant simply could not acknowledge.

The death of an illegitimate newborn was an event the courts saw as regrettable but not particularly serious, provided that its demise was caused by the mother acting alone. Administering poison or any instrument to procure an abortion was a felony with a maximum sentence of life in prison. Providing the instruments to procure an abortion was a misdemeanor punishable by up to three years in prison. Only four abortion cases were heard in Kentish courts between 1859 and 1880, and very little information is available in two of the cases. In one, Jeremiah Reader was indicted for "administering various substances in an attempt to procure a miscarriage"; he was acquitted at the spring assize in 1859. In the other, Ann Emery was convicted at Central Criminal Court in 1875 and sentenced to twelve months for administering a noxious herb to procure miscarriage. In a third case heard at quarter sessions in March 1874, William May, a sawyer, was charged with giving savin, "a noxious herb known to procure miscarriage," to his girlfriend, Sarah Demeza. She had not taken the herb and May had been ordered to pay child support for an infant born in December 1873. Three months later Demeza's father brought charges against May for having given her the drug. At the same quarter sessions Mr. Demeza also charged May with assault, and the court heard a long story about a feud between May and Demeza over a poaching incident. May was convicted and sentenced to six months for providing the means to procure a miscarriage, but there is little evidence of judicial enthusiasm for such proceedings.[53]

The heaviest sentences were given in a case heard at Central Criminal Court in 1869. Henry Timson was accused of "using a certain instrument to procure the miscarriage of Rosina Bush," and William McGrath was charged with "feloniously aiding and abetting Timson." The editor of the Sessions Papers felt the details were unfit for publication, but the *Maidstone and Kentish Journal* reported that Bush, "an innocent and respectable-looking girl of seventeen," had been seduced by McGrath, her cousin's husband. McGrath had sent her to Timson, "a laborer but recently acting as a doctor," who performed the abortion. The first trial ended with a hung jury, but at the second the jury convicted both men. Justice Brett sentenced Timson to ten years and McGrath, whose behavior he described as "base and cruel," to seven years. He also took the opportunity to speak out against abortionists, "who undertook for filthy lucre to assist young women to conceal the immorality of which they had been guilty, and which often led to the worse offense of destroying their children before birth."[54]

Presumably Brett preferred that unwed mothers deal with their problems on their own. In the two concealment-of-birth cases Brett heard in Kent, he gave sentences of two months and nine months. The latter was a case in which the mother had put the child's body in a box and nailed it shut. Brett said it was the worst case he had ever seen. His views on abortion may not have been typical, however; his biographer describes him as having a strongly conservative bias and being "more strong than discreet."[55] Certainly the small number of cases prosecuted indicate there was little judicial concern about abortion.

In addition to abortion and infanticide a third option existed for women, especially domestic servants, who could not keep their infants. Baby farmers were persons who, for a fee, would keep children in their homes. Some baby farmers were trying to provide a much-needed service, others were negligent, and a few were willing to accept a lump-sum payment from the mother with the tacit understanding that she did not wish to see the child again. In 1861 in Tonbridge the twenty-one-month-old illegitimate son of a domestic servant died while in the care of a baby farmer. The child's mother had suspected he was being abused, as his body was covered with bruises and neighbors had reported hearing screams. The baby farmer and her common-law husband were indicted for manslaughter. As was often the case when children were victims, the response of the public was much harsher than that of the courts. After the hearing, "on leaving the court the crowd of persons gathered outside the hall gave loud expression to their indignation against the woman and the two policemen found it so difficult to protect her from violence that it was thought advisable to take her to the railway station in a fly." At the assize the defendants claimed that the child had died from a fall. Since there was no indisputable evidence to the contrary they were acquitted of manslaughter. They were found guilty of assault, however, and sentenced to one month each.[56]

Parliament considered the need to regulate baby farmers in the early 1870s after it was learned that a baby farmer at Brixton had killed sixteen infants. But the M.P.s were cautious, since regulation might reduce the number of places available. If a woman could not find affordable child care her only option might be infanticide. The Infant Life Protection Act of 1872 required registration of persons who kept more than one infant under the age of one year in their homes for more than twenty-four hours, with local authorities setting regulations regarding numbers and facilities. The owners of registered facilities were required to keep a record of the name, age, and sex of all infants in their care and the names and addresses of their parents. The maximum penalty for failure to register or for failing to notify the coroner of the death of an infant in care was six months. Even these strictures were considered too harsh by some. The Committee for Amending the Law in Points Where It Is Injurious to Women argued that "The responsibility for the child in infancy, as in later life, lies with the mother, and we emphatically deny that the state has any right to dictate to them the way it should be fulfilled."[57] One of the major sponsors of the bill, Dr. Lyon Playfair, argued that protecting infants was good economics in the long run. "It would surely be right to inspect the upbringing of helpless children who by neglect might become so weak and stunted in frame that they would fill our hospitals and workhouses in future life, and yet who by care might be so nurtured as to become useful members of society." But in the short term the value of such children was virtually nil. As one M.P. pointed out, "when they advertised for a nurse to adopt an infant for life at a premium of from £5 to £10 and got some 300 answers, as witnesses had stated, clearly the speculators in adoption know that the value of the life was uncommonly small."[58]

That this was so was demonstrated again in Kent in 1879 when Charlotte Martin, a baby farmer at Gravesend, was charged with manslaughter. A two-year-old girl had died while in her care. The child's mother, Eliza Collyns, a domestic servant separated from her husband, paid Martin £2 8s. per month to care for her three children. The Collyns child had died from an inflammation of the brain caused by vermin. The workhouse doctor said it was the worst case he had ever seen: "The death of the child resulted from sheer neglect." More disturbing was that the police had become aware of the death only because no local physician would sign a burial certificate. After Martin was charged with manslaughter it was discovered that she had previously been fined for failing to register and that four other children had died in her care during the previous twelve months. At the assize she was convicted of manslaughter and sentenced to eighteen months.[59]

However horrifying such cases might be, authorities were unwilling to become more actively involved in the problems of unwed mothers and their children. Despite Playfair's arguments about the long-term impact, such children were a burden the state refused to accept on philosophical as well as moral grounds. Hence when a mother chose infanticide or a negligent baby farmer, the courts felt it only fitting that the penalties be fairly light.

The other category of crime in which children were most often victims was sexual assault. Only one man was charged with sexual assault on a male child in Kent between 1859 and 1880: a forty-two-year-old soldier was sentenced to five years' penal servitude for an assault on a six-year-old boy (no further information about the case is available).[60] The law against sexual assaults on a male person did not specify age, so the laws dealing specifically with child-molesting refer only to female children. Little girls who were the victims of sexual assaults were subject to some of the same suspicions and contradictions as adult victims. The law presumed that girls under the age of twelve were too ignorant to understand the nature of a sexual assault and were therefore incapable of giving consent. This presumption was double-edged. It might be assumed that if little girls had no knowledge of sex, an indecent assault would have no meaning for them and would therefore leave them relatively unscathed. In some circles in the eighteenth century the faith in childish innocence was taken to such grotesque extremes that sexual intercourse with a child was recommended as a cure for venereal disease.[61]

In addition to diminishing the perceived gravity of the offense, the assumption that girls under the age of twelve could not understand the nature of a sexual assault undermined the credibility of children as witnesses. When a schoolmaster was tried for indecent assaults on four students, "the case rested entirely on the evidence of the children and at the conclusion of the case for the prosecutor, before defense, his Lordship put it to the jury whether it would be safe to convict under such circumstances. The jury considered it would not and he was acquitted." Ironically, at the same time that a child's sexual ignorance lessened the offense, children were often suspected of fabricating details or encouraging their assailants. In 1867 the sentence of a man charged with the attempted rape of an eight-year-old girl was reduced because the judge believed the child had provoked the assault.[62]

Between 1859 and 1880 at least thirty-nine charges of sexual assaults on girls under the age of twelve were heard and handled summarily by magistrates, who dismissed the charges in nine of these cases and heard the remainder as aggravated assaults. Since the maximum sentence a magistrate could give was six months, such cases tended to be met with verbal outrage but light sentences. In one case the chairman of the Tunbridge Wells petty sessions described an assault on a four-year-old girl as "horrible and wicked, the worst thing a man could be guilty of," and then sentenced the offender to only four months.[63] Only ten men received the maximum sentence of six months, and another ten served less than six weeks or were merely fined.

The reluctance to send cases to trial did not always indicate magisterial indifference. Unless there was a very strong likelihood of conviction it was often thought best not to expose a very young child to the strain of a public trial. Most of the men brought to trial had long reputations as child-molesters. In reporting the arrest of sixty-seven-year-old John Haynes at Dartford, the newspaper added: "It may be mentioned here that this is the third time the old beast has been charged with the same offense, independent of the other acts of indecency towards children when their friends, from feelings of delicacy, refused to prosecute." Often the child was so traumatized she could not testify. In 1862 charges against an elderly man had to be dropped because his seven-year-old victim was "too frightened to give an account of the transaction." In what was widely regarded as divine retribution the accused dropped dead of a heart attack on his way home from the trial.[64]

Neither the leniency of the law nor the light sentences given by magistrates reflected public opinion on the subject. Many child-molesters were captured as the result of constant surveillance by neighbors who knew their reputations. In one case two men saw a known offender approach a little girl and lead her away. The men sent a woman to inform the child's mother that her child was with a man "who takes liberties with children." Meanwhile they followed the man and his intended victim to a field where they "caught Smith in a very indecent position" and handed him over to the police. In other cases vigilant local citizens received rewards or commendations for apprehending molesters.[65]

Once captured, offenders often required police protection. When a known offender was tried at Dover a crowd of five hundred mobbed the courthouse. After he was sentenced to six months' hard labor, "There were cries of 'Keel-haul him! Hang him! He ought to have twelve!', and several efforts were made by some females to get a grab at the prisoner's head as he stood in the dock." In another case after an elderly man was released because the court believed his ten-year-old victim had consented, "upon leaving the courtroom he was hissed."[66]

Though the magistrates may have been more lenient than the public wished, when a prisoner was bound over for trial the conviction rate for sexual assaults on children was almost twice as high as for those involving adults and adolescents. Judges also tended to give slightly longer sentences for sexual assaults on children. Justice Hawkins told one offender whose several prior convictions had always resulted in light sentences that "he felt it his duty for the protection of society, the protection of women and especially for the protection of young children who could not protect themselves to send him to penal servitude for a long time." He then sentenced the man to fourteen years. Justice Brett sentenced another man to fifteen years for the rape of a nine-year-old girl: "The children of the poor must be protected, as they had no servants to take care of them when out as well-to-do people had." The protection had come slowly, however; the man had over ten prior convictions but had never served more than six months.[67] Table 4-2 gives the conviction and sentencing rates for all sexual assaults heard by juries. In comparing sentences one must keep in mind that the maximum sentence for any indecent assault on a child short of rape was two years.

Keeping the age of consent at twelve meant that adolescent girls were particularly vulnerable to sexual assaults. The age of consent for females had been twelve since the thirteenth century, and was taken quite literally. As Justice Anthony Cleasby explained to a grand jury, "since the victim was twelve years old the prosecution had to prove the rapist used violent force although there was certainly as much moral guilt whether the consent had been obtained or not."[68] The age of consent was raised to thirteen in 1875 but no charges involving girls aged twelve or thirteen were heard in Kent between 1875 and 1880. Between 1859 and 1880 Kentish grand juries brought indictments for rape in thirty-one cases in which the victims were between twelve and sixteen. In twenty-six of these cases the charges were dismissed, the defendant acquitted, or the charge and sentence reduced because the victims had insufficient marks of a violent struggle. Unless the victim had been severely beaten, judges and juries assumed that these girls had consented to seduction.

The social purity movement of the 1880s encouraged raising the age of consent to sixteen, but since the movement did not begin until 1880 it is not within the scope of this work. However, the above figures should be considered in assessing their proposals. In her article on the debate over the age of consent, Deborah Gorham has argued that "age of consent legislation is explicitly designed to deny a girl the right to make decisions about her sexuality if she is younger than the selected age."[69] This argument confuses victim and offender. Consent legislation makes it a criminal offense for *men* to have sexual relations with females under a certain age. The idea that such legislation is coercive to young women is not far

Table 4-2. Verdicts and Sentences for Sexual Assaults by Age of Victim

	Victim 12 years or under		Victim over 12 years	
Sentence	Number	Percent	Number	Percent
Convicted	73	72	144	52
6 months or less	13	18	36	25
7–18 months	24	33	64	45
2–5 years	26	35	12	8
More than 5 years	10	14	32	22
Total charges	101		277	

removed from the philosophy that justified dismissing rape charges if there were no signs of brutal violence. Both assume that girls between the ages of twelve and sixteen were capable of acting as free agents in deciding to become sexually active. The evidence from Kentish courts indicates that was rarely the case.

The most severe tests of the notion of consent to seduction came in cases in which adolescent girls were sexually assaulted by male relatives. Strangely enough there was no law against incest until 1908. Anthony Wohl has suggested that the very idea of incest was too great a challenge to the sanctity of the family even to be considered.[70] The only courts empowered to hear charges of incest were ecclesiastical, and by the nineteenth century such courts had lost all effective power to punish.[71]

The criminal courts in Kent treated incest cases just as they treated other cases of sexual assault. Five fathers were accused of sexual assaults on their daughters. In the three cases in which the daughters were teenagers the judges directed acquittals because the victims had shown "insufficient resistance" to their fathers' sexual advances. In one case Justice Byles directed an acquittal on the grounds of consent because the father admitted he had been having sex with his daughter for six years—since she was eleven. The acquittals were technically correct, as the victims were over the age of consent and there was no law against sex between father and daughter. The two cases in which fathers were convicted involved victims under the age of consent. In 1866 a father was sentenced to two years for the attempted rape of his eleven-year-old daughter.

The only man convicted of actually raping his daughter was a forty-three-year-old laborer who had assaulted his twelve-year-old daughter shortly after her mother's death. Justice Hawkins sentenced him to fourteen years.[72]

Four men were charged with raping stepdaughters under the age of fifteen. No bill was brought in one case, and two of the men were acquitted. The fourth case was an exception. The eleven-year-old victim had given birth to her stepfather's child and Justice Kelly said he felt the "situation was repugnant." He sentenced the man to ten years.[73] Three men charged with sexual assaults on their adolescent nieces were convicted. Since the familial relationship was not as strong it may be that the courts felt freer to interfere in these cases than in those involving fathers and daughters. Generally, in incest cases as with other sexual assaults, legal protection was virtually nil within the confines of one's home.

As offenders the position of children before the law was uncertain. The problems stemmed in part from the lack of a clear definition as to when childhood ended. Childhood was not defined by statute until 1908, and in the mid-nineteenth century there was considerable ambiguity. While persons under the age of ten were generally accepted as children, persons between the ages of eleven and twenty were subject to painful contradictions in terms of social and legal expectations, responsibilities, and restrictions. As Barry Smith has pointed out, "Adolescence is a rare word in Victorian society. . . . They were not being simply callous when they asserted that adulthood began at twelve or thirteen and that 'adults' should be permitted to protect themselves."[74] The 1861 census shows that 37 percent of males and 20 percent of females between the ages of ten and fifteen were employed. For persons between the ages of fifteen and twenty the percentages rise to 91 percent of males and 69 percent of females. That they should work and protect themselves may have been expected, but there is evidence that they were also expected to live at home or in domestic service until marriage.[75] Since only 3 percent of females and 1 percent of males under twenty were married, it would appear that the majority of adolescents were subject to some of the responsibilities of adulthood but little of the independence.[76]

Legally no act done by a person under seven years of age could be considered a crime, and if the accused were between the ages of seven and fourteen the prosecution had to prove criminal intent and knowledge.[77] Technically the only special consideration for persons over the age of fourteen was the Juvenile Offenders Act, which made all persons up to the age of sixteen who were accused of larceny subject to summary jurisdiction. In the criminal statistics in the Parliamentary Papers prisoners were divided into the age categories of under twelve, twelve to sixteen, and sixteen to twenty. The sentences for persons under the age of sixteen usually reflect some special consideration, but there were cases in which children as young as eight were held in adult prisons for extended periods of time.

Between 1859 and 1880 thirty-nine children between the ages of seven and twelve appeared before Kentish grand juries. Twenty-seven of them were convicted and seventeen of them were sent to the county jail for sentences of up to six months. The jails also held children who were simply awaiting trial. When an eight-year-old boy was arrested with his father for burglary in August 1865, father and son were both held at the Maidstone Gaol until the December assize. After four months in prison they were acquitted, as nothing had been stolen.[78] In addition to these cases an additional 974 persons under the age of thirteen were committed to Kentish prisons for summary offenses. People between the ages of seven and twelve constituted about 1 percent of the total prison population in Kent between 1859 and 1880. The prison rules included a stipulation that discharged prisoners be given train fare for themselves and for any children they had kept with them in prison.[79]

The treatment of juvenile offenders was of growing concern during the 1860s and 1870s. Reformers were concerned that prison would brutalize young offenders and that contact with older, more experienced criminals would be detrimental. Such concerns were not merely humanitarian. The surest way to prevent overcrowded prisons was to rehabilitate the young. "If they rescued young criminals from such a course before they arrived at maturity it was evident that in the course of time the number of habitual criminals would be greatly lessened."[80] But the county prisons were not equipped for such rescues. During the early 1860s the children in Kentish jails were treated just like the adult prisoners. Kept in unlit sleeping cells from 6:30 P.M. to 6 A.M., they worked on a treadmill or picked oakum ten hours a day. The diet was sparse and unappetizing; most adult prisoners lost between fifteen and thirty pounds during incarceration.[81] New rules in 1866 exempted children under the age of fourteen from hard labor but they continued to be fed and confined as adults.

The chaplain of the Maidstone Gaol told the Kent general sessions in 1863 that "we can only hope to save the younger and more inexperienced by means of reformatories, penitentiaries and homes, which though seemingly an expensive machinery result in a real economy." Under the Reformatory Schools Acts of 1854 and 1857, judges could have young offenders sent to reform school for two to five years after they served a short prison sentence. Though it was a criminal offense for a reformatory student to leave the grounds without permission, judges considered committal to the reformatory as "a sentence of kindness where boys might be saved from ruin."[82]

But very few children could receive such kindness. The prison chaplain complained that between 1859 and 1865 fewer than 15 percent of Kentish prisoners under the age of sixteen were sent to reformatories, "although many of the remainder had been previously in prison or were orphans, or destitute of good home influence." Between 1859 and 1880 in cases where children were convicted of indictable offenses, judges used the reformatory option in 26 percent of the cases involving children under thirteen and in 30 percent of the cases in which the offender was between the ages of thirteen and fifteen. Ironically, the youngest offenders did not qualify for the reformatory; in 1861 the Home Secretary informed the magistrates that the minimum age for admission to the reformatories was eleven. The problem was money. Private charities were encouraged to contribute to the reform schools and the county provided limited funds, but free spaces at the reformatory were rare. If the offender had living parents they were liable for his maintenance at the reformatory. Not only would this save the expense on the taxpayer, it might also "induce parents to use every means possible to prevent their children from committing crimes."[83]

Parents were responsible for their children even if they were themselves destitute or criminal. Chairman J. G. Talbot of the west Kent quarter sessions felt that "the root of crime lay in the systematic bringing up of children to a criminal course of life." But there were very few instances in which the state was willing to replace the parent as the responsible party. Most often, if the parents failed the burden fell on the children. In 1860 two teenage girls appeared before the Maidstone quarter sessions charged with theft. The girls explained that their mother had died and their father had turned them out of the house, whereupon they had stolen boots and clothes to pawn to buy food. The chairman sentenced them both to prison and advised them that when they got out they should earn their living "by honest industry instead of defrauding other people. He feelingly pointed out the misery and degradation into which they would fall if they continued a course of wickedness." One couple had their eleven-year-old daughter arrested for stealing from them in April 1871. She was held in prison until the July quarter sessions, when the judge sentenced her to one day.[84]

Some children were imprisoned for trying to provide for their families. Talbot felt that "one crime more detestable than any other was when a mother encouraged her child to steal. It must, of course, be visited with severe punishment." At Woolwich Police Court a boy was charged with obstructing a roadway in order to sell vegetables. He was the eldest of seven children and his father had sent him out to support the family. The stipendiary magistrate was unmoved by the story: "Well I'm sorry you have got such a bad father but I cannot allow such offenses to go unpunished, 10s. or ten days." Another magistrate sentenced a boy to two months' hard labor for stealing meat for his mother and siblings. The courts were not adverse to using the children's suffering to punish the parents. At Ashford in 1868 two children age seven and eight were locked up for stealing four sticks of firewood: "The magistrates told the mother they were sorry they could not punish her or her husband instead as they believed they had encouraged the children to pilfer. The screams of the poor infants when taken to the cells was terrific and the mother seemed to suffer much anguish."[85]

The problem of children with unfit parents was addressed in the Industrial Schools Act of 1866, which provided for children under fourteen who were homeless, destitute, or had parents in prison. Magistrates could also send a child to an industrial school if he were frequently in the company of reputed thieves or prostitutes, or if his parents could not control him or he were refractory at the workhouse. In 1867 the Kent general sessions agreed to pay for any child the magistrates sent to a reformatory or industrial school,[86] but there is little evidence that Kentish magistrates used this option very often. The ratio of juveniles to adults in Kentish prisons did not change between 1859 and 1880.

The concern for juveniles as a distinct group did raise other questions, however. Reformatories and industrial schools were reserved for juvenile delinquents (a term which quite suddenly began appearing frequently in Kentish newspapers in 1866).[87] The Kent Reformatory Association explained that "however desirous it might appear to give a young lad the advantages of an education at an establishment like Redhill Reformatory, it should be borne in mind that it was for the reform of the habitual criminal rather than the casual offender."[88] But if prison was too corrupting for delinquents, it was certainly inappropriate for first-time juvenile offenders. Local magistrates told Home Office officials that "[t]reatment of juvenile offenders should be made as far as may be disciplinary and correctional rather than punitive." Many of the magistrates advocated corporal punishment as less brutalizing than prison. The suggestion of sending juvenile offenders to the workhouse was ruled out as being unfair to honest paupers.[89] The actual disposition of juvenile offenders after jury trials indicates the variety of options. Of the thirty-nine offenders under the age of thirteen, twenty-seven (69 percent) were convicted. Of those convicted five were released to their parents' custody, five were sentenced to be whipped, seven were sentenced to prison and reform school, and ten were given regular prison sentences of less than six months. Offenders aged thirteen to fifteen were more likely to be sent to prison. Of the ninety-seven persons in this age group who appeared before grand juries, seventy (72 percent) were convicted, and of those convicted forty-one or (59 percent) simply were sent to prison. Of the remainder five were sent home, three were flogged, and twenty-one were sentenced to prison and reform school.

Pamela Horn has suggested that until the justice system developed special procedures for young offenders, many people viewed extra-parental chastisement as a humane alternative to criminal prosecution.[90] Several incidents in Kent indicate that this idea was still accepted in some quarters. A charge of assault against a gentleman at Canterbury was dropped after a respectable witness assured the magistrates that it had been "a matter of a slight chastisement."

In another case charges against a farm bailiff for beating an eleven-year-old girl were dismissed. The child had been caught stealing apples and he had "merely given her a couple of stripes." Extra-parental chastisement might even be excused when the offense was not criminal. In 1870 a J.P. told a boy who had been knocked down for saying "Holloa Mr. Cole you are off to cricket" that he had brought the assault on himself by being impertinent.[91] In describing his childhood in Dover at the turn of the century, Steve Tremeere indicated that the tradition had continued throughout the nineteenth century. "Old people was always respected. If you was saucing one and somebody come along and heard you, it wouldn't matter if you was their boy or not, they'd clip your bloody ears."[92]

Though the magistrates recognized the right to chastise, even traditional authority figures did have to keep within certain limits. In 1879 the Reverend Thomas Candy, the rector of Swanscombe, was summoned for assaulting a page. When the boy had refused to make tarts, saying it was not his job, Candy had struck him in the throat with his cane. At the hearing Candy challenged the boy's right to testify, arguing that he could not understand the nature of an oath. He also called the headmaster of the boy's school to give evidence of the boy's general sauciness. Instead the headmaster gave the boy an excellent character. In desperation Candy then argued that he had not meant to hit the child in the throat; he was aiming for his mouth. The magistrates told Candy "the assault had been clearly proved and was quite unjustifiable" and fined the outraged clergyman £2.[93]

To be excused by the courts, extra-parental chastisement had to be both moderate and deserved. After fining a sexton for striking a boy in the face for laughing in church, the bench explained that some chastisement had been justified but not the use of the cane. In 1859 two gentlemen from Beckenham were involved in a dispute over some straw. One of the men called the servant of the other a liar, to which the boy replied, "You are as big a liar as I am." The gentleman then attacked the boy with his whip. After being charged with assault the man argued that he had been provoked by the boy's impertinence, but the magistrates ruled the excuse was insufficient and fined him £1. In 1860 a seven-year-old boy was charged with trespass but could not appear in court because of the bruises he had received from a beating by the complainant. At the next session the boy was fined 1d. for sliding on the grass and his assailant was fined 11s. for assault. In another case, which indicates the ambivalence of the courts, a beer-house keeper who kicked a boy for throwing stones at his dog was fined 20s. "The Bench considered it a very aggravated case and one in which the greatest possible injury might have been inflicted perhaps maiming the boy for life." The bench's actual concern may be measured by the fact that in the next case they sentenced a farmer to two months in prison for cruelty to a dog.[94]

Ironically, limited judicial tolerance for extra-parental chastisement combined with the growing concern about juvenile offenders may have increased the likelihood of police interference in "normal" childhood activities. In 1860 an M.P. complained that children were being jailed for nothing more than playing games in the street.[95] John Gillis found that around the turn of the century the new concern about juvenile offenders led to an increase in arrests and prosecutions for minor offenses.[96] While the number of juveniles in Kentish prisons did not increase during the 1860s and 1870s, children were being arrested for such offenses as sliding on wet grass and ice, playing tip-cat, throwing snowballs, whistling at respectable persons, ringing doorbells, and playing ball in the street, all of which were offenses under the Police Acts. But Tremeere remembered from his own childhood that "we kids always respected a policeman. . . . [W]e used to get a clip round the ear off them. But you had to be really bad before they took you in."[97]

The punishment of children charged under these acts varied according to the location. Rural magistrates usually fined young offenders, while those in Kentish London more often opted for brief jail sentences. The social status of the accused and his parents also made a difference. A twelve-year-old boy with "respectable connections" was sentenced to one day for stealing a horse and van, as it had been "only a lark." But an eleven-year-old serving-girl who stole clothes from a line to get money to go to an amalgamated fete was sentenced to ten days in jail and four years in a reformatory even though the things she had stolen for her lark were "not very valuable."[98]

Of the children under twelve who appeared before grand juries in Kent, 46 percent were charged with theft, 20 percent with arson, and 13 percent with church-breaking. Arson, church-breaking, and obstructing the railway were the only indictable crimes for which these children represented more than 1 percent of all those accused. Most of the arson cases were the results of pranks or accidents. Church-breaking and placing things on railroad tracks or throwing things at passing trains appear to have been popular pastimes among the young; only three persons accused of these offenses were over the age of eighteen. The children accused were usually sentenced to less than one month. The crimes of thirteen- to sixteen-year-olds were more like those of their elders, though five were charged with church-breaking and five with railway offenses. One hundred and ten (65 percent) were charged with theft. This group was responsible for 5 percent of all indictable thefts, 7 percent of all arson, and 2 percent of all unnatural sexual offenses. Predictably the types of crimes and the length of sentences for sixteen-year-olds were much more like those of adults than those of younger children. Only 4 percent of indicted sixteen-year-olds were sent to the reformatory.

Having discovered juvenile delinquency and accepted, at least in theory, that education and supervision were its remedies, the need for more and better educational institutions was obvious. For financial as well as philosophical reasons most authorities preferred that such places be administered and financed privately rather than by the state, but two incidents in Kent in the 1870s demonstrated the hazards of leaving such places unregulated. In 1873 two "decently clad boys were brought up on suspicion of absconding from the Working Boys Home at Peckham." The boys, aged twelve and fourteen, had come to the Dover police station in "a state of destitution." They produced a letter from the director of the home complaining that the boys were not sending him enough money. Upon investigation the magistrates learned that the director regularly sent his charges out for weeks at a time with instructions to sell spoons and send the money back to him. After pronouncing the arrangement most improper the magistrates sent the boys to the workhouse. The magistrates were not alone in their opinion. An editorial in the *Maidstone and Kentish Journal* lamented that: "Every principle contended for, and every end sought by the establishment of these places is violated and ignored by sending across the country a lot of poor little fellows to lead a vagrant life, sleep at common lodgings, and come into contact with the class of people whom they meet in their wanderings. It is the very way to ruin." The courts and the press could only express disapproval since no law had been broken. But the reaction does reflect some change in attitudes. Both of the boys were adolescents who in earlier times might have been expected to be self-supporting. In 1873 they were perceived as children who required adult care and supervision. The question now was who would pay for such care and who would supervise those who provided it.[99]

The dangers of not supervising the caretakers was tragically illustrated in 1879 in Deptford. Laura Addiscott, a young woman, had established "A Home for Friendless Girls." She travelled throughout Kent, lecturing on her noble mission and soliciting funds for its support. When some ladies who had contributed asked to see the home, however, admission was denied. Alarmed at the secrecy, the local vicar recruited a police constable, the relieving officer, and the coroner to help him force his way in. The men found seventeen girls between the ages of two and eleven, all of them diseased and emaciated. They also discovered that the girls were not orphans. In addition to the donations Addiscott solicited, the parents of the girls were paying Addiscott to care for them. Scandalized by the pitiful condition of the girls, the local board of Poor Law Guardians decided to prosecute Addiscott.[100]

Addiscott was tried at Central Criminal Court for assault and for the manslaughter of two children who had died in her care. Much of the evidence indicated a widespread apathy towards poor children. At the trial postal workers testified that they had seen the children eating grass and garbage, though they had not felt it was their place to report it to the authorities. Worse, the physician who had signed the death certificates of the two who died had sworn that they were victims of a rare intestinal disorder that had left them incapable of digestion. "I noticed the children looked very bare—it never occurred to me that such a thing as starving was going on." Under cross-examination the physician admitted that he had never seen the corpses. He had simply gone to the home, glanced at the other children, and signed the death certificates, supplying a diagnosis that fit Addiscott's specifications.

Addiscott's defense attorney argued that the conditions at the home were no worse than those of private residences in the neighborhood. The relieving officer's reply to this suggestion provides a fascinating illustration of a Victorian bureaucrat's views on poverty, respectability, and human misery:

> It is a poor neighborhood; there is frequently great distress there. I don't think there are places in which the furniture would be such as in this house. If you speak of respectable working men there is not a house in Deptford District that is not furnished. I only find that when they are drunken, worthless people neglecting their duty—there is no respectable home so bad as this was—we have respectable working poor and their very respectability keeps them in the state that they would be ashamed to see a broken pane of glass.

Addiscott was convicted on nineteen counts of assault and sentenced to eighteen months (she was acquitted of manslaughter as there was no evidence of intent).[101]

For many observers Addiscott's greatest fault appeared to have been her failure to perform her task efficiently. An editorial complained that she had been a poor manager: "That miserable and misguided woman appeared to have had no particular system of management or any special scheme on which to build or maintain a home of any kind. There was never in fact, anything so loose, disorganized and incomprehensible as the whole affair." Her failure threatened to undermine the public's faith in private institutions. She was also guilty of embarrassing the community. "The sooner the whole affair is put away, except as a warning, the more comfortable we will feel, for it is not pleasant to know such cruelties were suffered by so many at our doors, as it were, and not any notice taken." The one glimmer of light in all this was that the Greenwich board of Poor Law Guardians had successfully prosecuted "the woman who, through her errors or ignorance or greed or vice or cruelty [had inflicted] these tortures."[102] One might suspect that her sins are listed in order of importance.

The demonstrated need for efficient, well-regulated, and well-managed institutions for poor children helped fuel enthusiasm for national education, as did the sense of inequity in that juvenile delinquents were eligible for free education but innocent children were not. One magistrate expressed his concerns in a charge to a grand jury. "The poor but honest child of the poor but honest man finds no sympathy—no assistance is extended to him to enable him to educate his child in the habits of industry. It is a grave mistake to protect the guilty and neglect the innocent. The astounding blunder has been made of making crime the qualification for the benevolence of the state." Most magistrates believed that education for the working classes would be beneficial for society as well as for the children themselves. Chairman Talbot of the west Kent sessions was sure that "education will do more to repress crime than any amount of law to punish it."[103]

But education had to be carefully controlled. Talbot warned that, "Unless education were based upon religion he thought it would prove more a curse than a blessing." Secular education could be counter-productive. "There would probably be less robbery with violence; and fewer cases of direct abstraction of money from the person. But that is little satisfaction to a man just imposed upon by a clever knave who could write a clear enough hand to forge a signature."[104] There was no guarantee that the newly literate would limit their reading to the morally uplifting. The "penny dreadfuls," stories of action, crime, and mayhem geared to an audience of adolescent boys, were sometimes considered particularly hazardous, as they made a life of crime sound enticing. Patrick Dunae has argued that though the stories themselves probably rarely inspired crimes, "youthful offenders were all too adept at claiming extenuating circumstances which they believed would elicit sympathy from magistrates and police officers."[105]

At least one crime in Kent was inspired by a penny dreadful, but the results indicate that any juvenile offender who took them seriously would need sympathy. In May 1877 William Henry Hodgson, an assistant solicitor with the treasury, was riding from Woolwich to Lewisham when his hired carriage suddenly stopped near Blackheath. A masked man appeared at the window, pointed a pistol at the astonished Hodgson, and said, "Your money or your life." Assuming this was a drunken prank, Hodgson told the man to go away. When a second armed man appeared, Hodgson gave them some change and told the driver to move on. At this point one of the robbers cocked his pistol and calmly announced that he would blow Hodgson's brains out if he did not hand over his purse. No longer amused, Hodgson gave them his purse and they allowed the carriage to pass on. The robbers, teenagers from Cornwall, were new to the game. Hodgson's purse contained two easily traceable treasury notes that they used to pay their landlady in Greenwich. The police who came to arrest them three weeks later discovered pistols, cartridges, and a book, *Claude Duval, the Dashing Highwayman.* Both bandits were sentenced to seven years.[106]

While literacy posed some hazards, the more serious debate concerning national education was over whether it should be compulsory. During the campaign for a National Education Act, A. J. B. Beresford-Hope, a Conservative M.P. from Maidstone, gave lectures in a number of Kentish towns warning that compulsory education was "revolting to the best feelings of the heart, the best feelings of manly independence."[107] The National Education Act of 1870 was a model of compromise, requiring that public education be available but leaving the decision of whether attendance should be mandatory to the local school boards. Attendance was not made compulsory nationally until 1880.

During the 1870s various school boards in Kent began compelling attendance. It was soon apparent that a number of parents agreed with Beresford-Hope. Thirteen cases of truancy were prosecuted in Canterbury during the first petty sessions after the school board began requiring attendance. Non-compliance was not always passive. In February 1880 a laborer at Canterbury was sentenced to two months' hard labor after he assaulted school board officers who came to ask why his children were not in school. At Tunbridge Wells two boys and their parents were fined for swearing and using abusive language towards the master of the national school and his wife. The schoolmaster said "he had been subject to continued insults from the boys and some of the other inhabitants." The headmaster at Sittingbourne complained that "the Education Act was resisted by parents and the children followed it up by obstinately refusing to learn."[108]

In addition to compelling chlidren to attend school against their parents' wishes, schoolmasters were also granted the right to chastise their students. Even before education became compulsory the courts supported corporal punishment in schools even when the parents objected. In 1864 charges against a schoolmaster who had kicked a boy for mistakes in spelling were dismissed, as "there was no more violence used than was absolutely necessary to correct an obstinate boy." Even socially prominent parents could not overrule schoolmasters. In 1861 the headmaster of King's School in Canterbury was summoned for assaulting the sixteen-year-old son of a member of the town council. The school, founded by Henry VIII, had a long tradition of flogging slow learners, and the boy had been given stripes for failing to recite his Greek lesson properly. The magistrates angrily dismissed the charges and apologized for wasting the headmaster's time; the chairman, an alumnus of King's, added that he was delighted the current headmaster was following the old tradition of flogging. Compulsory education apparently led headmasters to resort to physical chastisement even more often. In November 1879 the headmaster at Sittingbourne was summoned for assaulting a ten-year-old student. The defendant angrily complained that "If he had not conquered the boy, the whole school would have mutinied. Their worships drove this class of children into school, but they little knew the difficulty there was in dealing with them when they were there." The magistrates expressed their sympathy for the schoolmaster and dismissed the case.[109]

The National Education Act represented a profound change in the position of the government vis-à-vis parents. Even more than compulsory vaccination, compulsory education established the principle that the state could compel parents to raise children in ways that were deemed most beneficial for society as a whole. It is worth remembering that compulsory education came at the end of the period under investigation and met with considerable resistance. For the courts and citizens of mid-Victorian Kent, government interference between parent and child was both rare and unwelcome.

The law and the men who enforced and administered it preferred to leave children to their parents, intervening only when there was a clear threat to the public interest. The courts could and did protect public welfare by compelling parents to have their children inoculated against contagious diseases, but whether they could force parents to provide medical treatment for non-infectious diseases remained a moot point. If they were financially able, parents were legally obligated to provide food and shelter for their children. They were not allowed to kill or permanently injure them intentionally, though physical chastisement was allowed so long as the action and instrument were deemed moderate. If parents abrogated their responsibility to keep their children from committing crimes, the police and courts could arrest, prosecute and, if necessary, send the child to prison, a reformatory or an industrial school. Within these broad limits parents were free to exercise their own judgement. Parliament and the courts, though not necessarily the neighbors, took very little notice of what went on in private between parent and child. A creed that honored the sanctity of the family and the right of every man to rule in his own home made further intervention unacceptable.

If they were victims of crimes children could only prosecute through their parents, guardians, or the local Poor Law board. They were considered unreliable as witnesses and their testimony was not usually accepted without adult corroboration. While judicial skepticism in dealing with children is understandable, skepticism in combination with the lack of precision in defining the limits of childhood was particularly harmful for adolescents. The following exchange between a magistrate and a relieving officer illustrates this point. The relieving officer sought a summons against a couple who had abused a fifteen-year-old servant. The magistrate asked if there was any evidence to support the girl's claim that she had been beaten. The relieving officer replied: "Only the evidence of the marks upon her body." The magistrate then said, "I think it would be better to get up the case in such a manner as will be sure to lead to a conviction before you take out a summons." The relieving officer warned that the girl might die and that "it was most important that the Poor Law Board should prosecute in some way because of the stigma that would be attached to them if she did." The magistrate answered that he did not think there was a chance of conviction without corroboration: "The girl, who is fifteen, was quite old enough to take care of herself and complain to the neighbors." He refused to issue the summons.[110] In the courts children were usually deemed either too young to be trustworthy or old enough to take care of themselves, and sometimes, as in this case, most painfully both.

5

Outlaws

> The jury must not attach too much importance to the consideration of the crimes being charged being first offenses, because it might well be that they had been in the company of bad characters and that though they happened to escape from the law they might not really belong to what might be called the innocent part of the community.[1]
>
> Chairman, west Kent quarter sessions, January 1871

To the merchants, artisans, and farmers who sat on Kentish juries there was a clear distinction between the innocent part of the community to which they belonged and the "criminal class"—persons who lived outside the bounds of respectable society and were inherently guilty. Such people were not necessarily criminals in a legal sense, that is, they might never have been convicted of violating the law, but they were always suspect and were in a sense outlaws. The term "outlaw" had originally referred to persons who had been expelled from the community for criminal behavior. Outlaws were those who lived outside the law—they neither obeyed it nor were protected by it. In the nineteenth century the legal status of outlaw was no longer recognized, but policemen, judges, and juries still responded quite differently to persons who were accepted as members of the innocent part of the community and to those who were perceived as being outside that community. The outlaws were "the criminal, vagrant and suspected classes."[2]

The existence and definition of the Victorian "criminal class" has been a topic for intense historical debate. In his pioneering work on crime in nineteenth century England, J. J. Tobias, using "contemporary description" and literary sources, concluded that there was, in fact, a distinct criminal class "which lived a life of its own separate from the rest of the community, members of which were usually easily distinguishable by their clothing and habits and lived wholly or largely on the proceeds from crime." Inspired by Dickens, Tobias wrote that "criminals were Fagin and the Artful Dodger and 'crime' was what they lived by."[3]

In the past twenty years scholars have found that the persons accused of crimes in the police and courts records were neither as colorful nor as skilled nor as distinctive as the fictional criminals created by Dickens.[4] In his study of crime in the Black Country, David Philips found that only 10 percent of crimes were committed by professional criminals. "The great majority of the criminal offenses seem to have been committed by people who were not full-time criminals, who worked at jobs normally, but also stole articles on some occasions or became involved in a fight or a robbery." Rather than the organized cadres of Fagin, Philips found "casualness and lack of professional planning, small amounts of property taken by poor men or women carried out with little planning."[5] Jennifer Davis reached similar conclusions in her study of London, and V. A. C. Gatrell wrote in 1980 that "the error of ascribing most Victorian crime to a professional class is now well-established."[6] Most recently George Rude concluded that "even in London, for all its reputation as a center of professional crime and 'dangerous deviants', the case for the existence of a definable 'criminal class' has not been made."[7]

The fact that a distinct professional criminal class as described by Tobias may not have existed does not completely resolve the issue. Literary sources and contemporary description may not be accurate presentations of reality, but as G. M. Young wrote, "the real central theme of history is not what happened, but what people felt about it when it was happening."[8] There is substantial evidence that judicial authorities and the general public believed that criminals were a distinct and threatening breed apart. The Penal Servitude Act Commission concluded in 1863 that "there is a class of persons who are so inveterately addicted to dishonesty and so averse to labor, that there is no chance of their ceasing to seek their existence by depredations on the public unless they are compulsorily withdrawn."[9]

Kentish authorities believed the career criminals of London were a constant threat. When the London police began a campaign against habitual offenders in 1872, the *Maidstone and Kentish Journal* complained that they were "driving those who made a profession of crime from the metropolis and large towns into the more rural districts and almost nightly there are robberies committed."[10] The fears were groundless; burglaries in Kent dropped by 50 percent after the crackdown by the London police, perhaps because the rural police tightened security in response to the perceived threat.

Local officials were careful to stress that the career criminals they feared were outsiders. After completing his annual report of "known thieves," the recorder for Gravesend was careful to point out that "these persons were not necessarily resident in the borough; their character might be perfectly well-known although they came from a distant part of the country." Gathorn Hardy, chairman of the west Kent quarter sessions, warned of "the practiced London pickpocket." Unwelcome invaders from London were especially dreaded during special events such as militia parades and royal embarkations. After a reception for the duke and duchess of Edinburgh at Gravesend a special petty sessions was held. Thirteen persons were convicted as pickpockets, three were jailed for loitering in preparation to commit a felony, and twenty-three were ordered out of town as suspicious characters.[11]

The belief in a criminal class made up largely of persons from "a distant part of the country" was both useful and comforting, however inaccurate it may have been. It made the distinction between good and bad, guilty and innocent seem absolute. The chaplain of the Maidstone Gaol assured the general sessions that "[i]t is to be expected that there should be a considerable number of vagrants, drunkards and prostitutes, who have grown up in such confirmed habits of laziness and vice, that nothing can raise them during their constantly recurring period of short imprisonment . . . and further that there should be a smaller body of professional thieves whose connections scarcely give them a chance of reformation." If some persons were inherently and irretrievably criminal while others were inherently innocent, the whole problem of crime might be solved by ridding society of the incorrigibles. By this logic it was a positive sign if most offenders who came before the courts had criminal records. As the chairman of the west Kent quarter sessions explained, "It was very satisfactory to limit crime to a certain number of the criminal class whom it was impossible to reform."[12]

The criminal class as perceived by judicial officials specialized in property crimes. According to the *Judicial and Criminal Statistics* of 1859: "The following crimes are chiefly those which may be ascribed to the existence of a criminal class: Burglary and house-breaking; robbery on the person; cattle, horse and sheep stealing; embezzling; fraud; arson; forgery; coining; treason and sedition and felonious riot."[13] Some inferences may be drawn from conviction rates and sentencing patterns for various types of property crimes. The numbers are problematic, however. Property crimes were increasingly subject to summary jurisdiction. By 1859 persons accused of stealing goods worth less than 5s. could be tried by two J.P.s, as could persons who pleaded guilty to stealing more than 5s., though the accused had the right to demand a jury trial. The number and types of non-violent property offenses that could be tried summarily were increased again in 1869 and 1879. As a result the vast majority of non-violent property offenses by first offenders were not heard by juries. The records from the Criminal Registers and the courts therefore only include a small proportion of such cases. Forgery, arson, burglary, and robbery with violence could only be heard at an assize. Hence the records used here reflect a disproportionate ratio of non-violent to violent property offenses.

Despite these limitations the figures are interesting and suggestive. Table 5-1 gives the conviction rates and sentencing patterns for various property crimes heard at the assize and Central Criminal Court. A few points stand out. Conviction rates are close to the overall average of 74 percent. The lowest rates are for thefts of food and livestock. One explanation is that it was more difficult for witnesses to positively identify particular items in these categories. While at first glance one might suspect that juries were showing mercy to those who stole to avoid starvation, that was rarely if ever the case. The persons indicted for stealing food, with the exception of ex-convicts who could not be tried summarily, were usually stealing mass quantities of food. For example, one case involved the theft of four hundred oranges, another fifty pounds of butter, others hundreds of pounds of meat. Obviously someone who stole perishable items in such large quantities was stealing to sell for profit.

Table 5-1. Convictions and Sentences for Property Crimes

	Percent total charges of property crimes	Percent convicted	Sentences (percent)	
			18 months or less	2 years or more
Livestock	4	64	92	8
Food	7	66	83	17
Purse	2	70	72	28
Jewelry	8	74	76	24
Tools	6	74	84	16
Money	8	78.5	82	18
White collar	10	79	85	15
Household	6	79	82	18
Burglary	20	80	68	32
Clothes	13	83	83	17
Counterfeiting	7	84	77	24
Other	9	77	79	21

Heavier sentences were also given for thefts that implied a certain degree of skill and hence an element of professionalism. Burglars, pickpockets, jewel thieves, and counterfeiters were all thought more likely to be involved in full-time criminal pursuits than persons who stole tools or household items. The light sentences for thefts of livestock reflect a long-term shift in values from earlier centuries when the theft of animals was among the most serious of offenses. In the seventeenth century 95 percent of horse thieves were executed, but during the late eighteenth century the percentage hanged had fallen to 13.2 percent.[14] The change certainly reflects changes in attitudes towards the death penalty. (Though such changes were not unanimous; as late as 1862 the Earl of Romney was complaining bitterly that sheep stealers who would have been hanged in his day were now getting off with light prison terms.[15]) But the decline in sentences may also reflect the fact that even though livestock was still valuable property (and horses and sheep were among the items stolen), the economy was becoming less dependent on agrarian wealth and transportation no longer depended solely on the horse.

The value of the items stolen was considerably less significant for sentencing than the record and reputation of the accused. That ridding society of career criminals was a higher priority than simply protecting property was made explicit in 1875. The grand jury at the spring quarter sessions complained that it was a waste of their time to hear cases involving paltry thefts. The total value of all the goods stolen by the six persons presented for indictment was a mere £29. The sessions chairman explained that prior records and circumstances were far more important than monetary value. He then underscored his point by sentencing three of the men to ten years' penal servitude and the others to seven years each.[16]

Obviously the connection between a record of prior arrests and professional criminality was not absolute. A number of arrests for theft could simply indicate serious ineptitude. One weary nineteen-year-old man told a judge "This is the fifth time I've been caught. I have had enough and shall give it up."[17] Conversely a truly skilled criminal might never be caught. But it was much more agreeable to believe in a few readily identifiable incorrigibles than to accept the idea that crimes might be committed casually by people who were not already clearly designated as criminals.

How to deal with the incorrigibles once identified was a particularly painful problem for the Victorians. In earlier times criminals had been disposed of through the process of outlawry, through capital punishment, and most significantly through judicial discretion. Cynthia Herrup has pointed out that in the seventeenth century "the general category of the criminally culpable contained only a few individuals who were considered to be truly criminals."[18] But the reforms of the early nineteenth century had changed the rules. The operating principle in the mid-nineteenth century was "that every discoverable offense should be automatically followed by prosecution."[19] Further, the acceptable forms of punishment had changed. Incarceration had become the standard, which created an enormous demand for places to house criminals.[20] During the first half of the nineteenth century transportation to Australia had provided a means of disposing of offenders, but the Penal Servitude Act of 1857 abolished transportation except for a very few places in western Australia, and by 1867 transportation had completely ceased. The state was now responsible for the financial support of members of the criminal population during incarceration either in county jails or for longer periods of penal servitude in the national convict prisons, one of which was located in Chatham.

The proper treatment of convicts was (as it still is) a topic of considerable debate. While many magistrates suggested that criminals were beyond reclamation, Major General Sir Joshua Jebb, the surveyor general of prisons until his death in 1863, was a firm believer in reform and reclamation. He hoped that moral and religious training and isolation from the contamination of fellow inmates would lead prisoners to a better way.[21] Predictably many people complained that penal servitude was being made so attractive that persons were tempted to commit crime just so they could receive its benefits. Justice Bramwell argued that those who designed the penal servitude system were unaware of the realities of life outside. "Penal servitude is not so dreadful to the vast majority who suffer it as it would be to those who provide it. Labour and subjection to the orders of others is the lot of the greater numbers of those who come within the scope of the criminal law. What would horrify a person of education and refinement, viz. the association with those who are the bulk of the convicted, is inoperative on those who constitute that bulk."[22] Despite the obvious implications of Bramwell's observations, the parliamentary commission did not consider inviting an ex-convict for an inside view. Such a view is available, however, in the depositions from the murder trial of James Fletcher, an inmate of the Chatham Convict Prison. As punishment for fighting with another prisoner, prison guard James Boyle had put Fletcher on bread and water for two days. Fletcher, who was 6′3″, had already lost twenty pounds during his first month at Chatham. The next time Fletcher saw Boyle in the prison yard, he smashed his head in with a hammer. At his preliminary hearing for murder, Fletcher gave the following deposition:

> The reason I did it was the officer was regular taking advantage of the men. There's men constantly dying in the prison now, Sir, with hunger and starvation. The men's regularly eating candles and soap and tallow, 'tato peeling or anything they can get hold of. The principal warder here, when I was in the cells said he would make my head and the wall come together so the brains would fly out—I thought when I got out I would do this and get shut of my life altogether—I was sick and tired of it.

Fletcher was convicted and hanged.[23]

The convict prisons that housed persons who were sentenced to penal servitude for two or more years were perceived as far more humane than the county jails. Justice Bramwell refused to sentence anyone to more than eighteen months in county jails as he felt it would be physically impossible to survive a longer term.[24] County officials purposely kept the conditions intolerable as they felt that career criminals should be in convict prisons, not in county jails where they were burdens on Kentish taxpayers. "We can but hope to keep them out of prison by making it as laborious and irksome to them as possible." Unlike the convict prisons where the inmates were trained to perform some nominally useful trade, the hard labor at the county jail was purposely designed to be both futile and tedious. At Maidstone prisoners worked on a treadmill from six in the morning until six-thirty in the evening. Dividers on the wheel kept the prisoners from communicating with each other. After work they were locked in unlit individual cells for the night.[25]

But if life in prison was grim, life after prison may have been even worse. If criminals were perceived as inherently different from other people, an ex-convict could not possibly be accepted into the community. Rehabilitation was not universally accepted as a goal of criminal justice. Viscount Raynham assured his colleagues in Parliament that "it was not a function of criminal jurisprudence to consider the after conduct of the convicted man; but only how he could be made sufficiently to suffer, so that others might be deterred from the commission of a similar offense."[26] In a charge to the grand jury at the winter assize in 1862, Justice Byles urged that transportation be reinstated. It was too expensive to keep criminals in prison and once released it was impossible for them to obtain employment. "What, in the present state of the labour market, is to be done with the prisoner after the expiration of his sentence? Who does not prefer to employ men of untainted character? I am afraid we invite, I had almost said compel, him to commit crime again."[27] If he did, the police and courts were ready. On at least nine separate occasions ex-convicts in Kent were sentenced to ten years' penal servitude after being convicted of stealing small amounts of food.

The law was designed to protect citizens from career criminals. If the value of an item stolen was over 5s. the maximum sentence for a first offense was three years regardless of the value of the property. If the defendant had a prior conviction the maximum sentence was ten years. At the west Kent quarter sessions in July 1877 two men were convicted in separate cases of stealing small shovels. One man, who had no prior record, was sentenced to two months; the other, who had four previous arrests, was sentenced to eight years. In 1878 a woman with a history of petty theft was sentenced to ten years' penal servitude for stealing an apron valued at 10s. Ex-convicts and those designated as "known thieves" were subject to constant surveillance. After one man was fined 20s. for hitting a policeman who had stopped him and searched his belongings, the press reported: "The prisoner who is well known to the police suggested that they might as well hang him at once."[28]

The Penal Servitude Act Commission had acknowledged that the crime rate was not simply a function of the treatment of known criminals. "The number of crimes committed at any given time in the country is probably less affected by the system of punishment which may be in use than by various other circumstances, such as the greater or lesser welfare of the population, the demand for labour, the state of the police and the manner in which justice is administered."[29] While insisting that the truly innocent would not steal regardless of their poverty, some authorities did recognize a connection between economic hardship and property crime. In 1876 Justice Pigott told the grand jury that "the abundance of employment was telling upon the lower classes of society. Their earnings are such as to remove them from the necessity or the temptation to commit offences against person or property." But other judges believed that the lower orders were more fractious when they had money. The chairman of the west Kent quarter sessions assured a grand jury that a decrease in crime could be attributed to a lack of money since prosperity led to intemperance. Despite the opposite conclusions both theories implied that the poor bore careful watching.[30]

In keeping with these theories the police often extended their surveillance from known offenders to the poor generally. There was a certain logic to this suspicion. Geoffrey Best has described "the rough underside of the mid-Victorian economy where in the last resort, only the Poor Law or 'private' charity or crime came between you and starvation."[31] Under these circumstances the criminal class might include not only skilled professionals but all those whose very existence depended on supplementing legitimate earnings through theft. Jennifer Davis argues that "one vital question to be asked about those individuals who were involved in the criminal justice system is not how often they had been arrested, but rather how much of their time was spent not in crime, but as participants in the legal economy."[32] The distinction between a class of career criminals and the poor who stole to survive is further blurred by the fact that both were most likely to commit crimes against property. As Gatrell concludes, "the criminal class merged imperceptibly with the wider class of which they were a part, and who provided them with their covers as well as their largely silent victims."[33]

Though the poor were often the victims of crime, the Kentish police tended to view them almost exclusively as suspects. Two men charged with assaulting a constable in 1880 were released after the constable testified that he had suspected them because they were "near a gentleman's house." To many police constables and J.P.s it seemed suspicious that any poor person should be in possession of valuable goods. The chairman of the west Kent quarter sessions explained that "it was in accordance with all the laws of common sense and common honesty that a man should be bound to give account of how he became possessed of property." In 1864 a prisoner, so weak from illness he was brought in on a stretcher, was charged with possessing a hassock and being "unable to give a satisfactory account. The law naturally inferred that he was a guilty party." The man died in jail. In December 1863 Thomas Holland was stopped by a police constable who inquired about a goose Holland was carrying. Holland explained that the goose was his Christmas dinner. The constable decided that Holland did not look as if he could afford a goose and arrested him. Holland remained in jail until the January session at Central Criminal Court where the judge dismissed the case. In another case Emma Pattison, "a hard worked looking woman," was arrested for having nine cabbages in her possession. A widow with several small children, neither the police nor the magistrates could believe that anyone would have given them to her. She was held in prison for four days while the police waited for a report of stolen cabbages. When no victim turned up, they reluctantly released her.[34]

Those who stole to survive were most likely to be tried by magistrates who rarely accepted starvation as a justification for theft. In 1859 the mayor of Maidstone heard the case of a man who had stolen a cape: "He pleaded guilty and said that he had been searching for work but could not obtain any. He had nothing to eat for days previously, and he took the cape to prevent himself from starving." He was sentenced to six weeks' hard labor, and the mayor "observed that if he were in such distressed condition his proper course would have been to have applied to the relieving officer." In 1865 a man died of consumption in the county jail while serving a nine-month sentence for stealing a loaf of bread.[35]

Some J.P.s did claim to consider poverty a mitigating factor. The Reverend G. Davis, a Rochester magistrate, sentenced a "distressed looking woman, deserted by her husband" to a month's hard labor for stealing a gown and pawning it to buy food. He explained that he had been lenient and given her one month instead of three because of her poverty. Other magistrates spoke of leniency when they imposed fines instead of jail terms for thefts of food or fuel. Such mercy was of little practical use since those who could not afford food could scarcely afford to pay fines, and default meant at least fourteen days in jail. In one typical case "Mary Ryan, a miserable looking woman, with an infant in her arms pleaded guilty to stealing turnip tops of J. L. Edwards. There was the usual plea in extenuation that her husband was always seeking for work, and that she with her three children were in starving condition." She was fined 12s. and then sentenced to fourteen days' hard labor for defaulting on the fine.[36]

While authorities may have suspected all of the poor, the concept of the poor but honest was staunchly defended. In a report to the Kent general sessions, J. G. Talbot, M. P. and quarter sessions chairman for west Kent, pointed out that "mixed up with the great bulk of the idle and the worthless, is invariably found a small proportion whose misfortune and not their fault it is to be poor. Misfortune will occasionally overtake the most provident and industrious."[37] Distinguishing between the deserving poor who preferred starvation to crime and the non-deserving was an important and useful way to avoid unpleasant realities, as became clear in the late 1860s. The dockyards at Deptford and Woolwich, which had "offered the most substantial and sustained ship-building employment" in Kentish London, were closed during the winter of 1867.[38] The effects were catastrophic. In January 1867 unemployment in Deptford and Greenwich was nearly 25 percent. The unemployed were men who had been regular and dependable wage-earners, and their suffering created considerable cognitive dissonance for those who preferred to believe that the able-bodied poor were idlers rather than victims.

Economic self-reliance was the cornerstone of respectability for the artisans of Kentish London as well as for the middle classes. The dockyard workers resented being forced to ask for charity and the system was ill-equipped to provide for them. A bread line at Deptford was the only available relief for the able-bodied unemployed. When the supply ran out those left standing in line ransacked the local bakeries. According to *The Times*: "One baker's shop they completely plundered, and proceeding along High-Street, Deptford, they came to the shop of another baker, and were about to make a forcible entry, when the proprietor called upon them to desist from destroying his property, promising them that he would give them the whole of the bread he had remaining unsold. This had the desired effect. Only two charges were brought before the magistrates." Despite this relatively peaceful conclusion the relieving officer hastened to assure the public that the deserving poor had not been involved. "The applicants who attended to seek relief were not of the class who joined in the lawless proceedings, the latter being mere roughs and idlers . . . many of them guilty of frauds upon the relieving officer." A letter to *The Times* reported that "notwithstanding the great distress among the mechanics and artisans, not one of those classes was to be seen in the so-called bread riots. . . . These riots were got up by roughs and juvenile thieves that were strangers to the locality."[39]

Another London newspaper lamented that "these ruffians had never learned the lesson of first earning by hard labour the food given them to eat." Lest anyone think him insensitive the editor hastened to explain, "[I]n writing this our readers will readily infer that these remarks are not directed against that class of the industrial poor who have been thrust out of their ordinary occupation through unforeseen circumstances." As proof that none of the rioters were from the ranks of the deserving poor, the paper noted that one of the rioters had raided a tobacco shop.[40] Since self-sufficiency was crucial for respectability, anyone who applied for relief was already suspect. Those who became disorderly when they did not receive aid were obviously not deserving. This circular argument salved a great many consciences.

The belief in self-reliance was not merely the rhetoric of the middle class. In his interviews with elderly residents of Kent, Michael Winstanley found that "poverty itself was no disgrace if brought about by misfortune." But going to the workhouse, becoming dependent on state charity, was not respectable. As one man told Winstanley: "I suppose they thought that charity's a gift. That's free. But they wouldn't apply if it was to the workhouse. They'd got it in their heads—the workhouse was a disgrace. It was planted in us—save something. You must save so that you don't, in your old age, have to go to the workhouse. . . . Well it's so ingrained in me, that if I was starving, I wouldn't ask for public assistance."[41] It was better to starve and some literally did. In 1864, in reporting the death from starvation of a twenty-four-year-old woman, the paper noted that "the family had been respectable but had fallen on hard times." According to the coroner's verdicts recorded in the *Judicial and Criminal Statistics*, at least forty-one people in Kent died of "want" between 1859 and 1880.[42]

Despite the faith in self-reliance, the fact was that during economic crises many people were unemployed, homeless, and devoid of any legitimate means of helping themselves. Arrests under the Vagrancy Act, as well as those for petty theft, rose during periods of economic crisis and fell during periods of prosperity. Most vagrancy offenses involved little more than being poor. It was, for example, a crime to be homeless. Being found sleeping out of doors with no visible means of support was a crime punishable by up to three months in prison. Other offenses included neglecting to maintain one's family, returning to the parish after being ordered to leave, trading without a license, riotous and indecent behavior by a prostitute, begging, causing a child to beg, using false pretenses when applying for relief, fortune telling, and loitering with intent.

Clearly the Vagrancy Act could be used to harass any person unfortunate enough to be unemployed and homeless. But the system had obvious flaws. For the homeless, a prison sentence could be desirable. In 1860 a man charged with breaking a street lamp explained to the bench that he had done it deliberately so he could go to prison and have a place to sleep. Outraged, the magistrates refused to sentence him. There was also concern that a prison sentence might be inhumane. In 1869 the *Maidstone and Kentish Journal* ran an editorial discussing the "great problem . . . how to deal with the criminal tramp so as not to press too hardly upon those whose crime is only that of being poor."[43] A combination of financial and humanitarian considerations led many Kentish magistrates to release homeless local women and children with a caution, though able-bodied men might be sentenced to three months' hard labor and poor women and children from London were escorted out of town.

But none of these actions solved the problem. Some Kentish communities attempted to deal with poverty and unemployment in a systematic way. In Maidstone efforts were made to establish night schools to teach the unemployed new skills. The *Maidstone and Kentish Journal* also suggested that laborers be sent to the colonies and that employers stop hiring women. Local officials in Sevenoaks gave seventy-eight unemployed men jobs in public works. In Gravesend the Mendicancy Society planned to organize charity according to two principles: "I. The suppression of professional begging and the relief of the destitute. II. Help rendered to persons in temporary difficulty arising from the loss of employment." But the poor had to remain in their place and not become a nuisance. One boy was fined for "annoying passengers at the Gravesend Railway Station by looking for a job."[44]

A major goal for authorities was to limit the number of persons being supported at rate-payers' expenses. The heaviest sentences under the Vagrancy Act were given to those accused of leaving their families chargeable to the parish.[45] Admission to the union workhouse was usually reserved for the constant poor—the aged, the sick, widows, and orphans. In 1866 Dr. Edward Smith reported to the National Poor Law Board that "Workhouses are now asylums and infirmaries, and not places where work is necessarily exacted in return for food, clothing and shelter, and so generally is this appreciated, that the very term 'workhouse' has fallen into disuse, and the word 'Union' has been familiarly substituted for it."[46]

Conditions in the workhouse were purposely designed to be so unpleasant that only the truly desperate would want to apply. Residents sometimes intentionally broke workhouse regulations in order to be transferred to jail. In 1865 a tramp assured the Rochester magistrates that a month's hard labor in the local jail was "far preferable to going to the workhouse."[47] Misbehavior by a workhouse inmate, a misdemeanor punishable by twenty-one days in prison, included refusing to work, drunkenness, playing cards, gambling, smoking, possessing matches, making noise when ordered to be silent, using obscene or profane language, insulting any person, threatening any person, not duly cleansing oneself, feigning illness, refusing to go to the proper yard, climbing a fence, misbehaving during divine service, returning late from leave, insulting the master, matron, or guardians, disobeying orders, striking another person, damaging property, writing indecently, or endeavoring to excite other paupers to acts of insubordination.[48] Magistrates in Kent heard an average of one hundred cases per year of misbehavior by workhouse inmates.

But fewer than 20 percent of paupers receiving relief actually lived in the workhouse. Outdoor relief was cheaper but far more controversial. Not only did it increase the likelihood of fraud, it undermined the spirit of self-reliance; the working poor should fend for themselves. The National Poor Law Board concluded in 1870 that:

> To extend the legal obligation beyond the class to which it now applies, namely the actually destitute, to a further and much larger class, namely, those in receipt of insufficient wages, would be not only to increase to an unlimited extent the present enormous expenditure but to allow the belief in a legal claim to public money in every emergency to impede in a further portion of the population, the full recognition of the necessity for self-reliant thrift.[49]

While talk of self-reliance was very popular, the fact remained that a number of people did not have sufficient means to survive. Begging was against the law, but authorities found it less objectionable than theft or an increase in the parish relief rolls. Most towns had periodic crackdowns, but enforcement waves only called attention to unpleasant realities. In 1861 after hearing complaints about beggars, the superintendent of the Rochester police arrested a seventy-year-old blind woman who had been begging for forty years. When the magistrates complained that the arrest was inhumane, the superintendent explained that in accordance with the expressed wishes of the public he had ordered his men to arrest all beggars and they were doing so at the rate of fifteen arrests a day. Horrified, the bench dismissed all the cases involving the disabled or elderly. The police, having made their point, returned to business as usual, that is, tolerating local regulars and ordering strangers out of town.[50]

Begging was more successful and less likely to result in arrest if the beggar were disabled as a child. Five persons were indicted for stealing children to use them as props for begging. In a rather bizarre twist, one of the accused men pleaded that his wife had died and he needed money to feed his own children. He was sentenced to eighteen months—the maximum sentence.[51] Children found begging were usually released with a caution. If absolutely necessary they were reluctantly admitted to the workhouse but not without a struggle.

While local beggars were tolerated, authorities were a good deal more alarmed about the transient poor. After the Poor Law modification of 1865 paupers were no longer required to establish a parish of residence. Many citizens felt that the travelling poor had no moral claim on local funds and suspected that professional vagrants kept lists of the most desirable and undesirable parish relief systems. David Jones has found messages written on workhouse walls advising fellow travellers of the most advantageous routes.[52] In 1871 the authorities in Maidstone devised a plan whereby vagrants were given tickets to obtain food at five-mile intervals. Each ticket could only be used at its designated location. The plan was to "keep the mendicants on the move. So long as he is fed once every five miles, he can have no reason to complain."[53]

Beyond the expense to local rate-payers, authorities were also concerned that many adult vagrants were criminal. "The number of respectable vagrants bears a very insignificant proportion to the great total of 142,000 which now come annually to our county." By statute and practice vagrants were liable to arrest on suspicion. The fear of criminal vagrants apparently increased during the 1870s. In 1880 quarter sessions chairman Talbot complained that the number of tramps being arrested was increasing. "The possibility exists that tramps are of a more generally criminal class than their predecessors. The considerable increase in the number of idle and vicious tramps deserves serious consideration."[54] His conclusions seem to reflect a self-fulfilling prophecy. It is true that more tramps were being arrested and that they constituted a larger percentage of all persons being arrested. In 1870 12 percent of the persons arrested in Kent were tramps, and in 1880 the figure was nearly 20 percent. But the increase was in arrests under the Vagrancy Act, which authorized the arrest of anyone a constable suspected was about to commit a felony, misdemeanor, or breach of the peace, as well as anyone loitering or whose name and address was unknown. In other words, having been labeled as criminal types, tramps were being arrested as suspicious characters. During the period 1859 to 1880 tramps were accused in only 2 percent of indictable offenses. Though more vagrants were being treated as criminals by the police, there is little evidence that their actual behavior had changed.

As Table 5-2 indicates, arrests for summary offenses such as petty theft, begging, and misdemeanors related to the Vagrancy Act and Poor Law increased markedly during times of economic crisis, such as the harsh winters of 1861 and 1862 and especially the years of severe unemployment in Kent between 1867 and 1873. In addition to relatively minor offenses such as petty theft and begging, another more serious crime was related to periods of economic distress. Of the 216 cases of arson heard in Kent between 1859 and 1880, 27 percent occurred between 1861 and 1863. Sixty percent of the men tried for arson between 1861 and 1863 told the judge that they were starving and had started the fire in hopes of being arrested and sentenced to penal servitude. For an able-bodied unemployed man, penal servitude might be the only source of food and shelter. Many arsonists claimed they had no idea whose property they had burned; they merely wanted a ticket to prison. David Jones found similar cases in his research, including incidents in which men pleaded guilty to arson even though they were clearly innocent.[55]

Such cases created serious tensions for judicial authorities. In one case a justice told a sixteen-year-old boy who had confessed to firing a stack: "That is a circumstance now become so common that it is necessary to visit the offence with considerable punishment. You are very young and you say you were in a state of destitution at the time. The law cannot possibly recognize that as any excuse for such malicious mischief." He sentenced the boy to five years' penal servitude, though definitions of rewards and punishment were becoming seriously muddled. Justice Blackburn suggested that arsonists should be flogged so that prison would seem less attractive. Justice Pigott concluded that "There are no means of dealing with motives like these except by those who perpetrate them being taught that they must have recourse to any mode of satisfying their hunger, rather than that of destroying the property of other

Table 5-2. Theft, Vagrancy, Workhouse, and Begging Arrests by Year*

Year	Theft	Vagrancy	Workhouse	Begging
1859	772	442	69	200
1860	863	362	68	129
1861	994	448	91	190
1862	955	481	102	259
1863	1104	457	131	211
1864	1098	437	67	215
1865	1173	428	90	195
1866	1114	439	101	170
1867	1288	477	94	212
1868	1395	474	123	271
1869	1175	611	154	297
1870	1390	713	170	410
1871	1284	629	109	378
1872	1104	546	119	330
1873	1170	462	144	237
1874	1284	433	74	191
1875	1042	345	66	171
1876	959	380	65	143
1877	1080	412	70	214
1878	1208	426	99	209
1879	1101	464	84	231
1880	1312	388	114	200

*Average number per year: Theft = 1130; Vagrancy = 466; Workhouse = 97; Begging = 230.

people." If Pigott implied that theft was preferable, Justice Wightman made his view explicit. He told a grand jury that it was better to be a highwayman than an arsonist, as arson "was a crime utterly unprofitable to those who committed it, who must therefore be actuated by malicious motives or be reckless of consequences."[56]

Of course, arson was not always unprofitable. At least eight persons were charged with arson to defraud insurance companies. Despite Wightman's comments on profit, arson to defraud was not viewed more favorably than other kinds. All those convicted received lengthy sentences of penal servitude. As A. J. Peacock has pointed out, arson could have many causes, including pyromania, personal animosity, and carelessness.[57] In Kent, court records and newspapers make it possible to discern at least the expressed motive in 80 percent of cases (Table 5-3). Arson was clearly considered a

Table 5-3. Arson by Motives and Sentences

		Sentence					
	Percent total	Convicted		Under 18 months		Over 2 years	
Motive	arson charges	Number	Percent	Number	Percent	Number	Percent
Accident	10	5	21	1	20	4	80
Fraud	4	7	87	0	0	7	100
Lark	7	6	40	6	100	0	0
Poverty	37	59	73	11	19	48	81
Revenge	5	9	82	2	22	7	78
Soldier	17	21	58	1	5	16	95
Unknown	19	17	39	4	24	13	76
Total		124	58	25	20	99	80

very serious offense, with 80 percent of those convicted sentenced to at least five years' penal servitude. The only cases not punished severely were those involving youngsters setting fires during Guy Fawkes or other celebrations. One motive which did not appear needs to be mentioned. Historically arson has often been used as a form of political and social protest. In Kent between 1859 and 1880 this was not the case. There were no cases of arson during the agricultural laborers' strike of the late 1870s, and the cases involving revenge as motive involved family disputes or romantic triangles. Most of the men who set fires to escape poverty claimed that they did not know whose property they had burned. While poverty influenced the rate of arson and was cited as a motive, the issue was personal need, not social or political protest.

One of the most disturbing facts about arson was that 17 percent of the cases involved soldiers, most of whom claimed they preferred prison to the army. Soldiers were also accused of 10 percent of indictable theft, 12 percent of indictable assaults, and 10 percent of sexual assaults. Kent had more military installations than any other county, and residents of garrison towns sometimes felt they were at the mercy of the troops. In Rochester in 1860 local citizens complained that "some of the soldiers in our garrison form themselves into regular marauding parties for the purpose of committing thefts from the persons." In Dover where troop ships unloaded men just arrived from abroad, liquor salesmen sometimes boarded the ships before the men disembarked. The soldiers concluded drinking bouts by ransacking local shops. Justice Willes said he believed that one of his duties was "to protect the public from the violence of soldiers in such a place as Dover."[58]

There are at least two explanations for the high crime rate among soldiers. Some genuinely believed that prison was better than life in the army. After being sentenced to seven years' penal servitude for robbery one soldier told Justice Byles, "Thank you my Lord; that is better than ten years soldiering." Frustrated, Byles told another arsonist who claimed his motive had been to escape from the army, "I'll make you a slave instead, penal servitude for life."[59] The desperate wish to escape military service is not surprising in light of the recruitment methods used by the nineteenth-century army. Brian Bond has described how the recruiting officers preyed on young, under-educated men and "neglected to make the terms of service crystal clear." After learning the realities of his commitment—twelve years' sevice for those recruited before 1876—a young soldier might welcome any escape. The desertion rate in the 1870s was five thousand a year. If army life was grim, it was also true that the ranks were not filled with Britain's finest: "The 'scum' of the population, unemployed agricultural laborers and Irishmen, criminals and ne'er-do-wells, were inveigled into the Colours by the dubious incentives of drink, bounties, and rosy descriptions of Army life."[60] Once in the army many of the soldiers stationed in Kent found little better to do with their spare time than wreak havoc on the locals. In addition to crimes against the civilian population, soldiers also committed a great many crimes among themselves: "At no time between 1856 and 1899 was there an average of less than five hundred soldiers confined in military prisons in Britain; not infrequently the figure was twice this amount, a number equal in size to two regiments of cavalry."[61] This figure is particularly striking when one realizes that unless all persons involved were military, charges against soldiers were usually heard by civilian authorities. Soldiers made up 11 percent of the male residents of Kent county jails during the 1860s and 14 percent during the 1870s.

Policemen and soldiers in Kent were particularly at odds. The superintendent of the Kent County Constabulary assured the magistrates that "the police endeavored to steer clear of the military as much as possible." When a soldier was arrested, his comrades almost invariably attempted to rescue him. In 1860 two police constables in Deptford were stoned by soldiers. When the constables ran into a shop to escape, the soldiers entered and ransacked the place. Eventually the confrontation involved twenty soldiers and eighty police officers. In 1874 five soldiers stationed at Woolwich were indicted for beating and cutting a constable outside a pub. The soldiers had been harassing a woman and the constable had tried to stop them.[62] Soldiers in Kent were indicted in fifteen cases of assault on police between 1859 and 1880 and a great many similar cases were heard summarily.

Officers as well as enlisted men were involved in disputes with the police. In 1873 Lieutenant Francis Johnson of the Dragoon Guards broke a street lamp in Maidstone. The local constable stopped him and asked his name. Johnson, feeling it would be a great joke to arrest a policeman, ordered a sergeant and four enlisted men to take the constable and lock him in the guardhouse. After his release the constable charged Johnson with assault. Johnson assured the magistrates it had been an "inspired joke." Unamused, they fined Johnson £10. Although Johnson's joke was probably inspired by liquor, there was also an underlying tension between army officers who had been the last resort against crime and disorder for centuries and the police force that had usurped that authority. In 1861 when a policeman tried to clear a pub at closing time, the army officers present claimed he had no authority over them. When the constable arrested an officer, he was mobbed. The army officers were fined £5 each despite their complaint that the police had been "haughty."[63]

Some of the most violent confrontations involved Irish soldiers. Between 1859 and 1860, when the Donegal militia was stationed at Deptford, twelve Irish soldiers were indicted in three different assault cases. A policeman testified that the soldiers marched into Deptford pubs waving their belts and shouting, "We will kill the bloody English!" The ornamental belts were particularly hazardous, prompting magistrates to recommend that soldiers be prohibited from wearing them when off duty. But the assaults on persons and property continued. In 1879 three members of the Irish Royal Artillery went on a rampage in a pub at Sheerness after the owner refused to serve them. They destroyed one hundred drinking glasses, fifty bottles of liquor, fifty cigars, three jars of bitters, a quart decanter, two mahogany tables, five chairs, a fender, ten spittoons, a door, and other property worth £30.[64]

Alan Skelley found that a high proportion of the men in military prisons were young, Catholic, and Irish.[65] The same disproportion was found in civilian prisons in Kent. Only 4 percent of adults living in Kent were Irish-born, yet Irish men made up 10 percent of the males in Kent county prisons, and Irish women accounted for 16 percent of female prisoners. Most of the Irish in Kent had been part of the enormous migration from Ireland that had occurred in the 1850s. Lynn Lees has pointed out that "for a society that had received no large-scale migration since the Norman Conquest, this influx of Irish amounted to an invasion." The Irish immigrants did not blend into the English community. Lees found that "rather than adopt the beliefs and customs of their host population, they adapted their Irish heritage to life in foreign cities." In her study of the Irish in London, she found that "the Irish held certain streets in Central London and the East End. . . . Although working class neighborhoods were shared, neither geographic nor social assimilation took place."[66]

The Irish in Kent were heavily concentrated in certain sections of Kentish London and in areas of Chatham, Elham, and the Isle of Sheppey. In Kentish London the Irish may have served as an extra layer in the social hierarchy. Geoffrey Crossick found that in Friendly Societies whose membership consisted exclusively of unskilled workers, Irish men were routinely barred from membership. He asks, "[A]re we observing the assertion of status consciousness by that section of the English working class that could at least pride itself on not being Irish?"[67] The exclusive policy was probably based on economics as well as pride. The Irish invasion was particularly threatening to the unskilled members of the English working class. Eleven percent of those employed in London were unskilled laborers and over 50 percent of the Irish were in unskilled jobs.[68]

The Irish were also perceived as a threat by English workers in extra-metropolitan Kent. In 1864 the railroad hired Irish workers for construction on the Isle of Grain. On April 14 a mob of about fifty locals attacked the house of an Irish worker. "The mob said they would drive all the Irish out of the Isle of Grain. . . . [W]itnesses proved various acts of rioting and savage assaults on Irish people." Seven men identified as having led the assault were indicted at the summer assize for felonious and tumultuous rioting. By chance, the presiding judge was James Willes, the son of a Cork physician and a graduate of Trinity College, Dublin. Justice Willes sternly informed the defendants that there was no doubt of their guilt. "They must remember that every person, whether a Scotchman, an Englishman, or an Irishman, had a right to seek for employment and to enjoy the liberty extended to every subject of the Queen. But as they had been in prison some time [three months] he thought they had been punished sufficiently for irregular conduct." He ordered the men released on a £5 recognizance.[69]

In addition to economic concerns, the Irish were suspect on other grounds as well. They were foreigners (technically they were British subjects but it would take a brave soul to address them as such), they were Catholic, they were suspected of political radicalism, and most of them had no aspirations to English respectability. The gap between the Irish and the respectable English was widest over the question of the proper use of the public streets. Lees points out that for the Irish, "streets served as extensions of cramped interiors, playgrounds for children, draping areas for laundry and meeting places for neighbors."[70] For respectable English and the constables who served them, people who were on the street without a specific purpose and destination were a nuisance at best and suspected felons at worst.

At first glance the judicial and criminal statistics would appear to justify the fear of Irish thieves and beggars. In 1874 the *Judicial and Criminal Statistics* noted that "while persons of Irish birth in England and Wales were only one-fortieth of the population, they appeared in the commitments to prisons as one-seventh of the total. It was thence assumed that they were much more criminal than the other inhabitants of the towns or parts of towns in which they resided." A special study done by the Home Department clarified this assumption. The Irish accounted for 15 percent of those convicted summarily (that is, tried and sentenced for a minor offense without a jury), but they constituted only 8.1 percent of those tried for indictable offenses.[71] While the fact that Irish crimes were usually minor is significant, an understanding of Irish criminality also requires consideration of the types of crimes committed and the motives most frequently cited. Though the vast majority of all indictments were for property crimes, the Irish excesses were in assaults and riotous behavior. In Kent the Irish committed only 4 percent of indictable thefts, a figure nearly proportionate to their numbers in the Kentish population. However, they were involved in 12 percent of indictable assaults, 31 percent of cases of indictable riot, and 22 percent of assaults on police officers.[72]

The figures for assaults on the police are particularly interesting. In Kent assaults on police officers comprised 31 percent of indictable assaults by Irish men as opposed to only 9 percent of all assaults. One possible explanation would be that the police were particularly suspicious of the Irish and were therefore quicker to act against them.[73] However, the reality in Kent seems to have been more complex. Clashes between the police and the Irish most often involved differences over limits on public behavior. For example, the Irish of Deptford frequently gathered on Saturday night for street dances. If local merchants complained, the police came in to disperse the dancers, with predictable results. The Irish resisted police interference, a brawl broke out between the Irish and the police, and at least one Irishman was arrested as an example. At the trial after one such incident a policeman testified, "there were over fifty most disgraceful characters there, I saw the prisoner in the crowd but did not see him do anything." Nevertheless the man was convicted and sentenced to twelve months for assaulting a police officer.[74] In a clash between the police and the Irish the courts were obligated to support the police.

Given the divergent views on proper public behavior it is perhaps surprising that the police and the Irish did not clash more often. Generally the police appear to have preferred to leave the Irish alone since even benign interference might spark violent resistance. In one case Archibald McNair, an Irish soldier, was found lying in the street at 1:30 A.M. When a policeman told him to move on before he was run over, McNair beat him up. Though "the prisoner put in a written defense saying he was drunk and therefore not answerable for his actions," McNair was convicted and sentenced to nine months. It is certainly possible, however, that the Irish did not have a monopoly on overreactions. In another case James McNulty of Crayford charged two policemen with assaulting him. After six hours of unpublished testimony the judges dismissed the charges and fined McNulty £2.[75]

In addition to their unconventional habits, the Irish were suspected of being more inclined to violence. One stabbing victim told a judge: "I laid my hand on the prisoner's shoulder and said 'Allow him to get up'—I did not give him a push because I knew there was a lot of Irish around and they would as soon take your life away as not."[76] Violence seems to have been endemic to the Irish slums. Though the Irish made up only 5 percent of the population of Kentish London, they were involved in 30 percent of the assault cases heard in the Kentish sessions at the Central Criminal Court. While high levels of violence are not unusual for urban slum areas, contemporaries suspected that violence was also an intrinsic part of the Irish character. Motives in Irish assaults were rarely mercenary. The Irish in Kent were involved in 38 percent of assaults cases stemming from brawls but only 4 percent of assaults with intent to rob.

According to English witnesses the Irish attacked out of sheer homicidal belligerence. Newspaper reports often implied that the Irish were savages given to sudden unprovoked attacks: "George Bennett was attacked by Irish and so brutally beaten and kicked that on Monday evening he died."[77] In most such cases the Irish claimed to have been provoked by being laughed at or insulted. In 1859 four Irishmen were accused of grievous bodily harm to three men who had intervened to stop them kicking another man. One of the victims claimed the Irish turned on him saying, "That is the way we do it in Ireland." But James Dunn, one of the accused, said, "We had our bounty and we went to see a man; we could not see him and these men began to laugh at us." Though the jury recommended mercy on account of provocation, Dunn was sentenced to four years' penal servitude and his accomplices to fifteen to eighteen months each. In another case three Irishmen charged with malicious wounding claimed that their victim had begun the quarrel by saying, "You Irish beggars, you are drunk." The cycle of prejudice and violence can be seen in the following deposition:

> I, Ellen Connor of Greenwich, wish to give myself up; I admit that as John Taylor did call me an Irish cow and a bloody thing and told me to go away as a dirty old sow and then a few minutes later when he was passing me he said "Ho, ho, Pat!" two or three times, I then on the impulse of the moment picked up a trimming knife

> that was lying beside me and threw it at him, but did not know if it struck him or not.[78]

Though they committed fewer violent crimes than men, Irish women did not necessarily shrink from a fight. In one case Mary Riley and Bridget Hayes had been drinking together in a pub when Hayes decided to go home. Riley followed her and began banging on the door screaming that she wanted to fight. Hayes refused the challenge but when she went out the back door to buy beer for supper Riley attacked her. Riley was sentenced to six months for unlawful wounding.[79]

Irish women were far more likely to run afoul of the law than their English counterparts. Between 11 and 19 percent of the women in Kentish prisons were Irish-born (as were 16 to 23 percent of all women in English prisons). The high ratio of Irish women in prison reflects the fact that Irish women (like Irish men) were slow to accept English definitions of propriety. The Rochester correspondent for the *Maidstone and Kentish Journal* took great delight in reporting the disreputable behavior of Irish women such as Anne Daly, "a nice motherly-looking old lady just come out of Maidstone gaol, charged with being beastly drunk. She was liberated upon pledging her honour—the only thing she had to pledge—that she would quit the ancient city of Rochester within a quarter of an hour." Or an elderly Irishwoman who "evidently unacquainted with water or soap came for some purpose, but for what nobody could distinctly make out . . . but she didn't come there to be laughed at."[80]

Most public officials and journalists in extra-metropolitan Kent viewed the resident Irish as incorrigible ruffians. In the press the term "Irish" was shorthand for brutal, drunken, and generally disreputable. Reporters for respectable journals took great delight in satirical gibes. One article said simply, "The complainant was from County Cork, the defendant from Connaught and a witness from Donegal. Need we say more?" In another case the reporter said he had given up because "the prisoners were violent in their eloquence and unintelligible in their brogue." A story about a man who had violently abused his wife was headlined "AN IRISHMAN ENTIRELY." Stories frequently appeared with headlines such as "ATTACKED BY IRISH" followed by accounts describing the Irish as violent sub-humans.[81]

As L. P. Curtis concluded in his study of prejudice in Victorian England, "Paddy was made up of the following adjectives: childish, emotionally unstable, ignorant, indolent, superstitious, primitive or semi-civilized, dirty, vengeful and violent."[82] During the severe unemployment of the late 1860s *The Standard* felt it was necessary to note that "Doubtless many of the hapless mortals are Irish; but their misery is none the less real on that account." The adjective Irish could be employed even when no natives of Ireland were involved. In Brenchly in 1868 a crowd of angry locals smashed all the windows of a pub from which they had been evicted for drunkenness. Though all the participants were native-born Kentishmen the newspapers described the incident as "something very like an Irish riot."[83]

In addition to differences in behavior and custom, the Irish were alien in their religion. Catholicism was crucial to the identity of Irish immigrants, and both foreign and suspect to most of the English: in 1881 five-sixths of all Catholics in England were Irish.[84] Anti-Catholicism was a strong and virulent force in Kent. There was an active branch of the Association for Irish Church Missions to Roman Catholics—a society dedicated to "bringing truth to the Irish, laboring under the bondage and degradation of popish tyranny." An article on Englishmen who had converted to Catholicism was headlined "REMARKABLE PERVERTS." Despite the fact that over a third of the prisoners in Kent were Roman Catholic in 1864, the Kent general sessions voted not to hire a Roman Catholic chaplain nor even allow an unpaid priest to be on the premises full-time.[85]

The Irish were also suspect politically. Fears of the Irish as belligerent aliens reached fever pitch after the Clerkenwell explosion in London in December 1867. The Fenians, an Irish revolutionary movement, had set off a bomb by the prison wall in hopes of allowing a fellow Fenian to escape. The explosive was so powerful that it killed 12 persons, injured 120 others, and did £20,000 worth of damage to property. None of the casualties were prisoners and many were women and children. The English had not suffered civilian casualties on this scale for centuries. Reaction was swift: the government, which suspected the London police of negligence, appointed a secret special force to investigate. The force was to be kept secret from the Metropolitan Police and their commissioner, Sir Richard Mayne, who was launching his own investigation.

Meanwhile, throughout the country 113,674 men were appointed as special constables.[86]

In December 1867 when a group of Irishmen at Deptford marched in support of the Fenians, the Deptford police superintendent announced that he was convinced all the local Irish were Fenians.[87] To counteract the suspicions, a mass meeting of Irish Catholics at Woolwich passed the following two resolutions:

> 1. That as members of the Catholic Church and therefore obedient to her authoritative teachings, we cannot approve or be members of any association which our prelates condemn. The Irish are essentially a loyal people, loving Her Majesty the Queen, submissive to the law, and despising all treasonable and nefarious acts. . . . Fenianism did not spring from real Irishmen, whether in Ireland or England, but from unscrupulous Americans.
>
> 2. As Irishmen, we love to see the evils of Ireland removed or redressed by lawful constitutional means; but we hereby express our abhorrence against violence and resisting the civil power, convinced that such resistance of evil, and that evil must not be done, whatsoever good may come of it.[88]

Despite these assurances, the secret force, the Metropolitan Police, and the special constables were all convinced there were Fenians in Deptford. Under the circumstances arrests were inevitable. At a meeting of four Fenians in late December three of the four men present attempted to arrest each other—each was a special constable on a self-appointed undercover mission. The fourth man was a London Police detective gathering evidence. Despite the over-abundance of *agents provacateurs* all three were indicted for trial at Central Criminal Court. After a long and embarrassing trial all three were acquitted.[89]

Many residents of extra-metropolitan Kent feared that all Irishmen were Fenians, and hundreds of special constables were appointed. With so many amateur detectives and very few, if any, Fenians the results were chaotic and at times comic. A special constable at Ashford was sentenced to twenty-one days for assaulting a "respectable inoffensive man" he thought looked like a Fenian. At Tunbridge Wells local residents notified police of a Fenian threat when a group of strangers dressed in black appeared. In fact they had come to attend the funeral of a local tradesman. Even the professional police were not immune to the hysteria. The superintendent of the Kent County Constabulary arrested a man "he thought possessed the appearance of a Fenian" only to discover the man was the respectable English guest of a prominent Faversham family.[90]

By April the Home Office, perhaps suspecting that the special constables were more of a menace than the Fenians, disbanded them. The panic ended with eighty-one civilians in English prisons as Fenians and a great many very embarrassed would-be detectives. No civilian in Kent was ever convicted of Fenianism. By February of 1869 the government felt it was safe to release forty-nine of the remaining prisoners as "young hot-headed men who had been dupes and tools of the leaders." By 1874 all but four of the Fenian prisoners had been released.[91]

Though the local Irish were apparently not revolutionaries, they were still perceived as dangerous. Anti-Irish sentiments were particularly strong during the harvest season when hundreds of Irish migrant workers from Kentish London arrived to help with the hop harvest. Though not all hoppers were Irish, the *Maidstone and Kentish Journal* usually added an ethnic slur to its complaints about the migrant workers: "We are informed by the numbers that swarm in our streets that the annual invasion has taken place of the Emerald Islanders. . . . [T]hey are at best an unwelcome set of individuals." Not only strange and disorderly, they were suspected of being infectious as well: "The uproar in which they throw the neighborhood and the drunkenness and vile language which abound so long as they remain, are not only a great nuisance but must give rise to serious moral harm amongst the rural poor who are forced into contact with these degrading influences."[92]

The arrest rate for assaults and drunkenness usually soared during the hop season. On August 31, 1868 the newspapers reported that 14,000 hoppers had arrived in the past two weeks: "Their advent is marked by the usual numerous cases of felony and within the past week, no fewer than fourteen petty cases of housebreaking have been committed. All these robberies were committed at labourer's cottages in the absence of the occupants." Even those who were not criminals were potential burdens on the rate-payers, for migrant hoppers could also create a huge demand for relief. In 1870 they arrived a week before the crop was ready: "In consequence hundreds are in a half-starved state, sleeping at night in the casual wards and roaming about in the day in search of food and employment." The captain of the Kent County Constabulary said that during the hop season the police had to suspend the Vagrancy Act.[93]

Even after the season started the conditions for the hoppers were abominable:

> The conditions in most of the hop-picker camps were deplorable. Huts were badly ventilated and unsanitary, water had to be carried from the farmyard pumps, or more likely fetched from the nearest pond or ditch. Rubbish bins or incinerators were unheard of . . . there were no surgeries or first-aid posts, and if a death occurred the body had to remain in the hut until funeral arrangements could be made. For medical treatment the pickers had to walk to the nearest Poor Law doctor. Conditions on the railway were appalling. Pickers came crammed into cattle trucks in trains which often arrived in the middle of the night and left them without food or drink until fetched by the farmer the next day.

While such conditions were hardly conducive to cleanliness and good order, many suspected that the hoppers were incapable of appreciating decent living standards. A missionary warned, "[M]any of the visiting hoppers were lawless and vicious, the scum of London's East End. Drinking is freely indulged; foul language abounds; quarreling rages." One editor even warned against treating the hoppers too well: "Liberal earnings mean drunkenness and disturbance."[94]

The most severe problems came in years when the harvest was poor. In 1866 the hop crop was virtually wiped out, but fourteen thousand hoppers arrived anyway. The local workers, already suffering from the lost harvest, resented the invaders. Fights broke out frequently and the police were called in to stop major brawls in at least five different villages. Officials complained that the Irish hoppers were attacking the local citizens and police without provocation. No one mentioned that the migrants were stranded in Kent without jobs, food, or money for their return fare to London. The worst incident occurred in Hadlow, when eight Irish hoppers were arrested and held for trial at quarter sessions. The defense attorney complained "that although a serious riot had occurred not one of the inhabitants of Hadlow, who had taken part in the riot was brought here." The judge ignored the argument and sentenced the defendants to nine months' hard labor, adding that "it was not to be tolerated that persons should come into a quiet village and make a riot and disturb in the manner in which the prisoners had done. It was a monstrous proceeding."[95] The fact that the village farmers' income depended on these persons coming in was deemed irrelevant.

That it was outsiders—soldiers, Irish hoppers, vagrants, and practiced London criminals—who committed most of the crimes in Kent was accepted as an article of faith, even though the perception did not entirely square with the facts. But there were local residents who were not part of the innocent community. The most readily identifiable local outlaws were prostitutes. Twenty percent of the women committed to Kentish jails each year were prostitutes. This figure needs some explanation, as prostitution per se was not a crime. It was a misdemeanor under the Vagrancy Act for a "common prostitute to wander in the public highway and behave in an indecent or riotous manner," but only about a third of the prostitutes arrested each year were charged under the Vagrancy Act. More often prostitutes were charged with drunk and disorderly behavior.[96] So long as prostitutes kept quiet, however, officials generally limited their response to verbal disapproval. In 1859 the mayor of Rochester complained that some "women living at Flushing wandered the streets without cape or bonnet and conducted themselves in a very disreputable manner." He suggested such behavior might be suppressed under the Vagrancy Act, but little if any action was taken.[97]

Most statements by public officials reveal a good deal of ambivalence. Some magistrates simply preferred to seem unaware of the subject entirely. When three prostitutes came before the Tunbridge Wells bench on mutual assault charges, "the chairman said the Bench did not want to hear any more of the case, for the parties were all living a very bad, indecent and wicked life and they should dismiss it. The parties were all ordered to leave the court at once."[98] The mayor of Dover "expressed his astonishment at the wanton infringement of public decency" after hearing the following arrest report:

> Lydia Jarvis, an unfortunate, was charged with loitering, standing at the Five Points Lane in such a manner as to cause public annoyance. She was without a bonnet and was ostensibly engaged in knitting, but it was believed by the constable that her industry in this respect was only a feint. . . . Some other girls of her own class were near her, and it was supposed that they were congregated there for the purpose of luring victims of the opposite sex to some of their vile dens which are to be found at no great distance from the spot in question. Local tradesmen complained frequently of the annoyance occasioned by the lewd conduct of girls like the prisoner, who had been cautioned more than once against the practice of standing at that particular spot.[99]

The Dover arrest report is interesting for several reasons. The woman arrested is referred to as an "unfortunate." This was a standard euphemism for prostitute, used by policemen, judges, lawyers, journalists, and the women themselves. While the term would seem to imply an assumption that prostitutes are themselves victims, the common usage apparently blinded officials to the irony of referring to the "victims" of "unfortunates." Recent research has disproved the myth that mid-Victorian prostitutes were sacrificial victims used to protect the purity of middle-class women; most of the clients of working-class prostitutes were working-class men. But prostitutes were victims in another sense. In the Dover police report, Jarvis's knitting is described as "a feint of industry." The implication is that she has rejected an opportunity to do honest work. The fact is that some women may deliberately have chosen prostitution as the most acceptable option for working women. Judith Walkowitz points out that prostitution offered the best chance for working-class women to achieve the financial independence required for self-respect.[100]

Prostitutes had a degree of personal autonomy that few working-class women could match, for most of the prostitutes in Kent appear to have operated as free agents. There is little evidence that they were under the influence of their landlords; most brothel keepers were simply accused of knowingly allowing prostitutes to live in their houses. Only one man was charged with compelling a woman to prostitution. It may be that in working-class areas prostitutes did not need protection. Michael Winstanley found his working-class subjects remembered prostitutes as fully accepted members of the neighborhood. One man recounted the warmth and generosity the local prostitutes often showed for families in distress. "There was always a prostitute in the street. There was two in our street. Good as gold. Never interfered with anybody. . . . Prostitutes always had more money than anybody else. Some of them, ithey'd had a good time, they'd go and get things out of pawn for people and chuck it at them."[101]

While some magistrates were clearly uncomfortable with the subject, the justices at the assize usually took a businesslike view of prostitution. Justice Pollock pointed out that they were merely making a living. In the fourteen cases in which prostitutes were indicted at assize or Central Criminal Court for stealing from clients, the judges were always quick to ask the victim whether he had paid the woman for her services. In all ten cases in which the prostitute had not been paid, the defendants were acquitted. Even when large sums of money were involved, judges and juries saw the transaction as matter of business. In one case a young painter claimed a prostitute had taken £11 from him during his first visit to London. The woman swore he had given her the money and he admitted he had been too drunk to remember. The case was dismissed.[102]

In addition to protecting the earnings of prostitutes, officials usually tolerated the existence of brothels, at least during the 1860s. Police raids of disorderly houses often received little support in court. In 1863 the Dover quarter sessions chairman censured the police for detaining brothel keepers on "very insufficient grounds." An overzealous policeman had arrested a couple he found in bed at 3:00 A.M. The chairman explained that "[t]he law evidently pointed to the nuisance and annoyance which these houses created by acts of indecency, riot, noise and so forth and did not pretend to take cognizance of mere acts of immorality." At Woolwich, a prosecutor refused to argue a case against a brothel keeper; "knowing what must necessarily be the case in a town such as Woolwich, he did not wish to make a personal example of the prisoner."[103]

The independence of prostitutes and the *laissez faire* attitude of the courts were altered by the Contagious Disease Acts of 1864, 1866, and 1869. Designed to protect soldiers from venereal disease, these acts empowered special plainclothes police officers under the supervision of the War and Admiralty Offices to arrest any woman they suspected of being a prostitute. The burden of proof was on the woman. If she could not prove that she was not a prostitute she was required to undergo an internal examination for venereal disease. If evidence of disease was found, the woman was imprisoned in a locked ward until a doctor pronounced her cured. The law was originally limited to areas with large military populations; eight of the sixteen designated areas were in Kent. Woolwich and Chatham were specified in the legislation of 1864; Canterbury, Dover, Gravesend, and Maidstone were added in 1869.[104]

The acts also required that the woman arrested by the special police be registered and required to return for periodic check-ups. In her study of Plymouth, Walkowitz found local officials "warmly endorsed the Acts as a means of curtailing street disorders and disciplining the non-respectable civilian poor in their community."[105] But officials in Kent were not pleased. At protest meetings mayors, J.P.s, and clergymen all spoke out for their repeal. At a meeting in Gravesend the mayor and five J.P.s all signed a resolution calling the acts "logically absurd, monstrously cruel and unEnglish." At Dover local J.P.s and clergymen resolved that "for tyranny, cruelty and unconstitutional and diabolical actions these acts had no parallel." They also complained that the acts discriminated against the poor and that they were unchivalrous: "Englishmen had sunk to a new low and degraded condition when they could be got to spy on helpless women." Resolutions for repeal were endorsed by the Working Men's clubs of Chatham, Rochester, Brompton, Strood, and Gillingham. The petition for repeal was signed by nearly a quarter of the total population of Canterbury. Opposition cut across class lines but was overwhelmingly male. The strongest objections raised in Kent were on constitutional grounds. Any problems with local prostitutes should be dealt with by local authorities, not a secret police force sent from London by the War Office.[106]

While many groups in Kent protested against the acts the number of arrests of prostitutes under the Vagrancy Acts increased. In the 1860s the average number of arrests per year was forty-two; in the 1870s the average rose to sixty-six per year. There is also at least anecdotal evidence of a change in magisterial attitudes. In 1874 two pubkeepers were fined £5 each for allowing prostitutes to live in their houses. When the defendants complained that police had entered the bedrooms of the prostitutes without knocking, the mayor replied that he could not interfere with the police.[107] Instead of being perceived as unfortunates earning a rather disreputable living, prostitutes in this case were seen as outlaws to be hunted down.

Though ex-convicts, the poor, vagrants, soldiers, the Irish, and prostitutes (and combinations thereof) were all suspect, the people with the longest arrest records were habitual drunkards. In Kent between 1859 and 1872, when the laws against drunkenness were strengthened, an average of 1,067 persons per year were charged with drunk and disorderly behavior. The *Maidstone and Kentish Journal* kept a running tally of the number of arrests for well-known drunkards. In May 1861 the paper reported that Elias Pullen held the current record, with sixty-eight separate arrests for drunken and disorderly behavior since 1851.[108]

Habitual drunkenness was a common problem among all the outlaw groups but it was by no means limited to them. A number of those arrested for public drunkenness were identified in the press as "respectable." Several women either from "respectable families" or with "highly respectable husbands" were fined or imprisoned, and postmen and policemen were censured for being drunk on duty. In 1861 a West Malling farmer was sentenced to three weeks in jail for being intoxicated in church and disrupting the service. In another case a respectable man appeared at the Gravesend police station claiming he had murdered his family. After his report proved false, he was fined 5s. for public drunkenness.[109]

Under the Police Acts drunk and disorderly behavior was punishable with a fine of 40s. or seven days in jail, but the authorities were often lenient. In 1859 the Rochester bench dismissed a man charged with being drunk and disorderly with just a caution because "the defendant had lost a trowel while in that state" and they felt that was enough suffering. In another case a professional fly driver charged with driving while intoxicated was released after his employer assured the magistrate that drunkenness was the man's only fault. The Cranbrook police routinely first warned drunks to go home and arrested them only if they "became exceedingly boisterous or wandered about disturbing the people." The Maidstone police kept a wheelbarrow for escorting drunk and incapable persons to the stationhouse to sleep it off.[110]

During the 1870s attitudes changed and public drunkenness became less acceptable. The Intoxicating Liquors Act stiffened the restrictions and penalties for the sale of alcohol and for drunkenness. Being found drunk in public was now a misdemeanor (formerly the offense was drunk *and* disorderly behavior). Being drunk and disorderly or riotous, driving when drunk, and possessing a firearm when drunk were all punishable by up to a month in prison. In Kent arrests for drunkenness increased by 57 percent to an average of 1,888 per year between 1873 and 1880. In 1878 a wealthy farmer sentenced to three weeks' hard labor for driving while intoxicated was told that he had not been given the option of a fine because his crime was one that endangered the public. But the issue was still *public* drunkenness. In 1877 Justice Mellor ruled that a publican being arrested for being drunk after hours was not guilty. The pub was his home and "drunkenness in itself was not an offense." In Kent the distinction was particularly important. The chairman of the west Kent quarter sessions warned in 1877 that unless public drunkenness was curbed "there was a grave danger of prohibition."[111] Prohibition would have been a disaster for the hop farmers of west Kent.

In addition to the disorder caused by public drunkenness, alcohol was a factor in the majority of felonies. Drunkenness was offered as an excuse for assaults, muggings, burglaries, rapes, and even homicides. In one typical case Michael Dee was charged with stabbing a man in the throat. At his trial Dee explained, "I do not remember anything about it. I was drunk. If I was sober I should not have done it." John McCartney responded to a charge of unlawful wounding with "It is impossible that I could have struck the prisoner in the back of the neck. He was sober and I was drunk." Thomas O'Donnell, charged with assaulting a police constable, told the judge, "I was so drunk I could hardly see, I was not the cause of it." John Fitzgerald, who knifed a pubkeeper, explained, "I was drunk at the time. The drink took effect on me and I did not know about it until the policeman told me the next morning."[112] The chairman of the west Kent quarter sessions suggested there be a minimum sentence of six months for repeated drunk and disorderly arrests. As things stood he complained of constantly hearing prisoners say, "It is not me that did it, but the drink in me."[113] According to Justice Stephen, "if the existence of a specific intention is essential to the commission of a crime the fact that an offender was drunk when he did the act which, if coupled with that intention, would constitute a crime should be taken into account by the jury in deciding whether he had that intention."

But though drunkenness was sometimes offered as an excuse for crime, it was not seen in itself as a cause of crime. The authorities in Kent firmly believed that crime was caused by criminals, people completely different from themselves and other respectable Kentish men and women. Respectable citizens might occasionally be arrested and fined for public drunkenness. Under a drunken impulse they might even act in violation of the law, but they would not be criminals. Criminals were a breed apart and crime could best be prevented by removing or reforming criminals.

In principle the attack on the outlaw classes was two-pronged. An efficient police force and a stern penal system would capture and punish the hardened offenders. Educating the younger members of this class in morality, sobriety, and respectability would stop crime at the source. Theoretically the old criminals would die off and there would be no new young criminals to replace them. Justice Chanell urged members of the grand jury "representing wealth and intelligence, to give their individual countenance and support to all institutions having for their objects the encouragement of persons in distress and the diffusion of religious instruction."[114]

The hope was that over time the criminal classes would master their baser drives and voluntarily eschew crime and drunkenness. But in the present, preventing crime in Kent meant keeping soldiers, hoppers, the Irish, and other inherently criminal sorts from disturbing the respectable citizens of Kent; providing just enough relief to keep the deserving poor from starving while simultaneously instilling them with the creed of self-reliance; and persuading prostitutes and drunkards to keep their immorality off the public streets.

6

Class and Respectability

It was impossible for a gentleman like Mr. Russell to be guilty of such an offense.[1]

Defense attorney for a wealthy farmer accused of assaulting the police

Victorian justice was shaped by three of the central concerns of Victorian society: respectability, public order, and class. Although not synonymous, the three were intimately connected; each was measured on a scale determined by the other two. References to respectability are ubiquitous in the comments of attorneys, defendants, judges, policemen, and journalists. Persons identified as respectable were accused and sometimes even convicted of murders, rapes, robberies, theft, vandalism, riot, public drunkenness, and assault. Despite the belief that crimes were committed by criminals, many of the persons accused of breaking the law were not from the outlaw classes. According to the judicial statistics, 39 percent of the persons convicted of summary offenses and 18 percent of those indicted for serious crimes were of previous good character.

Respectable offenders could be dealt with in three possible ways. The charge could be dismissed on the grounds that it was impossible for a respectable person to have done such a thing. This option was used most frequently when respectable men were charged with assaults, especially sexual ones. Respectable dress would often help a case—a fact which should not be surprising to twentieth-century readers accustomed to seeing murderers appear for trial in three-piece suits. In 40 percent of the cases in which the *Maidstone and*

Kentish Journal uses the word "respectable" to describe a defendant, the reference is to dress or appearance. While appearance did not always suffice to sway judges and jurors, it certainly could help. For example, in December 1860 "James Cross, a respectably-dressed man, was charged with a violent assault on Mary Walsh, a young woman of indifferent character." Not only was the charge dismissed, but Walsh was ordered to pay Cross £2 to cover his court costs.[2]

A second possibility was that the accused could be deemed no longer respectable. The clearest example of this was the experience of Major Murton, a wealthy farmer who was convicted of beating his wife to death. Despite his income and record in the community, Murton's crime cost him his respectability. When he was released from prison he was ostracized. Thirty days after his release he was charged with threatening a neighbor. At the hearing Murton claimed there was a conspiracy against him: "Sir John Croft has said I shall not have a horse and should not have a glass of ale at the inn." The magistrate ignored Murton's complaint. "That has nothing to do with the case. The applicant swears that his life is in danger of you and we must bind you over—yourself in £50 and two sureties." When no one was found willing to provide the sureties Murton was sent back to jail. Though Murton's fall from grace was permanent, others who had forfeited respectability were encouraged to reclaim it. In 1872 a young woman who, while intoxicated, had attempted to drown her illegitimate child was discharged on the basis of having shown no criminal intent. The petty sessions chairman added that "It was sad to see a woman who might be respectable, and who appeared to have some means, letting herself down in such a manner."[3]

The third and most likely outcome was that, though the accused was convicted and given a light punishment, court officials and others would explicitly delineate the distinction between the behavior of the accused and similar actions by "real" criminals. "Murder" was a vile act committed only by monstrous criminals; if a respectable man beat a child or woman to death it was merely immoderate chastisement. "Rape" was the brutal act of a man no better than an animal; a respectable man who sexually assaulted a servant was merely guilty of "seduction." A rioter participated in behaviors that terrified reasonable men; no reasonable man could be terrified by the behavior of respectable people.

Theft by respectable people was slightly more difficult to reconcile. White-collar crimes could only be committed by people who appeared to be respectable.[4] As Justice Edward Vaughn Williams pointed out to a young man convicted of embezzlement: "In this case character was not of much assistance to the prisoner, as it was owing to his previous good character that he had been enabled to obtain a situation, which he had violated." The chairman of the west Kent quarter sessions told a convicted embezzler who pleaded for mercy on grounds of previous good character that "character and trust aggravated the offense all the more." But while he sentenced the embezzler to twelve months, at the same session he sentenced one ex-convict to ten years for stealing a loaf of bread and another to fifteen years for stealing a piece of meat.[5]

Persons accused of white-collar crimes were convicted in 79 percent of all cases, but sentences were slightly lower than for theft over all (Table 6-1). Judges sometimes chided white-collar offenders for stealing when they had no demonstrable need. Before sentencing a young postal clerk to three years for stealing from the post office, Justice Wightman told the woman: "I may say from your position of apparent respectability you cannot have had an inducement to commit this such as those who may want food."[6]

But the public reaction to white-collar offenders was often more sympathetic. When a nursery manager in Maidstone was convicted of embezzling over £1500, the following notice appeared in the *Maidstone and Kentish Journal*:

> To the Benevolent. The wife and large family of W. J. Epps (late of Maidstone and Ashford nurseries) have been placed in the

Table 6-1. Sentences for White-Collar Theft and Sentences for All Theft

	Type of theft (percent)	
Sentence	White-collar	All
6 months or less	43	33
7–18 months	42	46
2–5 years	11	10
More than 5 years	4	11

> greatest distress by the proceedings taken against her husband, which resulted in his imprisonment for six months. She does with great grief and pain respectfully ask your kind aid, as everything is taken from her, not even a bed being left to call her own, and for the last two months she has been dependent upon her friends for support. She is now necessitated to make this appeal having six children to maintain without any means whatever.

The notice was followed by an editorial urging readers to contribute. No one suggested that she try the workhouse, nor was any mention made of her husband's salary of £150 per year, which was roughly three times that of an agricultural laborer. When Epps was sentenced to four years' penal servitude the paper ran a touching account of his farewell to his son.[7]

Epps's wife and children were still accepted as members of the respectable community despite his conviction. Ironically, while the poor were being told it was more respectable to starve than beg or steal, similar behaviors by middle-class members of the community could be excused on the grounds of distress. At the west Kent quarter sessions a local merchant pleaded guilty to forging a £10 cheque but explained that he "was driven to it by distress." He was released on a recognizance. The next defendant was a little girl who had attempted to steal a pot of jam. She was sentenced to one month's hard labor and five years in the reformatory.[8]

Momentary distress might excuse one lapse but systematic theft was not excused even when the accused had respectable connections. In 1865 Samuel Greaves, the seventy-year-old actuary and secretary of the Canterbury Savings Banks, pleaded guilty to embezzling £9,300 since 1840. He had been keeping two sets of books and had been stealing systematically to supplement his salary of £200 per year. After confessing to the police, Greaves had sold his property in order to return £1700. At the sentencing at the Canterbury quarter sessions a memorial was presented asking for mercy on account of Greaves's excellent character. It was signed by eight clergymen, the sheriff of Kent, and numerous prominent tradesmen. The presiding judge rejected the plea for mercy. He explained that Greaves was a well-paid man who had taken the money of hard-working poor persons "little able to bear such loss." He was also guilty of systematic, long-term theft. Despite Greaves's list of respectable character witnesses, he was sentenced to six years' penal servitude.[9]

If theft by respectable men was disturbing, theft by respectable women seemed almost incomprehensible. The psychological implications of theft by middle-class women who had very little to do and virtually no control over their own lives escaped Victorian judges.[10] Eight women described in the press as respectable were charged with theft. Most often the designation was a function of their marriage to respectable men. Thirty-seven percent of all references to respectable women in the Kentish press are based on marriage or family connections. For example, in 1860 Sarah Russell, "an elderly lady-like woman," was charged with theft at a railway station. Her credentials were impeccable: "She had highly respectable connections. Her husband rented a well-furnished house and kept servants. He was a general agent and they had every comfort required." The judge said he "was surprised at a woman in her position committing such a paltry robbery" and sentenced her to four months' hard labor.[11]

Other respectable thieves were the sons of respectable families. Their crimes were most often deemed "larks," that is, thefts which were not serious because they were not committed out of need or avarice. Often the victim chose not to prosecute if the offender was from a good family. In 1864 a baker caught a fifteen-year-old boy stealing a loaf of bread from his cart. Though poor children were often jailed for such an offense, the baker told the court "he did not wish to prosecute as the boy was respectably connected." Identical actions could be deemed crimes or called larks according to the connections of the accused. In 1864 "a slovenly dressed young woman" was found guilty of stealing roses from a market gardener. "The Bench, determined to protect flowers and garden property from being injured, sentenced her to six weeks hard labor." But a year later when six young men were caught stealing roses worth £1, the gardener explained that "as the defendants all belonged to respectable families he did not wish to press charges."[12]

The same reluctance to prosecute sons of good families can be seen in vandalism cases. In 1874 the police arrested the teenaged sons of a Rochester J.P. for destroying £3 worth of hop binds. The victim refused to prosecute as it had been merely "a drunken freak." Neither the magistrate nor the police agreed with his assessment. The petty sessions chairman pronounced his opinion that "drunkenness was no excuse," and the superintendent of police complained that the victim had specifically asked for police protection for his property. The victim and the defendants' father left the courtroom arm in arm.[13]

If a member of a respectable family proved utterly incorrigible the family might be absolved of blame and the black sheep shorn of his immunity. A twenty-four-year-old man from a respectable family told the officer who arrested him in the act of church-breaking, "I suppose I've done it and shall have to get out of it as I did before." But this time he was sentenced to eighteen months. When a young woman from "a respectable family" was charged with being drunk and disorderly, the court had her removed from her mother's house. Some defendants tried unsuccessfully to argue that their crimes were the fault of their parents. At Central Criminal Court the thirty-seven-year-old son of a lieutenant general was tried for check forgery. His defense was that "his father never brought him up to any profession until he was twenty-four years of age, and that he had been accustomed to draw on his father for several years, and he had never made any objection." He was convicted and sentenced to five years' penal servitude. When a fifteen-year-old boy convicted of stealing a handkerchief from his father told the court that he had committed the theft because his father had turned him out, "The Chairman addressed the prisoner in a very feeling manner, and told him that in consideration of his father's respectable character, he should sentence him to one month."[14]

Respectability could and did influence judges and jurors. Though considerations of respectability were not completely in keeping with the spirit of impartial justice, they were also not completely unreasonable. Persons of good reputation with ties to the local community were less likely to become repeat offenders and could be readily identified and apprehended if they did. The notion that the well-dressed were more virtuous than others was absurd, as was the idea that persons thought to be respectable were inherently incapable of committing heinous crimes, but the belief that persons of good repute were both deserving of mercy and less likely to be a threat to the community was based on sound logic and precedents.[15] Even given the presence of a professional police force, personal behavior is regulated more by the standards an individual has internalized than by any external force. A man who appeared to have accepted the standards of respectable society was therefore less likely to violate laws that reflected those standards. Until and unless a man of respectable reputation proved that he had renounced society's standards on a permanent basis he was not perceived as an ongoing threat to the community. The courts might therefore take a charitable view of, as Justice Brett put it, "a sudden outbreak of wickedness" in a normally respectable man. The same allowances were made for public rowdiness or even riot by respectable locals. Kentish authorities were generally tolerant of raucous popular activities, probably because there were few signs of political or social hostility. This sense of security appears to have been true of England generally between 1850 and 1890 (though there were of course exceptions). In 1885 *The Times* observed: "The country was able without danger to act as if it were momentarily insane, because it felt itself essentially sane at the bottom."[16]

An average of 145 charges of breach of the peace were heard summarily each year, most of them punished by fines. Unplanned revelry by respectable local citizens usually met with a mix of understanding and caution. In Erith on Maundy Thursday, 1864, a group of men, all gainfully employed laborers and artisans with no criminal records, entered a bakery and began throwing flour at each other. When the proprietor and a customer tried to intervene they threw flour at them. They also accidentally broke a window. After leaving the shop, the men captured a policeman and planned to throw him off the dock as a lark. The constable escaped unharmed and ran for reinforcements. After tracking the culprits to a local pub, the police arrested everyone wearing flour.

Twenty-four men were arrested but only ten were held for trial. They were charged with riot and assault. The defense attorney argued that "what had taken place with regard to the bakery was really nothing more than a little amusement. . . . [T]here had been some little assault on the police but after all no great amount of violence was used. . . . [I]t was but the result of a spree." The quarter sessions chairman reminded the men that the assault on the woman customer in the bakery had been unmanly and "that in taking the flour they were committing a robbery," but noted that they were all respectable working men and sentenced them to from two to six weeks each.[17]

Sprees by upper-class citizens also met with stern words and light sentences. In 1872 the police attempted to arrest a man at the

Edenbridge steeplechase. A group of gentlemen gathered to watch and one of them, Captain Algernon Dawson of the Dragoons, knocked a policeman's helmet off with his umbrella, admonishing the constable to "Go it, Bobby!" The police superintendent arrested Dawson but offered to release him if he would give the police his name. Dawson refused and Richard Russell of Otford Castle told the superintendent that he could not arrest Dawson because he was a gentleman. At this point, according to the police, they were mobbed by six horsemen and two hundred gentlemen. At the hearing the police urged mercy for Dawson, who was fined £3. Russell and another gentleman were fined £1 each for resisting the police.[18]

Generally the definition of public order and the official tolerance for rowdiness depended on who was involved, whether any serious damage was being done to property or persons, and whether respectable persons were being annoyed as a result. As one Kentish J.P. pointed out, "[I]t was happily the case in England that a great noise was frequently made when very little was done." Some of the greatest noise was made by respectable residents in Plumstead in 1876. Plumstead Common belonged to Queen's College, Oxford. In 1866 a court order forbade any further encroachment on the common, but in 1876 the War Department leased the property for military exercises. When the military erected fences around the common, local residents pulled them down. On July 1–3 crowds of local residents gathered to protest the encroachment of the military. Three hundred policemen were called in and riots ensued. Several arrests were made but many local residents also lodged complaints about the behavior of the police. The local magistrate warned that "all respectable persons should keep out of the way of a riot, as their presence only gave countenance to the disorderly part of the mob." The president of the Commons Protection League announced that his group disavowed the riots and pledged "to endeavor to obtain their objectives by legal and orderly behavior." But he also announced that the League would establish a defense fund for all those arrested during the riots, most of them respectable young people.[19]

Eleven persons were tried at the west Kent quarter sessions for riot and malicious damage. Chairman Talbot explained the law on riot specifying that "criminality existed where terror and alarm had been caused as must necessarily affect the peaceable and quiet subjects of Her Majesty." He stressed that the issue was not the rightness of the rioter's cause but their behavior. He also noted that "people might come forward for the defense and say they were not frightened." Ten of the persons being tried were local residents accused of throwing stones and tearing down the fences. Eight of them were acquitted, one released on recognizance, and one fined. The eleventh defendant, John De Morgan, was identified as an outside agitator who had spoken to the crowds and allegedly encouraged them to riot. He was sentenced to one month and fined £50.[20]

The Plumstead rioters were respectable local residents protesting an illegal action by the central government, and so the Kentish courts were understandably sympathetic. But the courts were not so sympathetic when raucous behavior annoyed the respectable citizens of Kent. The mayor of Canterbury warned a boy charged with whistling at a local man that "boys could not be allowed to annoy respectable inhabitants in the public street. . . . [T]hey would be liable to a fine of 20s." The fines increased with the age of the offender and the respectability of the victim. In 1861 at Great Chart Miss Emma Ellen Fry accused a local man of insulting her. "A policeman was sent for but happened to be out." There was no witness to the incident, but the bench announced that they assumed Miss Fry told the truth and pronounced sentence of £2 or one month.[21]

The fact that the person doing the annoying had a legitimate grievance did not lessen the offense. A woman at Gravesend was sentenced to one week in prison on bread and water for "annoying conduct at the house of Mr. Franklin, the relieving officer." The most extraordinary case of harassment involved a young postal clerk at Dover. The man, George Hook, had fathered the illegitimate child of Hannah Squires, a local married laundress whom Hook now charged with waiting outside the post office to chase him home. He also claimed that on one occasion she had thrown the child at him. His attorney argued that "under no circumstances could the defendant have any possible right to annoy and insult the complainant in the public streets." Squires's defense was that "he had broken up her home and made her an unhappy woman for the rest of her life." The magistrate ruled that "it was admitted that there had been an unfortunate connection between complainant and defendant but that was no excuse for such conduct as this which might lead to the loss of the complainant's situation." He fined Squires 20s. A month later Hannah Squires was tried at quarter sessions for assaulting Hook with a wine bottle. At the trial it was learned that Hook had fathered two children by Squires during a four-year affair but had broken off the relationship when Squires prosecuted her husband for abusing her. The jury found Squires not guilty, perhaps feeling that justice had been served as Hook deserved the blow. The Chairman reprimanded them both for unseemly behavior and urged them to stay out of his courtroom.[22]

Disorder in the public streets was particularly upsetting for respectable tradesmen, and the courts were usually sympathetic to their complaints. In the late 1870s the Salvation Army launched a campaign to shame shopkeepers into closing on Sundays. One shopkeeper complained that they had gathered twenty people outside his door and publicly announced that he and his wife were damned forever. The group had also prayed aloud that God would kill and exterminate all their enemies. In 1880 the Tunbridge Wells Improvement Commission had the Salvation Army summoned for "unlawfully causing an obstruction to the annoyance of residents and passengers." They reported that a crowd of three hundred had blocked the main streets for twenty minutes. "These people sang hymns to popular tunes and the crowd generally joined in. Some were singing hymns, others singing songs and tin kettling. No one could have got through the crowd while they were in the street. The defendants and others were preaching and singing. They were a regular nuisance to the people in the town." The magistrates warned that "these things might lead to very serious riots," and fined all those involved.[23]

Judicial concerns about public order sometimes extended to the festivals which were holdovers from earlier times.[24] Each November Mock Mayor's Night was celebrated in several Kentish towns. Descended from the medieval festivals of Misrule in which the social hierarchy was overturned, the festival had largely lost its political and social significance and was now simply an occasion for drunken merriment.[25] In 1859 the magistrates at Maidstone warned local pub owners that they would lose their licenses if they encouraged "these mock mayors to be got up at their houses. The practice had been an intolerable nuisance." In 1860 the Gravesend magistrates heard sixteen charges stemming from Mock Mayor's Night, many of them involving respectable people. A civil engineer was fined for "being disguised by face blackened and false moustache."[26]

Fairs could also present problems. In 1859 the *Maidstone and Kentish Journal* complained about the Whitsuntide Fair with "its usual attendants, drunkenness and profligacy. It may be stated to the credit of the police that there was as much quiet as could be expected among such an assemblage." The paper also implied that the fair did not enjoy local support or participation. "Fortunately it is not held where the inhabitants can see, hear and be annoyed by it, or some steps would doubtless be taken to abolish the nuisance." But more often such festivals were encouraged or at least tolerated. One magistrate dismissed a man charged with drunk and disorderly behavior on May Day "as it happened on a day which is one of enjoyment to your class."[27]

Though authorities showed some tolerance for drunken revelry, private efforts were being made to train the working classes to seek higher forms of amusement. The clergymen of Sevenoaks met in 1861 to discuss ways to "elevate the labourer's condition both socially and intellectually." They recommended better housing, shorter working hours, better leisure facilities and the proper education of women to keep their houses tidy. They met again in 1866 this time inviting local gentry and farmers to a private meeting to consider "the condition of the working classes, with a view to their general improvement." In 1870 a Temperance Society was founded in Kent, which included among its stated goals: "to institute measures for the establishment of some benefit societies unconnected with the public house; for the promotion of village flower and industrial shows; and for the assistance of parochial efforts to win people to sobriety and rational amusements."[28]

But before the poor could be elevated the worst elements had to be sanitized. In 1863 a Society For the Suppression of Vice was formed at Maidstone "to abate that class of public offenses which consists in acts of indecency, prostitution, cruelty to animals, drunkenness, profanity and open Sabbath-breaking." According to the *Journal* the majority of those present were working men but there was also "a large sprinkling of tradesmen." The idea was that the respectable working-class members of the community would correct the behavior of the roughs. The association had no official role, but "thousands of eyes of private individuals were waiting to inform the magistrates of every breach of the law, and there were some offenses which no human law could reach and which a proper display of public opinion could alone effectively reach." Seven months later the press reported that deputations had been sent to all the shops in Maidstone that were open on Sunday. Of 117 shopkeepers, it was reported that only 26 wanted to continue Sunday trading. "Let it not be said that the interests of the majority are disregarded for the sake of an unreasonable minority."[29]

Sunday trading was a problematic issue however, as it might affect some of the very shopkeepers who supported the society. A stronger and perhaps more acceptable campaign was launched against prostitution. The leaders of the society assured its members that "the social evil was a vice which was doing more than any one other sin to lead souls to hell. The sights which were to be seen and the words that were to be heard in our public streets could not but have a baneful influence upon all classes of society." Kent already had a penitentiary for fallen women "as no respectable person will give them employment until they have been in some degree purged from the pollution in which they have lived."[30]

It is impossible to estimate how much real support the Society for the Suppression of Vice actually enjoyed. Groups that advocate morality tend to believe they represent the majority whether they do or not. Neither the police nor the courts were willing to launch an all-out campaign against prostitution, as it was neither legally nor financially practical to do so. When a member of the society wrote to the *Gravesend and Dartford Reporter* he clearly hoped to inspire his fellow citizens:

> Look at those who having once been betrayed, sacrifice their once prized honour and a priceless soul for illicit gain or a nefarious livelihood. The alleys and courts of the towns swarm with "unfortunates" whose obloquy and shame are manifest. Ruined, irretrievably ruined, the once fair daughters of our poor brethren resort to prostitution as a means to earn their daily bread! Shall we refuse a brother's sympathy to those who have fallen from virtue's highest estate by the passionate lusts of men?

The only replies to this plea were from angry residents of the working-class neighborhood the writer had cited as the home of these ruined women. The residents assured him that they were every bit as respectable as he was and they would thank him to mind his own business.[31]

This incident is significant as a reminder that despite the overheated prose of some reformers, Victorians were no more of one mind on matters of sexual morality than their twentieth-century descendants are. In 1977 F. Barry Smith described the current state of knowledge regarding Victorian sexuality as "a promising state of uncertainty." At that point Smith argued that the stereotype of "male dominance in the family, strict differentiation of sex roles, separate standards of morality for males and females, female coldness in marriage and general silence about sexual matters, all of it tainted by hypocrisy" had not been substantiated outside of the works of novelists and eccentric social reformers.[32] In Victorian Kent male dominance received judicial support as did the double standard, but attitudes towards other aspects of sexual morality were more ambiguous. It is true that judges often cleared women and children from the courtroom before hearing cases involving brothels or sexual assaults, and the *Central Criminal Court Sessions Papers* often reported that evidence in such cases was not fit to print. But the same judges also warned that such cases should be heard. "However much they might wish to spare the court the recital of objectionable details, if it was undesirable that such cases should be tried, it was still more undesirable that they should be allowed to proceed without being checked."[33]

The attitudes of judicial officials towards matters of public decency were usually pragmatic and businesslike. Judges showed little sympathy for excessive prudery. When Dover magistrates heard complaints about men bathing without a bathing machine after 7 A.M. one alderman joked about "people who were over-fastidious and sentimental" and climbed up in the window with a telescope in order to be offended. The interrogation of rape victims was usually brutally matter-of-fact and judges did not indulge displays of "Victorian" sensibilities. In a well-publicized slander case between a vicar in Tonbridge and a woman parishioner, the judge told the jurors that her testimony suggested "a lurid imagination such as were frequently to be found in low novels." He warned them not to receive such evidence without corroboration and "to guard against the influence of a pretty face in the witness box." The jury ruled against the woman and the judge assessed £10 damages.[34]

But one category of sexual offense was truly horrifying. Though the courts were pragmatic if misogynistic about sexual assaults on women, sexual acts between men or between men and animals were literally unspeakable. The Criminal Registers and the *Central Criminal Court Sessions Papers* indicate charges of bestiality, buggery, and sodomy with ellipses: b-st-y, b—y, and s—y. Blackstone had refused to define "the crime not to be named. I will not act so disagreeable a part to my readers as well as to myself, as to dwell any longer upon a subject, the very mention of which is a disgrace to human nature."[35] In 1860 Justice Williams warned a grand jury considering two cases of bestiality and two of homosexual sodomy:

> The cases are not only serious and painful but of a revolting kind. With respect to these I have to make a remark which has no doubt often been made to you, and it is that public investigations of this kind are not only extremely shocking, but very mischievous, and tending to increase such crimes by suggesting them to other persons of depraved minds who may be present. If, therefore it is possible with propriety to throw out the bill, it is better to do so. . . . In these cases you ought to employ more than ordinary care to see that the evidence is likely to lead to a conviction.

Justice Huddleston echoed these sentiments in 1876 when he told a grand jury that "in cases of disgusting character, they would, if there was reasonable doubt do well to spare the Court the consideration of revolting particulars."[36] Grand juries failed to indict in 15 percent of bestiality cases and 24 percent of cases involving homosexuality.

Besides wishing to avoid discussing such matters, judges and juries sometimes suspected the motives of those who brought the charge. "Accusing or threatening to accuse of an infamous crime to extort" was a felony punishable by life in prison. At least three cases in Kent were dismissed when it was learned that the charges had been brought by an angry ex-employer. Even disinterested witnesses were viewed with suspicion. In 1875 Justice Brett dismissed a case because he felt the constable had stood and watched the crime for an inordinate amount of time before making an arrest. In another case Justice Hawkins sentenced the offender and then rebuked the witnesses for their unseemly curiosity.[37]

Despite the reluctance to consider such charges, sodomy, the legal term for both bestiality and homosexual intercourse, was a very serious offense. It had been a capital crime continuously since the sixteenth century. Prosecutions had increased during the early years of the nineteenth century; in 1806 more men were hanged for sodomy than for murder. But the Victorians were less harsh. The last execution for sodomy was in 1835,[38] and in 1861 the death sentence for sodomy was abolished. However, the minimum sentence was ten years' penal servitude. The harsh punishments for sodomy reflected the belief that sodomy was particularly abominable as an offense against God. The form of the indictment indicates that this was a crime unlike others:

> The jurors for our Lady the Queen upon their oath present that John Farrance upon a certain mare feloniously did lay his hands and then and there feloniously, wickedly, diabolically and contrary to the order of nature have a venereal affair with the said mare and the said mare then and there feloniously, wickedly and diabolically and contrary to the order of nature did carnally know and that detestable and horrid crime called buggery with the said mare then and there feloniously, wickedly, diabolically and contrary to the order of nature did commit and perpetrate to the great displeasure of Almighty God and to the Great Scandal of all human kind.[39]

Even allowing for legal hyperbole this is heated rhetoric. Other offenses were merely felonious and against the statutes.

In practice, judges and juries were able to soften the law somewhat. The conviction rate in cases involving bestiality or homosexuality was only 48 percent. Two death sentences given in 1859 were quietly commuted to five years each. Juries also were encouraged to convict defendants of the attempt rather than the act itself to allow for lighter sentences. Only eight of the fifty-five men accused of bestiality served more than five years and 59 percent of those convicted served less than eighteen months. In addition to problems with evidence, the light sentences may also reflect the fact that 35 percent of the men accused of bestiality were under twenty years of age. Charges of homosexuality were rarer than those for bestiality—only twenty-two men were accused of buggery together or sexual assaults on males. This subject was even more taboo than bestiality. In almost all cases no information was recorded beyond the names, dates, locations, and sentences. Sentences were higher than for bestiality. Seven of the eleven men convicted, or 63 percent, were sentenced to penal servitude for at least five years.

The most publicized case of homosexuality involved a curate who was accused of an indecent assault on a French valet he met in Folkestone. The incident occurred in November 1879 but was not heard until April 1880. It had been moved from the Kentish assize to Central Criminal Court. "The Vicar of Smarden and the rector of an adjoining parish gave him an excellent character for morality and honorable conduct." The defendant had been in prison from the time of his arrest until the trial four months later. Despite serving as character witnesses, both the clergymen had found new curates and apparently neither was willing to post bail. After half an hour's deliberation the jury found him guilty and sentenced him to an additional nine months.[40] The outcome is significant. The curate was a respectable man with excellent character references. Had he been charged with rape or child molesting the case might well have been dismissed as incredible. But despite his respectability he was convicted of an unspeakable crime. This offense, unlike most others, could not be rendered less offensive. It is an interesting commentary on Victorian justice that while assaults on women and children were easily ignored or dismissed as mere trifles, indecent assaults on adult males, once made public, could not be excused.

Victorian judges and juries considered the status of both victim and offender in determining verdicts and sentences. A criminal justice system that failed to recognize the distinctions among persons would have been seriously at odds with the social hegemony. The tenets of Victorian respectability were fundamentally incompatible with the notion of regularized and impartial justice. To a great extent respectability meant behaving in a manner appropriate to one's status—hence the standards had to differ and the courts responded accordingly.

But recognizing that behavioral norms varied according to class did not mean that the courts were ever willing to admit openly that rich and poor were not equal under the law. Blatant appeals to class interests were considered offensive. In 1875 a colonel charged with indecent assault requested a special jury as he felt a prejudice existed against him "among the classes of which common juries are usually composed. I am desirous of a special jury which composed as it would be of the same rank of society as myself will look with a more impartial view." Justice Brett would have none of it. He announced sternly that "according to the law of this country the jury is not to be altered with reference to the rank of the parties. All persons are equal in the eyes of the law." But at the same time references to the reality of class were common and understood. *The Times* continued this report by noting that the jury for the case was "of a highly respectable class—all substantial tradesmen of independent means, not merely the lower class of those qualified but jurors of the better class."[41]

Although class might be considered, it grew increasingly important that legal issues be couched in terms of respectability rather than class. In 1860 a poulterer had been fined for insulting a customer. Twenty years later a clerk from the Ecclesiastical Commissioner's Office was charged with assault for having slapped a stationer for calling his remarks "absurd." He explained to the magistrate that "it was not a very nice observation for a tradesman to use to a customer and some people were more sensitive than others. He would not mind if it came from a gentleman but he could not bear it from a tradesman." The magistrate told him he was insufferable and sentenced him to £3 or one month.[42]

Though rowdy young gentlemen could safely expect to receive very light punishments, if any, they did well not to mention their class or social status to the magistrates. Tolerance of youthful exuberance was not limitless, and arrogance was particularly objectionable. In 1867 at Margate the son of a peer assaulted a waiter who had tried to eject his drunken friend. He admitted guilt but explained to the magistrate that he "had been held incarcerated in a cell for many hours, sufficient degradation for any man occupying a respectable position in society." The magistrate replied that his being a gentleman made the offense worse and sentenced him to twenty-one days. Magistrates were also unsympathetic toward the drunken pranks of upper-class tourists. In 1870 a gentleman from London and his friend decided to disembowel a first-class railway carriage during the ride from Tunbridge Wells to Dover. They ripped out the seats and elbow rests and threw them out the window, leaving a trail of furniture to mark their route. Upon their arrival at Dover, they offered the conductor £100 for the Railway Workers Benevolent Fund if he would forget the incident. The conductor refused the bribe and the railroad prosecuted. The quarter sessions chairman said such behavior was inexcusable for gentlemen and sentenced them to one month's hard labor without the option of a fine.[43]

The connection between class and justice in Kent was criticized from both sides. The Conservative newspaper complained that authorities went too far in their efforts to appease the working man. "Your only pampered aristocrat nowadays is your labourer or artisan. If he honestly pays his way everybody joins in flattering him to the echo. If he happens to have a taste for beating his wife, guzzling his wages at the alehouse, or herding his family like pigs into the sty, there is an equally unanimous conspiracy to coax him, to lecture him and to bribe him into better behavior."[44] But this view was far from unanimous. In 1874 the Chatham police found a man lying in the road bleeding from the mouth. They took the man to the police station and locked him in a cell. The next morning they discovered he was dead. The police surgeon reported that he had been "a victim of intemperance who died, under distressing circumstances, of a hemorrhage of the stomach caused by drink." A week later an angry letter appeared in the Chatham newspaper asking why the man had not been taken to a hospital. "I think it is most unfortunate for anyone to be taken ill in the street unless he has a good coat to his back and plenty of money in his pocket—as perhaps that might make a little difference. A man found with a white jacket and guernsey, who has to earn his living by the sweat of his brow in such a condition seems to have little chance of any better treatment."[45]

Complaints about unequal treatment were always met with assurances of impartiality. As Chairman Talbot pointed out after sentencing two men accused of burglarizing the cottages of local laborers during hopping season, "without the police and the courts the property of the poorer classes would be absolutely defenseless." It could also be argued that the courts protected consumers, rich and poor. In the summer of 1868 shopkeepers were warned that persons who sold unfit food to hoppers would be prosecuted, and at the October quarter sessions a merchant was sentenced to two months' hard labor for this offense. Butchers, grocers, and pub-keepers were all fined for using unfair weights and measures, but the punishments were still meted out on the basis of status. For example, one magistrate fined a baker 10s. for using false weights and then sentenced a laborer to three months for stealing a loaf of bread.[46]

Protection for consumers, even respectable ones, was sometimes considered less important than the perceived need to protect the independence and reputation of respectable merchants. In February 1869 the twenty-one-month-old daughter of G. R. Cobham, a builder, died after a Gravesend chemist confused strychnine with saccharine while preparing her teething powder. The chemist explained to a coroner's jury that he had realized his mistake but "he did not send a cryer round as it would disgrace him." The child lived three hours after taking the poison. After a twenty-three-minute deliberation, the coroner's jury ruled that it was death by misadventure rather than criminally negligent homicide. They did, however, tell the chemist they thought it was "reprehensible to mix poisons with other ingredients."[47]

The issue of class and justice was also raised in cases concerning domestic servants. Magistrates, who usually employed servants themselves, took a keen interest in disciplining the servant class, and historically were empowered to do so. Until 1867 servants were liable to criminal prosecution for failing to fulfill their master's requirements. The law was blatantly inequitable: masters accused of breach of contract were only subject to civil actions, while servants who failed to fulfill a contract, whether written or verbal, were liable to criminal prosecution and three months' hard labor. Masters could be sued for cruelty, dismissal without adequate notice, or failure to pay wages due, and the burden of proof was on the servant. A servant who disobeyed orders not only lost his job, he also forfeited his right to wages already earned. The legal precedent was that a year's contract implied that a year's work must be satisfactorily completed before any wages were due.[48] Contracts were almost always verbal and magistrates usually accepted the master's recollection as to their contents, even allowing retroactive provisions. At Tunbridge Wells in 1859, a man who had been fired without wages or notice sued for breach of contract. His employer said he had been late for work. "Both parties stated that no particular hour was agreed on. The employer did not deny this, nor did he feel the employee had robbed him of his time." Nonetheless the magistrates ruled in favor of the master.[49]

In addition to imposing financial losses, magistrates were willing and eager to imprison the disobedient. In one case at Rochester a wagoner had refused to follow his master's instructions to use a three-horse team instead of four and had insulted his master by saying that he knew more about horses. When the employer decided to withdraw the charge, "the Bench told the wagoner if it had not been for his master's forbearance they would certainly have sent him to the tread-mill for his conduct." At Ashford the magistrates sentenced a man to a month's hard labor for disobeying his master's order to eat his rhubarb pudding. Another laborer was sentenced to ten days for being, according to his employer, "a downright lazy fellow."[50]

The broad definition of criminal behavior in servants may be observed in the testimony of Captain Frederick Gedden who charged his footman, George Carter, as follows:

> He has on two occasions been unfit for his duty and more particularly on Saturday last when he refused to bring the dinner at the proper time and would not do so until it suited him. This led to remonstrances on my part, and I afterwards found him giving vent to violent and threatening language against myself. On Saturday week last on Mrs. Gedden's presenting herself at the carriage door for admission, the prisoner opened it with a pipe in his mouth. I found that he was unfit to be entrusted with the reins, and was under the necessity of driving home myself. When I gave him leave to quit my service, I was met with a volley of filthy language.

For these crimes, Carter was sentenced to a month's hard labor. In saying he had given Carter "leave to quit" Gedden was not being rhetorical. Leaving service before the agreed time was a criminal offense. After sentencing a servant who had attempted to resign his position one magistrate told the defendant, "he seemed to entertain an opinion that he could engage himself as a servant and leave when he liked, but that was a mistake." Nor was there any protection against double jeopardy in such cases. The offense of breach of contract could be punished repeatedly. At Ashford the magistrates warned a young maidservant that she must either return to work or go to prison for two months, and after her imprisonment she would have to return to work or be jailed again; this cycle would continue until she yielded.[51]

The Master and Servant Act of 1867 was designed ostensibly to correct the worst inequities. It protected employees from immediate arrest and made both parties liable to a summons, but once the summons was issued the servant was not much better off than before. The magistrate could impose a fine of £20 with a three-month prison sentence in case of default. Further, if two J.P.s agreed that the employee's behavior had included aggravated misconduct or misdemeanor they could impose a three-month prison sentence. In his treatise on the act, James Edward Davis acknowledged that it was not equitable for employees to be treated as criminals when employers were not, but since workers could not afford to pay damages the only practical expedient was to jail them. Davis also argued that absconding servants committed a crime against society. "There is something of a public wrong considering how many persons, often fellow workmen in the same class of life, suffer from the sudden neglect of work. Imprisonment may be viewed as a mode of compelling the performance of contracts."[52]

Though both parties were criminally liable in cases of aggravated offenses, magistrates in Kent imposed criminal sanctions only on servants. During the same month that the press was hailing the Act for guaranteeing equal rights, the Tunbridge Wells magistrates sentenced a farm laborer to seven days for absenting himself from work. "The Bench did not wish to be hard on a Working Man but felt it necessary to make an example as a warning to others." Throughout Kent, magistrates continued to jail absconding servants regularly. The Tonbridge magistrates also claimed that they had no power to help unpaid workers obtain wages due them, despite the fact that the legislation had specifically given workers the right to sue their employers.[53]

The Employers and Workmen Act of 1875 repealed the Masters and Servant Act, but despite the attitudinal change indicated by the new title the inequity persisted in Kentish courts. By law, breaches of contract were completely removed from criminal jurisdiction and both parties were liable only to civil action.[54] In practice absconding employees were still jailed. In July 1877 a brickmaker who left service without notice was given six weeks' hard labor. Technically he was imprisoned for defaulting on the damages his employer had won in a civil suit, but the magistrates announced that the sentence was intended "to show the working people that they could not absent themselves as they chose."[55]

Though magistrates did not always follow the letter of the law, judicial attitudes toward the relationship between master and servant did show some evolution toward equity. Kentish magistrates were increasingly reluctant to acknowledge a master's right to chastise. In 1878 an elderly farmer who struck a maidservant for oversleeping was fined 10s. and threatened with jail and hard labor if it ever happened again. In another case a man who had struck the cook after his wife complained that she was dawdling was told, "[T]he Bench was prepared to admit the behavior of the complainant was undoubtedly bad, but anything like the use of hands, whether open or closed, especially towards a woman could not be allowed."[56]

While judges were at least nominally concerned with protecting servants from employers, they considered it a primary duty to protect employers from servants. When Justice Bramwell heard a case in which an employer had incited a maidservant to poison her mistress, he explained, "[W]hen he considered how much people were at the mercy of their servants, he felt he should not be doing his duty if he did not sentence her to three years penal servitude." In another case the chairman of the east Kent quarter sessions described theft by servants as "a most heinous crime, it was the duty of servants to protect their master's property rather than steal it." To prove his point he sentenced a girl to six months' hard labor for stealing her master's shawl and told her he had been lenient because of her previous good character. The next case he heard was a stabbing that he described as "a most savage attack resulting in serious wounds." Again the sentence was six months.[57]

Though the treatment of individual members of the working class was still a subject for debate, organized movements of workers were gaining strength. Despite or perhaps because of the lack of overt hostility, Kent was the setting for strong and successful labor organizations in both urban and rural areas. Nationally the legal position of trade unions altered considerably during this period. The Criminal Law Amendment Act of 1871 removed many of the restrictions on trade union activity, though it remained unlawful to use violence, threats, intimidation, molestation, or obstruction to coerce an employer or another workman.[58] The first major test of this legislation occurred in Kent in December 1872. The workers at the Gaslight and Coke Company in Beckton stopped work in an attempt to force their employer to reinstate a fellow worker who had been dismissed. Since the Gaslight Company supplied the City of London and most of the West End, the work stoppage blacked out much of the metropolis. George Trewley, the plant manager, warned the workers that they had no legal right to stop work but agreed to the reinstatement under protest. Five of the men who led the strike were indicted at Central Criminal Court for "unlawfully conspiring by diverse means and by threats and molestation to obtain and extort from Trewley . . . a promise contrary to his own free will." During the trial Trewley testified that "there was no violence of demeanour or threatening of any sort on the part of any of the men in my presence—what led me to reinstate Dilly was my anxiety to get the work performed." The defense argued that since no molestation or threats had been used the indictment was invalid; the men had acted under the law.

Justice Brett saw the situation differently. He defined molestation as "anything done with an improper intent which the jury would think was an unjustifiable annoyance and interference with the masters in the conduct of their business." He also referred to the common law and the Master and Servants Acts of 1867 to argue that regardless of the law of 1871, the defendants were still guilty of a breach of contract and of conspiring to coerce others to break their contracts. The jury returned a verdict of guilty of "conspiracy to break and to coerce others to break their contract of service." They also recommended mercy for the defendants "on account of their great ignorance, their being misled, and their previous good character." Justice Brett saw no grounds for mercy. He sentenced the men to twelve months each for conspiracy to coerce.[59]

Brett's ruling prompted union leaders to work for clearer legislation. In June 1875 the Conspiracy and Protection of Property Act declared that acts done by a combination of persons in trade disputes were not criminal if the said acts were not criminal when performed by individuals. The legislation also limited the sentence for molestation or breach of contract to three months. The first case heard under this legisation involved a strike by Kentish ironworkers in 1875. The Amalgamated Society of Engineers had a strike fund of £250,000, and its 170 members at Erith walked off the job in December 1875 with a good deal of confidence. Six weeks later the employers resolved "to hire and fill vacancies created by the strikers . . . as they saw no reason why workers should be exempted from the law of freedom of contract." The union met to discuss the employer's decision and resolved to "defend the rights of the working classes."[60]

After the strike was settled in April, nine of the workers were arrested for having molested a scab during the strike. At the July assize Justice Huddleston told the grand jury that the workers had the right to strike but not to molest others. The question was whether they had intimidated their replacements: "Intimidation, of course, of a character that would shake a well-regulated, and not merely a weak and feeble intellect." Huddleston also stressed that collective action was illegal only if the action itself was criminal. The grand jury returned a thirty-five-count indictment. Sensing a moral victory and eager to avoid further disturbances, the prosecutor refused to present a case and the men were released, leaving the limits on strike activities satisfactorily ambiguous.[61]

In addition to industrial disputes, Kent was the home of the most successful of the agricultural labor unions involved in "the revolt of the field." From the farmers' perspective relations in the 1860s were excellent. The Kent Agricultural Association held an annual competition in which farmers and landlords presented awards in such categories as best plowman, best shepherd, length of service, bringing up the most children without parish relief, most children in domestic service, most children in Sunday School, and other respectable accomplishments of the working classes. *The Times* complained in 1859 that such awards were patronizing, but the farmers insisted they promoted goodwill. Farmers bet on their employees and took great pride in having their people win the most awards. Whether the laborers enjoyed the festivities is less clear. After the competition the laborers were sent home while the farmers and landlords attended a lavish awards banquet.[62]

But the laborers were not as docile and full of goodwill as their employers hoped. In 1872 the Kent and Sussex Agricultural Laborers Union was founded, with Alfred Simmons as its president. The announced goal was to raise wages by decreasing the supply of laborers. (As early as 1864 the *Maidstone and Kentish Journal* had warned that the emigration of laborers to the colonies could lead to a shortage: "There is ample reason for supporting every new project calculated to induce them to stay.") During its first two years of existence the union raised enough money to send 2,200 workers to Australia, and claimed full credit when the average weekly wage in Kent rose from 10s. to 15s. For the farmers the changes seemed ominous. Conservatives warned laborers that if they insisted on wages based on supply and demand they would lose the perquisites of winter work, low rent, and discounts on foods. The *Journal* sternly warned that "the laborers who belong to the Union will not have any persons but themselves to blame if some portion of the annoyance which they have caused to their employers now recoils upon their own heads." In June 1873 the farmers organized in what they viewed as self-defense. At their meeting the farmers agreed that the workers had never had it so good. One speaker chastised the laborers for complaining about the high price of coal and meat when fifty years earlier they would have had neither. The Farmers Union, whose membership included several J.P.s and Poor Law Guardians, agreed to blacklist troublemakers.[63]

The Agricultural Laborers Union meeting in 1874 heard that some members had been fired or locked out in the eastern districts. But five thousand people gathered for the meeting and the treasury held £1,631. Some farmers began to speak of the workers' need for security and to warn their fellows that it was best to keep the workers happy. Good harvests and prosperous times kept things peaceful during the mid 1870s. The spirit of harmony was such that the President of the Agricultural Labourers Union was elected to the Poor Law Board of Guardians. At the May 1878 meeting of the Agricultural Labourers Union, the executive board reported that wages were sufficient; the next goal was sickness and funeral insurance. The union also sponsored a huge celebration at Canterbury that drew 30,000 for a day of bands, parades, baby shows, foot-races, and fireworks.[64]

But bad times struck in the fall of 1878. The price of wheat fell 30 percent. The union pledged to strike if there was any cut in wages. Despite the threat the East Kent Farmer's Club voted to cut wages by 1s.6d. per week. At a meeting in Maidstone fifteen thousand union members voted to strike. In east Kent six hundred workers were immediately locked out and threatened with eviction for refusing to accept the reduction, and some farmers began firing all union members. The *Kentish Express* discreetly observed that "some employers have gone beyond the bounds of the law," but the *Journal* blamed the workers: "Why should landlords and farmers bear the whole of the brunt of agricultural depression and the labourers go scot free? They should economize as much as farmers." By the end of November twenty-two farms in east Kent were involved in the strike/lockout. The December quarter sessions heard twenty-one eviction cases, but the magistrates at both Faversham and Canterbury delayed the cases until the spring session in hopes of a peaceful solution. On February 1, 1879 Simmons and 1,100 union members sailed for New Zealand. The farmers responded by importing laborers from west Kent and hiring soldiers to work the farms. In November 1879 the landlords reduced rents and the remaining workers returned at their old wages.[65]

Remarkably during the strike there was no significant increase in reports of arson or vandalism, the two traditional weapons of rural protest. While the press occasionally referred to outbreaks of vandalism, the judicial records indicate no increase. The *Journal* suggests that the solidarity among the laborers prevented the capture of the culprits, but the outcome of the only clearly strike-related case of vandalism heard by the courts indicates that the farmers were also reluctant to bring the law into the dispute. Two Faversham teenagers were fined 5s. each for throwing a plow down a well to protest the use of labor-saving devices during the strike. Their employer immediately told the court that he would pay their fine and that they could both keep their jobs. Apparently the successful application of the laws of supply and demand made farmers flinch at using the iron fist of the law. Neither the police nor the courts played any significant role in the revolt of the field in Kent.[66]

The revolt of the field symbolized a general shift in relations between employers and workers. Gradually paternalism was being replaced by negotiations based on supply and demand. This shift from paternalism and deference to businesslike procedures could also be observed in attitudes toward such traditional activities as gleaning and poaching.[67] In a study of nineteenth-century harvesters David Morgan wrote that "the villages had their own ways of attempting to regulate gleaning, deciding for themselves when gleaning should be allowed to start, keeping out strangers and deciding who had a right to glean in certain fields." The first ruling against gleaning, a practice recognized since biblical times, had come in 1788 when the Lord Chief Justice ruled it "inconsistent with the nature of property, destructive of the peace and good order of society and amounting to a general vagrancy." But the practice continued. "During the period of gleaning the fields no longer belonged to the farmers but to the villagers. The law decreed one thing, but the laboring poor went their way regardless."[68]

Kentish farmers in the last half of the nineteenth century usually insisted that workers had no right to glean, though as private acts of charity they might allow certain individuals to do so. The courts backed the farmers. In November 1859 a farmer prosecuted a woman "with babe in arms" for stealing 2d. worth of turnips after the harvest. He assured the court that "although he was always willing to give some to any poor person who applied in the proper manner" he felt obligated to press charges as an example. In Faversham during the same week that donations were being taken for poor relief, a man was sentenced to three months' hard labor for gleaning potatoes. The victim said that while the man had absolutely no right to the potatoes he would recommend mercy. The magistrates said they saw no grounds for mercy in a clear case of theft. The fields and the crops were private property and the courts protected private property.[69]

Poaching was another activity deemed illegal by the statutes but not necessarily perceived as criminal by either its perpetrators or the public. The idea that wild animals could be considered property had never been fully accepted by the public. F. M. L. Thompson writes that "the offense in poaching was in trespassing on private land in pursuit of game, not in the taking of a wild animal that could not have a legal owner." But if that were technically the case the law implied something more. The Poaching Prevention Act of 1862 gave the police the power to stop and search persons suspected of poaching even if they were found on public lands. While the ostensible purpose of the legislation was to prevent conflicts between poachers and gamekeepers by allowing police to intervene beforehand, its effect was to deepen suspicions that the police were aiding the propertied in the oppression of poachers.[70] Though by the mid-nineteenth century the laws against poaching were no longer as blatantly discriminatory as they had been in earlier times, they still bore the taint of class interest. When a gamekeeper was charged with assaulting a farmer he found in possession of dead rabbits, the magistrate sternly advised him, "We wish to impress on your mind that you have no business to go and take game or rabbits from anyone in such a position as Mr. Hayward, who was known to you and was on land of his own occupation."[71]

David Jones found that nineteenth-century poachers fell into two categories. On the one hand there were those who poached to feed their families. This type of poaching tended to increase during times of economic hardship. In Kent the number of poaching cases heard summarily tended to rise and fall at the same times as prosecutions for petty theft and begging. On the other hand there were the professionals who ran profitable large-scale operations. Jones found these professional poachers were impressive in their "intelligence, confidence and humor" and were often perceived as shrewd businessmen rather than criminals.[72] During the debate in the House of Lords on the poaching legislation of 1862, Earl Grenville argued that "it did not appear that persons engaged in poaching were habitually guilty of other crimes. Only 1 percent of persons convicted of felony had prior convictions for poaching."[73]

Magistrates in Kent heard an average of 184 poaching cases per year. As the charges were heard summarily there is no record of the sentences, but they appear to have been light. When a man with a wife and two children and no previous record was sentenced to two months for poaching, the editor of the *Maidstone and Kentish Journal* complained of the unusual and unwarranted severity of the sentence.[74] The only time poaching cases were heard by juries was when there had been a violent confrontation between poachers and gamekeepers. Thirty-nine men appeared before Kentish grand juries on charges of poaching combined with assault or manslaughter. Even in these cases the sentences were light. Though three gamekeepers were shot and killed, no one was convicted of manslaughter. Gamekeepers apparently were unpopular with both the public and the authorities. They were often ex-military or ex-policemen with dubious records and little regard for legal niceties.[75] Some Kentish magistrates viewed them as a hindrance to law and order. As one J.P. explained, "[T]here is a proper remedy [for poaching] attainable by summons and the magistrates will see that justice and not violence is done to the offender." The longest sentence imposed for assaulting a gamekeeper was two years. Often they were much lighter. In 1865 a story on an attack on a gamekeeper was headlined "ATTEMPTED MURDER." At the next quarter sessions the four men accused were convicted of assault and given sentences of three to six weeks each.[76]

Judges appear to have accepted poaching as a fact of life and limited their involvement to preventing bloodshed. As Justice Denman explained to a grand jury, "He did not give [poachers] a lesson against poaching as he knew they would take no notice of it. What he said to poachers was this: If you are found, run away. Do as little mischief as possible."[77]

Significantly, during the periods of economic hardship when the number of poaching cases was highest (1867–1871), there were no violent confrontations between poachers and keepers. The serious clashes between gangs and keepers occurred during prosperous years. Apparently those who poached to eat were not inclined to stand and fight while those involved in professional efforts were willing and able to defend what was a very profitable, albeit illegal, business venture. As David Jones writes, poaching, for all its businesslike elements, "was an extension of a traditional independent way of life, in which notions of rights and customs played a part."[78]

Conclusion

The traditional ways of right and custom and the related concern with community law were being challenged in mid-Victorian England, but they were far from moribund. One of the most remarkable things about the criminal justice system and the men who ran it in Victorian Kent was the sense of tradition and continuity. The citizens of Kent respected the rule of law. Even the working classes brought their complaints to court. When one magistrate complained of his heavy case load a laborer explained, "[T]hat was because they did not take Lynch Law here but brought disputes to the magistrates." But the law was determined as much by local tradition as by parliamentary statutes. As one magistrate told a lawyer who raised a technical objection, "we do not want any Old Bailey sharp practices here."[1]

In mid-Victorian Kent the respectable men of the local community defined crime and justice through the J.P.s who represented "wealth and intelligence" and the juries who made the law's abstractions concrete. The national government provided the statutes and the assize judges provided expertise and ceremony for the judicial process. The importance of these ceremonial elements became apparent when modern justices ignored them. When Justice Denman pronounced a death sentence in 1875 without first donning the black cap, the omission got more attention in the press than did the facts of the case. The differences between the efficient modern judges from London and the traditional local authorities were even more plainly displayed in 1879. The assize sessions had always opened with the mayor's procession, in which the mayor, beadles, chaplain, town clerks, aldermen, and common councilmen, all dressed in ceremonial robes, escorted the judge to the courthouse in a magnificent demonstration of the majesty of the law. But when it rained on the opening day of the July assize, Justice William Grove, described by the *Biographica Juridicia* as "an efficient judge," decided the procession was a waste of time. Despite the urgent pleas of the local sheriff, Grove left for the courthouse without his escort. When the soggy mayor's procession arrived at his lodgings to discover he was already gone, they were outraged at the snub. Grove might reasonably have argued that colorful parades had nothing to do with the efficient administration of justice, but the mayor and his party clearly felt otherwise.[2]

The efficient administration and enforcement of the statutes was only part of the task of the men who ran the criminal justice system. It was equally important to maintain and protect the safety, good order, and respectability of the local community. That these aims were best accomplished by honoring the idea of the law as an impartial entity while at the same time judging cases according to persons and circumstances is neither surprising nor even necessarily sinister. No two crimes are ever exactly alike, and a justice system that lacks the flexibility to consider such factors as malice, motive, and prior offenses would be blatantly unjust. As Justice Martin pointed out, the written definitions of crimes often sound more serious than the offenses appear in reality. "Burglary is a very great sounding word, but the majority of cases of burglary are as little heinous offenses as well can be. The great bulk of cases of burglary consist in people being hungry and seeing a window open or easy to be opened, put in their hands, or get in themselves, and take away from food or article of clothing, and it is very seldom indeed that you have a real case of burglary."[3] The gravity of an offense depended in part on who was involved and why. The fact that some of the priorities of the Victorian justice system are objectionable to twentieth-century consciences and were in fact objectionable to some contemporaries, does not mean that any justice system could or should operate without priorities.[4]

Impartial justice is always an abstraction. The way a society brings the law's abstractions to life provides important evidence about the fundamental values of that society. The principles and priorities of the Kentish justice system were conservative. Authorities wished to protect the respectable community of free-born Kentish men from the encroachment of legalistic bureaucrats as well as from the predatory activities of the criminal classes. For the men of Kent the preservation of local tradition was of enormous importance. In 1878 *The Times* warned: "Reformers all forget that they are dealing with the old English people. It is one of the oldest, strongest and most obstinate breeds in the world."[5] Justice administered through a local J.P., a jury of local men, and the occasional addition of rough music was perceived as a fundamental right by the old English people of Kent.

Kentish J.P.s and jurors defined crime and the law according to the standards of the respectable male members of the community. The criminality of interpersonal violence, homicide, sexual assault, child abuse and neglect, arson, vandalism, and even theft were measured at least in part according to the perceived significance and character of the victim and offender and the concomitant threat to the respectable members of the local community. Together the respectable men of Kent combined state and community law to protect their society. Respectable men were not to be assaulted, robbed, or insulted, nor were they to be harassed by judicial authorities. In sum the criminal justice system did what its constituents expected by providing considerable protection and autonomy for the persons, property, and sensibilities of respectable Kentish men.

Notes

Abbreviations

CCC *Central Criminal Court Sessions Papers*
MKJrnl *Maidstone and Kentish Journal*

Public Record Office (PRO)

ASSI Home Office, Assize Records

Parliamentary Papers

AC *Abstract of the Census of England and Wales*
CPC *Report of the Capital Punishment Commission*
JCS *Judicial and Criminal Statistics*
KGS *Report from Kent Annual General Sessions*
PSC *Report of the Penal Servitude Act Commission*
RPI *Report of Police Inspectors*
RSS *Reports to the Secretary of State for the Home Department*
SCP *Report of the Select Committee on the Police*

Introduction

1. See David Philips, "'A New Engine of Power and Authority': The Institutionalization of Law Enforcement in England 1780–1830," in *Crime and the Law*, ed. Gatrell et al. Also see Radzinowicz, Emsley.
2. Tholfsen, *Working Class Radicalism*, p. 17.
3. Young, *Victorian England*, p. 25.
4. Tholfsen, *Working Class Radicalism*, p. 218.
5. Young, *Victorian England*, p. 24. Also see Perkin, *The Origins*, chs. 7 and 8.
6. Crossick, "Labour Aristocracy," p. 306. See also Prothero, *Artisans and Politics*, pp. 26, 239, 328; Laqueur, *Religion and Respectability*, p. 231; Meacham, *A Life Apart*, p. 26.
7. MKJrnl, 24 September 1861; 6 February 1871.
8. Peter Bailey, "'Will the Real Bill Banks Please Stand Up?'," p. 338.

9. Crossick, "Labour Aristocracy," p. 306.
10. Winstanley, *Life in Kent*, p. 86.
11. Crossick, "Labour Aristocracy," p. 307.
12. Best, *Mid-Victorian Britain*, p. 269.
13. Thompson, *Whigs and Hunters*, p. 206.
14. Michael Winstanley, "Voices From the Past: Rural Kent at the Close of an Era," in *The Victorian Countryside*, ed. Mingay, pp. 633–34.
15. Jessup, *History of Kent*, p. 161.
16. Assistant Commissioner W. Little to the Royal Agricultural Commission, quoted in Winstanley, *Life in Kent*, p. 17.
17. Jessup, *History of Kent*, p. 142.
18. *Domesday Book*, ed. Baxter.
19. Jessup, *History of Kent*, pp. 142, 154, 170.
20. *County History*, ed. Page, vol. 3, p. 317; MKJrnl, 31 December 1859.
21. Crossick, *Artisan Elite*, pp. 199–200.
22. Winstanley, *Life in Kent*, p. 163.
23. Crossick, *Artisan Elite*, pp. 32–35.
24. Jessup, *History of Kent*, p. 170.
25. Jessup, *History of Kent*, pp. 169–170.
26. *Kent Directory and Gazette*.
27. Winstanley, *Life in Kent*, p. 164.
28. Winstanley, *Life in Kent*, p. 164.
29. Winstanley, *Life in Kent*, p. 24.
30. Winstanley, *Life in Kent*, p. 164; Jessup, *History of Kent*, pp. 176, 162–68. The fifth Cinque Port was Hastings in County Sussex.
31. Winstanley, *Life in Kent*, p. 163.
32. For a discussion of the problems and potential of the judicial and criminal statistics see V. A. C. Gatrell and T. B. Hadden, "Criminal Statistics and Their Interpretation," in *Nineteenth Century Society*, ed. Wrigley, p. 340ff. Also see Sindall, "Criminal Statistics," and Emsley, *Crime and Society*, ch. 2.
33. There were sixteen petty sessional divisions in Kent. The sessions and the site of hearings were Ashford (Ashford), Bearsted (Maidstone), Blackheath (Greenwich), Bromley (Farnborough), Cranbrook (Cranbrook), Dartford (Dartford), Elham (Hythe), Faversham (Sittingbourne), Home (Canterbury), Malling (West Malling), Ramsgate (Ramsgate), Rochester (Rochester), Sevenoaks (Sevenoaks), Tonbridge (Tonbridge), Tunbridge Wells (Tunbridge Wells), and Wingham (Dover).
34. The Central Criminal Court's jurisdiction in Kent included Charlton, Eltham, Greenwich, Kidbrooke, Lee, Lewisham, Mottingham, Hamlet, Plumstead, Deptford, and Woolwich.
35. The borough quarter sessions were at Canterbury, Deal, Dover, Faversham, Folkestone, Gravesend, Hythe, Maidstone, Margate, Ramsgate, Rochester, Romney Marsh, Sandwich, Tenterden, and Tonbridge.
36. Stephen and Stephen, *Criminal Procedure*, p. 123.

Chapter 1

1. Bruce Lenman and Geoffrey Parker, "The State, the Community and the Criminal Law in Early Modern Europe," in *Crime and the Law*, ed. Gatrell et al., p. 23.
2. *Times*, 13 March 1868. Also see Green, *Verdict According to Conscience.*
3. Davis, *Criminal Law Consolidation Statutes*, p. xii.
4. CPC, pp. 32, 42, 254.
5. Stephen and Stephen, *Criminal Procedure*, pp. 17–21.
6. MKJrnl, 1 January 1859.
7. Landau, *Justices of the Peace*, p. 2.
8. Oke, *Magisterial Synopsis*, p. 716.
9. Saunders, *Summary Jurisdiction Act*, p. 46.
10. MKJrnl, 11 December 1871, 20 March 1865.
11. Oke, *Magisterial Synopsis*, pp. 21–24.
12. MKJrnl, 2 November 1868; PRO, ASSI 35, Indictments, Box 308 (Case of George Wright); MKJrnl, 21 December 1868.
13. *Kentish Express*, 6, 13, 20 April 1872.
14. *Kentish Observer*, 10 October 1867; *Kentish Mercury*, 20 August 1870; *Hansard's*, vol. 223 (March 19, 1875), c. 103.
15. MKJrnl, 24 September 1877.
16. *Kentish Express*, 22 January 1859.
17. *Tonbridge Telegraph*, 20 June 1866.
18. Thompson, "Eighteenth Century English Society," p. 154; Thompson, "'Rough Music'," p. 285; Ingram, "Ridings."
19. Storch, "Policeman as Domestic Missionary," p. 490.
20. MKJrnl, 1 September 1863.
21. MKJrnl, 15 October, 1861.
22. *Tonbridge Telegraph*, 9 July 1864; PRO, ASSI 36, Depositions, Box 11 (Case of Thomas Cole et al.); *Tonbridge Telegraph*, 30 July 1864.
23. MKJrnl, 1 August 1864; PRO, ASSI 36, Depositions, Box 11 (Case of Thomas Cole et al.); *Tonbridge Telegraph*, 12 December 1867.
24. *Gravesend Free Press*, 21 May and 4 June 1859.
25. *Gravesend Reporter*, 18 June 1859.
26. *Gravesend Free Press*, 18 June 1859.
27. MKJrnl, 11 August 1866; *Tonbridge Telegraph*, 11 August 1866; MKJrnl, 13 August 1866; PRO, Criminal Registers, HO 27, vol. 143.
28. *Kentish Observer*, 29 January 1863.
29. JCS, 1862, vol. 56, p. vi.
30. RPI, 1859 (ses. 1), vol. 22. The total manpower of the Kent County Constabulary was 236 from 1859–1862; 262 from 1863–1867; and between 300 and 305 for the period 1868–1880. The borough forces were in Canterbury, Deal, Dover, Faversham, Folkestone, Gravesend, Hythe, Maidstone, Margate, Ramsgate, Rochester, Sandwich, Ten-

terden, and Tunbridge Wells. On the distinctions between county and borough forces see Steedman, *Policing the Victorian Community*, pp. 41–47.

31. SCP, p. 16.
32. MKJrnl, 15 January 1870.
33. RPI, 1859, vol. 22; 1866, vol. 58; 1867, vol. 57; 1872, vol. 50.
34. MKJrnl, 21 March 1870.
35. *Kentish Express*, May–November 1875.
36. Meacham, *A Life Apart*, p. 18.
37. CCC, vol. 68, September 1868.
38. RPI, 1859, vol. 22; 1866, vol. 58; 1867, vol. 57; 1872, vol. 50. For a fuller discussion of wages and salaries of the Victorian police see Steedman, *Policing the Victorian Community*, p. 109.
39. *Kentish Express*, 2 October 1869; CCC, vol. 81, April 1875.
40. *Rochester Gazette*, 14 May 1861; MKJrnl, 29 October 1870, 17 April and 29 July 1871, PRO, ASSI 35, Indictments, Box 311 (Case of George English).
41. Gash, *Aristocracy and the People*, p. 36. Also see Radzinowicz, *A History of English Criminal Law*, vol. 4, p. 105; Philips, "A New Engine," in *Crime and the Law*, ed. Gatrell et al., p. 161; R. Quinault, "The Warwickshire County Magistracy and Public Order, c. 1830–1870," in *Popular Protest and Public Order*, ed. Quinault and Stevenson.
42. MKJrnl, 14 January 1860.
43. SCP, p. 21.
44. Jones, *Crime*, p. 31.
45. Barbara Weinberger, "The Police and the Public in Mid-Nineteenth Century Warwickshire," in *Policing and Punishment*, ed. Bailey; also see John Field, "Police, Power and Community in a Provincial English Town: Portsmouth 1815–1875," also in Bailey; Storch, "Plague of Blue Locusts"; Philip Thurmond Smith, *Policing Victorian London*.
46. CCC, vol. 83, December 1875. On police violence also see Emsley, "'Thump of Wood.'"
47. MKJrnl, 10 July 1860, 4 December 1871.
48. MKJrnl, 14 March 1870; *Tonbridge Telegraph*, 18 March 1871.
49. Stephen and Stephen, *Criminal Procedure*, p. 61.
50. MKJrnl, 26 May 1860.
51. *Gravesend Reporter*, 7 November 1863.
52. *Gravesend Reporter*, 21 and 28 November and 5 December 1863.
53. *Gravesend Reporter*, 16 January 1864; PRO, Criminal Registers, HO 27, vol. 137.
54. *Gravesend Reporter*, 18 November 1864.
55. MKJrnl, 7 November 1864. Robert Storch found similar variations in his study, "'Please to Remember the Fifth of November': Conflict, Solidarity and Public Order in Southern England, 1815–1900," in *Popular Culture*. Also see Bushaway, *By Rite*, pp. 64–74.

56. CCC, vol. 70, August 1869.
57. Steedman, *Policing the Victorian Community*, pp. 18–21.
58. *Chatham Observer*, 19 June 1875.
59. Accounts of the events of election day and the petty sessions appeared in MKJrnl, 5 December 1868, and *Tonbridge Telegraph*, 28 November 1868.
60. *Tonbridge Telegraph*, 5, 12, and 26 December 1868.
61. Richter, "Role of Mob Riot," p. 23.
62. *Times*, 4 December 1868, p. 10. Also see Emsley, "'Thump of Wood,'" p. 128.
63. Philips, "A New Engine," in *Crime and the Law*, ed. Gatrell et al., p. 156.
64. Stephens and Stephens, *Criminal Procedure*, p. 20.
65. Jennifer Davis, "A Poor Man's System," pp. 309–35.

Chapter 2

1. CPC, pp. 621–22.
2. CPC, pp. 25, 38, 78.
3. CPC, p. 32.
4. CPC, pp. 33, 38; MKJrnl, 26 February 1877.
5. PRO, ASSI 36, Depositions, Box 21 (Case of Thomas Fordred); MKJrnl, 8 April 1876.
6. MKJrnl, 26 February 1877.
7. MKJrnl, 27 November 1865; CPC, p. 79.
8. MKJrnl, 9 April 1859, 14 April 1863; CPC, p. 37.
9. CPC, pp. 97, 27.
10. MKJrnl, 14 April 1863, 12 January 1867.
11. For an excellent account of the panic and its aftermath see Jennifer Davis, "The London Garotting Panic of 1862: A Moral Panic and the Creation of a Criminal Class in Mid-Victorian England," in *Crime and the Law*, ed. Gatrell et al., pp. 190–213.
12. RSS, p. 29ff.
13. *Gravesend Reporter*, 15 November 1879; MKJrnl, 1 February 1859, 5 December 1864, 15 March 1873; *Kentish Express*, 10 January 1876; *Dover Express*, 7 February 1863. For the traditional code of honor and its resistance to change see Davidoff, *Best Circles*, p. 36, and Andrew, "Code of Honour."
14. Jervis, *Archbold's Pleading*, p. 764.
15. MKJrnl, 10 December 1861.
16. *Tonbridge Telegraph*, 15 March 1873; CCC, vol. 84, August 1876; vol. 66, October 1867.
17. CCC, vol. 61, November 1864.
18. MKJrnl, 10 December 1861.
19. Radzinowicz, *English Criminal Law*, vol. 1, p. 704.
20. Philips, *Crime and Authority*, p. 250.

21. *Kentish Express*, 24 February 1877; MKJrnl, 24 February 1877.
22. *Times*, 10 December 1878, p. 3c.
23. PRO, ASSI 36, Depositions, Box 23 (Case of Stephen Gambrill).
24. *Times*, 15 January 1879; MKJrnl, 16 and 25 January and 3 February 1879.
25. MKJrnl, 16, 19, and 23 April 1859; *Hansard's*, vol. 157 (March 16, 1860), c. 731.
26. MKJrnl, 12 April and 1 August 1864; PRO, ASSI 36, Depositions, Box 11 (Case of Richard Miles and James Batchelor).
27. MKJrnl, 29 June and 3 August 1867.
28. PRO, ASSI 36, Depositions, Box 15 (Case of Alfred Lawrence). MKJrnl, 2 August 1869.
29. CPC, p. 36.
30. CCC, vol. 74, July 1871; MKJrnl, 15 and 17 July 1871.
31. MKJrnl, 16 July 1877.
32. The trial transcript is in CCC, 1877, vol. 86. The events are also covered extensively in the *Maidstone and Kentish Journal* and *The Times* from April through November 1877. The terms of the commutation are in the Parliamentary Papers, 1878, vol. 79, p. 7.
33. CPC, p. 131.
34. MKJrnl, 24 March and 14 April 1863.
35. Skelley, *Victorian Army*, p. 166. On the problems of recruitment see Bond, "Recruiting," p. 335.
36. CCC, vol. 62, September 1865.
37. *Kentish Observer*, 31 March 1864; MKJrnl, 25 December 1865.
38. Olive Anderson, *Suicide*, p. 368.
39. MKJrnl, 4 December 1880.
40. Olive Anderson, *Suicide*, p. 368.
41. *Times*, 29 November 1861, p. 9c, 3 December 1861, p. 10a; CCC, vol. 55, November 1861.
42. Macdonald, "Secularization of Suicide." Also see Olive Anderson, *Suicide*.
43. *Chatham Observer*, 13 September 1879; *Kentish Observer*, 31 March 1864.
44. MKJrnl, 3 August 1867, 7 March 1868.
45. MKJrnl, 15 January 1866.
46. Anderson's second chapter deals extensively with the age and gender of suicide victims.
47. *Kentish Express*, 13 March 1869; MKJrnl, 20 October 1860, 7 October 1872.
48. MKJrnl, 12 January 1874.
49. CPC, p. 25; *Times*, 28 November 1861; Oke, *Magisterial Synopsis*, p. 742; MKJrnl, 22 December 1873. For an overview, see Walker, *Historical Perspective*.
50. MKJrnl, 10 December 1861, 15 September 1873; PRO, ASSI 35, Indictments, Box 313; Bligh, *This Was A Man*, p. 238.

51. MKJrnl, 4, 8, 11, and 15 September 1879. In 1834 Cockburn had been the defense attorney in the M'Naughton case that had set the precedent for the use of the insanity plea.

Chapter 3

1. *Tonbridge Telegraph*, 4 March 1865.
2. Blackstone, *Commentaries*, bk. I, pp. 442, 445.
3. See Katherine O'Donovan, "The Male Appendage: Legal Definitions of Women," in *Fit Work for Women*, ed. Burman, p. 138ff., and Lee Holcombe, "Victorian Wives and Property: Reform of the Married Woman's Property Law, 1857–1882," in *Widening Sphere*, ed. Vicinus, p. 4.
4. Oke, *Magisterial Synopsis*, p. 742.
5. See Crow, *The Victorian Woman*, p. 146; Lieck, *Justice and Police*, p. 49; and Holcombe, "Victorian Wives," in *Widening Sphere*, ed. Vicinus, p. 4. The problems in interpreting this law are discussed in Branca, *Silent Sisterhood*, p. 9.
6. James Fitzjames Stephen, *Digest*, p. 17.
7. MKJrnl, 29 July 1871.
8. Charles Dickens, *Oliver Twist*, ch. 51.
9. CCC, vol. 57, January 1863.
10. Gatrell and Hadden, "Criminal Statistics," in *Nineteenth Century Society*, ed. Wrigley, p. 374.
11. Philips, *Crime and Authority*, p. 148.
12. Philips, *Crime and Authority*, p. 149.
13. MKJrnl, 16 August 1859, 29 January 1859.
14. For example see Nancy Tomes, "'Torrent of Abuse'," p. 342.
15. Bauer and Ritt, *Free and Ennobled*, p. 1, 3. On chivalry and its requirements see Harrison, *Separate Spheres*, p. 71; Sally Mitchell, "The Forgotten Women of the Period," in *Widening Sphere*, ed. Vicinus, p. 51; Clark, *Women's Silence*, p. 2; Davidoff, "Class and Gender," p. 118.
16. MKJrnl, 11 April 1877. Also see Tomes, "'Torrent of Abuse'," p. 342.
17. CCC, vol. 80, August 1874; vol. 73, April 1871; vol. 75, April 1872.
18. MKJrnl, 8 December 1863.
19. MKJrnl, 11 December 1871.
20. MKJrnl, 8 December 1863.
21. MKJrnl, 6 December 1873.
22. Blackstone, *Commentaries*, bk. 1, p. 444.
23. Henry John Stephen, *New Commentaries*, vol. 2, p. 276.
24. Based on Summary Jurisdiction Records for Kent in the Parliamentary Papers. On the merits of the records regarding enforcement of the Act as a guide to the incidence of spouse abuse see Tomes, "'Torrent of Abuse'," p. 338, and Ross, "'Fierce Questions'," p. 591.

25. *Chatham Observer*, 21 September 1872; MKJrnl, 3 July 1860, 9 January 1865; *Tonbridge Telegraph*, 20 August 1870.
26. *Hansard's*, vol. 158 (May 2, 1860), c. 533–534, 524.
27. MKJrnl, 7 August 1876; *East Kent Times*, 25 June 1859; CCC, vol. 50, June 1859; MKJrnl, 17 May 1859.
28. MKJrnl, 14 January 1860; PRO, ASSI 36, Depositions, Box 19 (Case of John Chatsfield).
29. *Times*, 3 March 1859, p. 11; *Tonbridge Telegraph*, 13 June 1874. Also see Tomes, "Torrent of Abuse'," p. 335.
30. Henry John Stephen, *New Commentaries*, vol. 2, p. 276.
31. MKJrnl, 24 May 1859; CCC, vol. 49, July 1859.
32. MKJrnl, 12 January 1867; CPC, p. 33.
33. Quoted in Jennie Kitteringham, "Country Work Girls in Nineteenth Century England," in *Village Life and Labour*, ed. Samuel, p. 129.
34. Quoed in Seccombe, "Patriarchy Stabilized," p. 55. Also see Weeks, *Sex, Politics and Society*, p. 68; Mitchell, "Forgotten Women," in *Widening Sphere*, ed. Vicinus, p. 51.
35. Leonore Davidoff, "The Separation of Home and Work: Landladies and Lodgers in Nineteenth and Twentieth Century England," in *Fit Work for Women*, ed. Burman, p. 76.
36. MKJrnl, 14 July 1863, 5 December 1864.
37. CCC, vol. 83, December 1875; MKJrnl, 26 July 1875, 8 February and 19 March 1859. On the acceptance of domestic violence see Ross, "'Fierce Questions'," pp. 591–93.
38. MKJrnl, 9 December 1862.
39. MKJrnl, 22 December 1863; PRO, ASSI 36, Depositions, Box 10 (Case of James Palmer).
40. Quoted in Kitteringham, "Country Work Girls," in *Village Life and Labour*, ed. Samuel, p. 129.
41. *Chatham Observer*, 7 September 1872; CCC, vol. 84, August 1876. This view of women was not unique to the Victorians. In 1571 Thomas Wolsey issued a proclamation that "no woman should come together to babble and talk, but all men should keep their wives in their houses." Quoted by Russell, *Crisis of Parliaments*, p. 76.
42. MKJrnl, 14 March 1870, 8 November 1879.
43. PRO, ASSI 35, Indictments, Box 213; PRO, ASSI 36, Depositions, Box 18 (Case of James Gorman); MKJrnl, 6 December 1873.
44. Much of the following discussion of rape appeared in a slightly revised form in my article "Rape and Justice in Victorian England," *Victorian Studies* 29 (1986): 519–34.
45. Henry John Stephen, *New Commentaries*, vol. 4, p. 78.
46. Quoted in Henry John Stephen, *New Commentaries*, vol. 4, p. 82.
47. *Kentish Express*, 12 March 1859; MKJrnl, 8 February 1859, 18 October 1873.
48. MKJrnl, 9 December 1872.
49. *Times*, 3 August 1875, p. 10.

50. PRO, ASSI 35, Indictments, Box 318 (Cases of John Goodwin, George Lilles, and Fredrick Allen). MKJrnl, 9 December 1872, 15 March 1873.
51. MKJrnl, 18 December 1865, 28 July 1871; *Dover Express*, 26 September 1863.
52. MKJrnl, 9 December 1872; PRO, ASSI 35, Indictments, Box 312 (Case of Alfred Ralph).
53. MKJrnl, 3 November 1879; *Chatham Observer*, 15 June 1878.
54. MKJrnl, 28 July 1866, 14 March 1870; *Kentish Observer*, 19 May 1866; *Canterbury Journal*, 9 November 1878.
55. MKJrnl, 25 July 1874; *Kentish Express*, 6 August 1870.
56. Jervis, *Archbold's Pleading*, p. 764.
57. MKJrnl, 27 January 1873.
58. *Kentish Express*, 19 July 1879; *Dover Express*, 26 September 1863.
59. *Gravesend Reporter*, 15 November 1879; *Tonbridge Telegraph*, 4 March 1865; MKJrnl, 8 April 1872.
60. MKJrnl, 7 May 1861; *Gravesend Reporter*, 7 May 1864; MKJrnl, 30 December 1872; *Dover Express*, 12 September 1863; MKJrnl, 9 March 1868.
61. MKJrnl, 24 October 1864; *Rochester Gazette*, 16 October 1864.
62. *Kentish Express*, 6 April 1872; MKJrnl, 24 July 1875, 3 September 1859; *Faversham Mercury*, 27 October 1860; *Times*, 3 August 1875.
63. *Gravesend Reporter*, 7 May 1870.
64. *Times*, 14 July 1864; MKJrnl, 9 June 1877; *Dover Express*, 3 September 1880.
65. Henry John Stephen, *New Commentaries*, vol. 4, p. 80.
66. MKJrnl, 22 March 1864, 17 July 1876.
67. Jervis, *Archbold's Pleading*, p. 764.
68. MKJrnl, 4 August 1863, 5 June 1875, 14 March 1874; PRO, ASSI 35, Indictments, Box 314 (Case of William and Frederick Divall).
69. *Kentish Express*, 20 January 1863.
70. PRO, Criminal Registers, HO 27, vol. 134.
71. Marcus, *The Other Victorians*, pp. xiii, 25. For Acton's reputation among his peers see F. Barry Smith, "Sexuality in Britain, 1800–1900," in *Widening Sphere*, ed. Vicinus, p. 182; Branca, *Silent Sisterhood*, p. 125; Weeks, *Sex, Politics and Society*, p. 39ff. Also see Peterson, "Dr. Acton's Enemy," pp. 579–90.
72. MKJrnl, 26 February 1877. On the ideology of rape as a natural urge also see Clark, *Women's Silence*, pp. 39, 88.
73. *Kentish Observer*, 4 July 1861; MKJrnl, 20 October 1873, 25 December 1865; PRO, ASSI 35, Indictments, Box 305 (Case of George Parkins).
74. *Canterbury Journal*, 9 November 1879.
75. MKJrnl, 19 December 1864; PRO, ASSI 35, Indictments, Box 304 (Cases of William Harrison and James Meadhurst).
76. *Times*, 3 August 1875.
77. Anna Clark and others have suggested that the fear of rape developed

as a middle-class myth used to terrorize women into staying in their proper place. See Clark, *Women's Silence*, p. 110, and Walkowitz, "Jack the Ripper." The evidence in Kent suggests that this argument, in its conspiratorial aspect, is seriously overstated.

78. *Times*, 3 August 1875.
79. *Kentish Express*, 18 January 1879; *Faversham Mercury*, 14 September 1878.
80. MKJrnl, 25 July 1868.
81. Stephen, *New Commentaries*, vol. 4, p. 78.
82. MKJrnl, 11 June 1870.
83. *Dover Express*, 12 September 1863.
84. *Hansard's*, vol. 215 (April 2, 1873), c. 481.

Chapter 4

1. CCC, vol. 86, October 1877.
2. AC 1861, p. 225.
3. Quoted by Pinchbeck and Hewitt, *Children in English Society*, vol. 2, p. 359. On the Victorian family see Weeks, *Sex, Politics and Society*, p. 25; Horn, *Victorian Country Child*, p. 180; Wohl, ed., *Victorian Family*, p. 201 and *passim*; Ruth Inglis, *Sins of the Fathers*, p. 23; Young, *Victorian England*, p. 150.
4. *Times*, 9 May 1872; CCC, vol. 76, May 1872.
5. CCC, vol. 80, August 1874; vol. 82, June 1875; vol. 84, September 1876.
6. Shurkin, *Invisible Fire*, pp. 184–211.
7. *Gravesend Reporter*, 21 August 1869; *Chatham and Rochester News*, 26 December 1874.
8. *Chatham Observer*, 6 March 1875, 5 January 1878.
9. On the question of state intervention and public health see Lambert, "Central and Local Relations," p. 121ff.; Henriques, *Welfare State*, and Brian Harrison, "State Intervention and Moral Reform," in *Pressure From Without*, ed. Hollis.
10. Quoted by Inglis, *Sins of the Fathers*, p. 23.
11. MKJrnl, 17 April 1860, 22 May 1865.
12. MKJrnl, 29 July 1871.
13. PRO, ASSI 36, Depositions, Box 23 (Case of Mary Pevy).
14. MKJrnl, 5 February 1861.
15. David Roberts, "The Paterfamilias of the Victorian Governing Class," in *Victorian Family*, ed. Wohl, p. 62.
16. *Chatham Observer*, 7 September 1872, 22 May 1875.
17. MKJrnl, 28 June 1859, 19 May 1860.
18. *Tonbridge Telegraph*, 14 April 1877; *Kentish Mercury*, 25 January 1862; MKJrnl, 14 August 1869.
19. *Dover Express*, 3 January 1863.
20. Jervis, *Archbold's Pleading*, p. 690.

21. MKJrnl, 11 July 1870.
22. MKJrnl, 16 January 1879; *Chatham Observer*, 7 September 1872.
23. Branca, *Silent Sisterhood*, p. 110.
24. MKJrnl, 26 July 1859.
25. Perkin, *Origins*, p. 185. Also see Behlmer, *Child Abuse*, p. 12.
26. Letter quoted by Pinchbeck and Hewitt, *Children in English Society*, p. 622.
27. *Tonbridge Telegraph*, 23 August 1879.
28. *Tonbridge Telegraph*, 25 March 1871; PRO, Criminal Registers, HO 27, vol. 164, Quarter Sessions, 1871.
29. MKJrnl, 3 February 1879.
30. *Chatham Observer*, 22 May 1875.
31. For a discussion of the debate see Sharpe, "Domestic Homicide," pp. 29–48. Also see Demos, "Child Abuse in Context," in *Past, Present and Personal*, and Pollock, *Forgotten Children.*
32. *Dover Express*, 3 January 1863.
33. MKJrnl, 18 August 1866; 21 and 28 October and 9 December 1867; CCC, vol. 58, September 1863; *Times*, 24 September 1863.
34. Elissa P. Benedek, "Women and Homicide," in *Human Side of Homicide*, ed. Danto et al., p. 150.
35. PRO, ASSI 36, Depositions, Box 12 (Case of Ann Lawrence); MKJrnl, 22 and 29 December 1866.
36. PRO, ASSI 36, Depositions, Box 14 (Case of Frances Kidder); *Kentish Express*, 4 and 11 April 1868.
37. CCC, vol. 81, March 1875; PRO, ASSI 36, Depositions, Box 21 (Case of James Parris); PRO, ASSI 36, Depositions, Box 23 (Case of Charles Brown); MKJrnl, 4 August 1863.
38. Danto et al., *Human Side of Homicide*, p. 10.
39. Inglis, *Sins of the Fathers*, pp. 116, 117.
40. *Times*, 3 April 1868; MKJrnl, 23 March 1868; *Chatham Observer*, 7 September 1872.
41. Sharpe, "Domestic Homicide," p. 46. Also see the lively debate between Sharpe and Lawrence Stone: Stone, "Interpersonal Violence," p. 22ff; Sharpe and Stone, "Debate," and Stone, "Rejoinder," p. 206ff. For statistics see Hoffer and Hull, *Murdering Mothers*, p. 87, and Lionel Rose, *Massacre of the Innocents*, p. 1.
42. CPC, p. 291.
43. Hoffer and Hull, *Murdering Mothers*, p. 87.
44. Jervis, *Archbold's Pleading*, p. 715.
45. CPC, pp. 22, 124, 274. For a discussion of the connections, both perceived and real, between illegitimacy and infanticide see Ann R. Higginbotham, "'Sin of the Age'.
46. Weeks, *Sex, Politics and Society*, p. 24.
47. Gillis, "Servants," p. 171.
48. *Dover Express*, 12 December 1863; MKJrnl, 4 December 1875, 29 January 1870.

49. *Kentish Observer*, 9 August, 29 November, and 20 December 1866; MKJrnl, 25 December 1876.
50. *Kentish Observer*, 9 August 1866.
51. Gillis, "Servants," pp. 166, 143, 159; also see Higginbotham, "'Sin of the Age'."
52. PRO, ASSI 36, Depositions, Box 9 (Cases of Eliza Bunyan and Mary Ann Hook).
53. MKJrnl, 28 March and 11 April 1874.
54. CCC, vol. 70, September, 1869; MKJrnl, 10 July, 21 August, and 27 September 1869; *Times*, 25 September 1869.
55. PRO, ASSI 35, Indictments, Boxes 316, 317 (Cases of Jane Carpenter and Jane White); MKJrnl, 26 February 1877. Foss, *Biographia Juridicia.*
56. MKJrnl, 2 and 9 April, 30 July, and 6 August 1861; PRO, ASSI 35, Indictments, Box 301.
57. Quoted in Pinchbeck and Hewitt, *Children in English Society*, vol. 2, p. 618.
58. *Hansard's*, vol. 209 (March 6, 1872), c. 1497.
59. MKJrnl, 20 March and 26 April 1879.
60. PRO, Criminal Registers, HO 27, vol. 155.
61. Bristow, *Vice and Vigilance*, p. 60.
62. MKJrnl, 8 January 1859, 21 October 1867.
63. MKJrnl, 4 December 1871.
64. MKJrnl, 18 August 1863, 12 December 1862.
65. MKJrnl, 3 June 1867, 19 May 1873; *Kentish Observer*, 30 June 1864.
66. *Dover Times*, 17 April 1863; *Chatham Observer*, 7 September 1872.
67. *Canterbury Journal*, 9 November 1878; MKJrnl, 26 July 1875.
68. MKJrnl, 25 July 1874.
69. Gorham, "'Maiden Tribute'," p. 365.
70. Anthony S. Wohl, "Sex and the Single Room: Incest Among the Victorian Working Class," in Vicinus, *Suffer and Be Still*, p. 201.
71. James Fitzjames Stephen, *Digest*, p. 103.
72. PRO, ASSI 35, Indictments, Boxes 299 (Case of William Standen), 308 (Case of Henry Comfort), 314 (Case of John Reader); MKJrnl, 30 July 1859, 14 December 1874, 13 March 1868; PRO, Criminal Registers, HO 27 vol. 143; MKJrnl, 5 March 1866, 28 October 1878; PRO, ASSI 35, Indictments, Box 318 (Case of James Baker).
73. MKJrnl, 16 January 1879. It is worth noting that even the legislation of 1908 did not include stepfathers in its ban. (Nancy F. Anderson, "'Marriage of a Deceased Wife's Sister'," p. 85.)
74. Smith, "Sexuality in Britian," in *Widening Sphere*, ed. Vicinus, p. 196.
75. Davidoff, "Home and Work," in *Fit for Women*, ed. Burman, p. 74.
76. On adolescence in Victorian England see Mintz, *Prison of Expectations*, p. 18; May, "Innocence and Experience."
77. James Fitzjames Stephen, *Digest*, p. 15.

78. PRO, ASSI 35, Indictments, Box 305 (Case of James and Thomas Webb).
79. KGS, p. 565.
80. Chairman J. G. Talbot to west Kent quarter sessions, quoted in MKJrnl, 11 March 1872.
81. Report to Kent general sessions, published in MKJrnl, 15 August 1864.
82. MKJrnl, 3 November 1863, 3 July 1865. For more on the reformatory schools see Horn, *Victorian Country Child*, p. 189ff.
83. MKJrnl, 24 April 1865, 5 November 1861, 8 January 1859.
84. MKJrnl, 11 March 1872, 3 January 1860, 1 July 1871.
85. *Kentish Independent*, 5 March 1879; MKJrnl, 4 January 1869; *Kentish Mercury*, 15 February 1868.
86. KGS, p. 29.
87. On the timing and causes of the new outlook on juvenile crime see Gillis, "Evolution"; Magarey, "Invention"; and May, "Innocence and Experience."
88. MKJrnl, 21 January 1860.
89. KGS.
90. Horn, *Victorian Country Child*, p. 194. Also see Gibson, *English Vice*, p. 193.
91. MKJrnl, 5 September 1870, 10 November 1879, 16 July 1870.
92. Winstanley, *Life in Kent*, p. 202.
93. *Gravesend Reporter*, 15 November 1879.
94. MKJrnl, 16 October 1869, 3 December 1859, 31 January and 7 February 1860, 3 February 1863.
95. *Hansard's*, vol. 157 (April 20, 1860), c. 2048.
96. Gillis, "Evolution," p. 98; also see Meacham, *A Life Apart*, p. 93; May, "Innocence and Experience," and Magarey, "Invention."
97. Winstanley, *Life in Kent*, p. 203.
98. MKJrnl, 24 October 1868, 24 July 1869.
99. *Dover Express*, 23 May 1873; MKJrnl, 2 June 1873.
100. *Greenwich Chronicle*, 26 April and 18 June 1879.
101. CCC, vol. 90, August and September 1879.
102. *Greenwich Chronicle*, 27 September 1879.
103. MKJrnl, 1 January 1861. On education as social control see Horn, *Victorian Country Child*, p. 59; Pinchbeck and Hewitt, *Children in English Society*, vol. 2, p. 516; Meacham, *A Life Apart*, p. 171.
104. MKJrnl, 5 July 1873, 10 January 1876.
105. Dunae, "Penny Dreadfuls," p. 141. Also see Emsley, *Crime and Society*, pp. 70, 71.
106. CCC, vol. 86, October 1877.
107. MKJrnl, 3 February 1868. Also see Harrison, "State Intervention," in *Pressure from Without*, ed. Hollis, p. 316.
108. MKJrnl, 6 July 1878, 9 February 1880; *Tonbridge Telegraph*, 21 August 1880. MKJrnl, 22 November 1879. Emsley cites sources claim-

ing that a half-million parents were prosecuted in England for non-compliance during the first twenty years after the National Education Act was passed. (Emsley, *Crime and Society*, p. 24).

109. MKJrnl, 14 December 1864; *Kentish Observer*, 12 September 1861; MKJrnl, 22 November 1879. Also see Meacham, *A Life Apart*, p. 171.
110. *Kentish Mercury*, 11 January 1868.

Chapter 5

1. MKJrnl, 7 January 1871.
2. JCS, p. xvi.
3. Tobias, *Crime and Industrial Society*, p. 11.
4. Though Dickens's criminals were fictional creations, he did have at least one encounter with the real thing. While lecturing at Chatham in 1859 he was robbed by a local man identified as a market gardener. MKJrnl, 8 January 1859.
5. Philips, *Crime and Authority*, p. 287.
6. Gatrell, "Decline of Theft and Violence," in *Crime and the Law*, ed. Gatrell et al., p. 265; Jennifer Davis, "London Garroting," also in *Crime and the Law*, p. 213.
7. Rude, *Criminal and Victim*, p. 125. For a further discussion of the existence and definition of the criminal class see Emsley, *Crime and Society*, ch. 6.
8. Young, *Victorian England*, p. vi.
9. PSC, p. 25.
10. MKJrnl, 15 January 1872.
11. MKJrnl, 1 January 1872, 23 October 1865, 14 March 1874.
12. MKJrnl, 3 November 1863, 7 January 1871.
13. JCS, p. xvi.
14. Herrup, "Law and Morality," p. 116; Emsley, *Crime and Society*, p. 213.
15. MKJrnl, 12 March 1862.
16. MKJrnl, 6 March 1875.
17. MKJrnl, 15 October 1861.
18. Herrup, "Law and Morality," p. 107.
19. Philips, "A New Engine," in *Crime and the Law*, ed. Gatrell et al., p. 158.
20. The best treatment of this transition in punishment theories is in Beattie, *Crime and the Courts*, chs. 9 and 10. Also see Emsley, *Crime and Society*, ch. 9.
21. For a cogent albeit controversial critical analysis of the nineteenth century penal system see Ignatieff, *A Just Measure*. Also see Radzinowicz, *English Criminal Law*, vol. 5, and Emsley, *Crime and Society*, ch. 9.
22. CPC, p. 620.

23. PRO, ASSI 36, Depositions, Box 12 (Case of James Fletcher).
24. PSC, p. 37.
25. "Report on Maidstone Gaol," Kent General Sessions, in MKJrnl, 3 November 1863, 15 August 1864.
26. *Hansard's*, vol. 158 (May 2, 1860), c. 519.
27. MKJrnl, 2 December 1862.
28. PRO, ASSI 35, Indictments, Box 317 (Case of Henry Godfrey). PRO, Criminal Registers, HO 27, vol. 179; MKJrnl, 7 January 1860. On the attitudes towards and treatment of habitual offenders see Peter W. Bartrip, "Public Opinion and Law Enforcement: The Ticket-of-Leave Scares in Mid-Victorian Britain," in *Policing and Punishment*, ed. Bailey, pp. 150–81; Stevenson, "The Habitual Criminal."
29. PSC, p. 23.
30. MKJrnl, 26 July 1873, 11 January 1869.
31. Best, *Mid-Victorian Britain*, p. 121.
32. Jennifer Davis, "London Garroting," p. 213.
33. Gatrell, "Decline of Theft and Violence," p. 265.
34. CCC, vol. 92, December 1880; MKJrnl, 7 January 1860, 12 July 1864; CCC, vol. 59, January 1864; MKJrnl, 19 February 1861. Also see Miller, *Cops and Bobbies*, p. 126.
35. MKJrnl, 4 January 1859, 18 September 1865.
36. MKJrnl, 19 February 1861, 29 January 1859.
37. MKJrnl, 1 November 1869.
38. Crossick, *Artisan Elite*, p. 50.
39. *Times*, 25 January 1867; MKJrnl, 28 January 1867; *Times*, 26 January 1867.
40. *Kentish Mercury*, 26 January 1867.
41. Michael Winstanley, "Voices From the Past: Rural Kent at the Close of an Era," in *The Victorian Countryside*, ed. Mingay, p. 633.
42. MKJrnl, 22 August 1864. Also, e.g., see MKJrnl, 8 June 1859, 28 August 1871, 13 May 1872, 1 March 1880.
43. MKJrnl, 17 January 1860, 28 January 1869.
44. MKJrnl, 28 May 1870, 6 September 1869.
45. On the subject of support requirements see Crowther, "Family Responsibility," pp. 131–45.
46. Quoted by Michael E. Rose, *English Poor Law*, p. 168.
47. MKJrnl, 20 February 1865.
48. Provisions under the Poor Law (33 Geo. 3, c. 55).
49. Michael E. Rose, *English Poor Law*, p. 160; Minutes of Poor Law Board 1869–1870, quoted in Michael E. Rose, *English Poor Law*, p. 226.
50. MKJrnl, 18 June 1861.
51. MKJrnl, 10 June 1867; PRO, Criminal Registers, HO 27, Vol. 149, Quarter Sessions, July 1867 (Case of Thomas Maundy).
52. Jones, *Crime*, p. 187; also see Vorspan, "Vagrancy and the New Poor Law," p. 59ff.

53. MKJrnl, 6 February 1871.
54. MKJrnl, 6 February 1871, 24 January 1880.
55. Jones, *Crime*, p. 202.
56. MKJrnl, 22 December 1863, 25 March 1862.
57. A. J. Peacock, "Village Radicalism in East Anglia, 1800–1850," in *Rural Discontent*, ed. Dunbabin, pp. 27–62.
58. MKJrnl, 20 March 1860, 25 July 1868.
59. MKJrnl, 8 December 1860.
60. Bond, "Recruiting," pp. 335, 334, 332.
61. Skelley, *Victorian Army*, p. 127.
62. *Rochester Gazette*, 4 June 1861; CCC, vol. 52, May 1860; vol. 81, November 1874.
63. MKJrnl, 14 July 1873; *Kentish Observer*, 4 June 1861.
64. MKJrnl, 7 January 1861, 16 December 1872; *Sittingbourne Gazette*, 25 June 1859; *Kentish Observer*, 27 November 1879.
65. Skelley, *Victorian Army*, p. 134.
66. Lees, *Exiles of Erin*, pp. 15, 18, 58, 63.
67. Crossick, *Artisan Elite*, p. 186.
68. Lees, *Exiles of Erin*, p. 98.
69. *Rochester Gazette*, 26 April 1864; MKJrnl, 1 August 1864; PRO, ASSI 35, Indictments, Box 304 (Case of Thomas Butler).
70. Lees, *Exiles of Erin*, p. 82.
71. JCS, vol. LXXXI, p. 282.
72. These results are similar to those found by David Jones for Merthyr in Jones, *Crime*, pp. 105–6; Roger Swift for Wolverhampton in "'Another Stafford Street Row': Law, Order and the Irish Presence in Mid-Victorian Wolverhampton," in *The Irish in the Victorian City*, ed. Swift and Gilley, p. 182; and Finnegan, *Poverty and Prejudice*, p. 143, though Finnegan found a higher incidence of theft.
73. Swift, in "Outcast Irish," p. 268, cites a number of local studies where police harassment was a factor.
74. CCC, vol. 73, April 1871.
75. CCC, vol. 60, July 1864; MKJrnl, 23 July 1866.
76. CCC, vol. 61, November 1864.
77. CCC, vol. 61, November 1864; MKJrnl, 1 October 1861.
78. CCC, vol. 93, December 1880.
79. MKJrnl, 16 August 1859; CCC, vol. 72, June 1870.
80. MKJrnl, 29 January 1859.
81. MKJrnl, 16 August and 10 December 1859, 11 September 1865.
82. Curtis, *Anglo-Saxons and Celts*, p. 53.
83. *Standard*, 29 December 1869; MKJrnl, 7 September 1868.
84. Arnstein, "Victorian Prejudice," p. 455. Also see Lees, *Exiles of Erin*, p. 212; Sheridan Gilley, "Catholic Faith of the Irish Slums, London, 1840–1870," in *The Victorian City*, ed. Dyos and Wolff, p. 837.
85. MKJrnl, 15 July 1867, 27 January 1868, 12 January 1864. Also see Arnstein, "The Murphy Riots."

86. Phillip Thurmond Smith, *Policing Victorian London*, pp. 190–96.
87. Crossick, *Artisan Elite*, p. 239.
88. *Times*, 24 December 1867.
89. CCC, vol. 67, February 1868.
90. *Kentish Mercury*, 15 February 1868.
91. *Hansard's*, vol. 194 (February 22, 1869); vol. 219 (March 27, 1874), c. 347.
92. MKJrnl, 1 September 1863, 25 September 1876.
93. MKJrnl, 31 August 1868, 29 August 1870.
94. West Kent Federation, *Old Days*, p. 42; MKJrnl, 25 September 1876.
95. MKJrnl, 15 October 1866.
96. On the link between prostitution and drunkenness see Finnegan, *Poverty and Prostitution*, p. 32.
97. MKJrnl, 4 June 1859. According to JCS, 1860, vol. 159, six prostitutes were arrested in Rochester under the Vagrancy Act during that year. Also see Walkowitz, *Prostitution and Victorian Society*, p. 14.
98. MKJrnl, 6 September 1869.
99. *Dover Express*, 25 April 1863.
100. Finnegan, *Poverty and Prostitution*, p. 115; Gorham, "'Maiden Tribute'," p. 355; Walkowitz, *Prostitution and Victorian Society*, pp. 19, 31.
101. Winstanley, *Life in Kent*, p. 199.
102. CCC, vol. 90, May 1879.
103. *Dover Express*, 17 October 1863; MKJrnl, 7 July 1863.
104. E. M. Sigsworth and T. J. Wyke, "A Study of Victorian Prostitution and Venereal Disease," in *Suffer and Be Still*, ed. Vicinus, p. 77.
105. Walkowitz, *Prostitution and Victorian Society*, p. 4.
106. *Gravesend Reporter*, 18 June 1870; *Chatham Observer*, 19 June 1875; McHugh, *Prostitution*, p. 156.
107. MKJrnl, 29 June 1874.
108. MKJrnl, 7 May 1861.
109. MKJrnl, 18 September 1860, 28 January 1861, 11 December 1865, 12 February 1866, 10 July 1869, 2 April 1861, 28 July 1863, 12 February 1866.
110. MKJrnl, 3 September 1859, 26 May 1860, 12 April 1864, 16 April 1861.
111. MKJrnl, 14 October 1878. CCC, vol. 86, June 1877. Brian Harrison has argued that drinking habits were undergoing class segregation during the Victorian period. "Respectable people tended increasingly to drink in private," while the working classes patronized the pubs. (Harrison, *Drink and the Victorians*, p. 319). The records for Kent are not complete enough to distinguish who was drinking where but the *Maidstone and Kentish Journal* reports a number of cases in which respectable people were arrested for public drunkenness. MKJrnl, 7 July 1877.
112. CCC, vol. 59, January 1864; vol. 56, May 1862; vol. 67, April 1868; vol. 72, July 1870.

113. MKJrnl, 7 January 1878.
114. MKJrnl, 21 December 1868.

Chapter 6

1. MKJrnl, 7 May 1872.
2. MKJrnl, 18 December 1860.
3. *Faversham Mercury*, 5 August 1865; MKJrnl, 17 August 1872.
4. On white-collar crime see Sindall, "Middle-Class Crime."
5. MKJrnl, 10 December 1859, 10 March 1863; PRO, Criminal Registers, HO 27, vol. 134.
6. MKJrnl, 24 March 1863.
7. MKJrnl, 24 November 1863, 1 August 1864.
8. MKJrnl, 13 April 1878; PRO, Criminal Registers, HO 27, vol. 179.
9. MKJrnl, 23 October 1865.
10. See Hartman, "Crime and the Respectable Woman."
11. MKJrnl, 24 January 1860.
12. MKJrnl, 16 February and 5 July 1864, 19 June 1865.
13. *Chatham Observer*, 20 June 1874.
14. MKJrnl, 18 March 1871, 29 January 1861; CCC, vol. 67, April 1868; MKJrnl, 22 November 1859.
15. On the significance of reputation and character in sentencing in earlier periods see King, "Decision-Makers," p. 48; Herrup, "Law and Morality," p. 119.
16. Quoted by Richter, "Role of Mob Riot," p. 28. Also see Jones, *Crime*, ch. 1, and Harrison, *Peaceable Kingdom.*
17. MKJrnl, 12 April 1864; PRO, Criminal Registers, HO 27, vol. 137.
18. MKJrnl, 6 May 1872.
19. MKJrnl, 23 October 1876; *Times*, 4, 5, and 6 July 1876.
20. MKJrnl, 23 October 1876; PRO, Criminal Registers, HO 27, vol. 173.
21. MKJrnl, 2 June 1860, 30 July 1861.
22. MKJrnl, 24 March 1860; *Dover Express*, 21 March and 11 April 1863.
23. *Chatham Observer*, 8 November 1879; *Tonbridge Telegraph*, 13 November 1880.
24. See Storch, *Popular Culture*; Cunningham, *Leisure*; Bushaway, *By Rite*, pp. 245–74; Yeo and Yeo, eds., *Popular Culture.*
25. For the traditional festivals of Misrule see Natalie Davis, "Reasons of Misrule."
26. MKJrnl, 19 November 1859, 17 November 1860.
27. MKJrnl, 18 June 1859, 7 May 1861.
28. MKJrnl, 2 April 1861, 8 January 1866, 31 January 1870. On efforts to improve the lower orders in Kent also see Jessup, *History of Kent*, pp. 160–61.
29. MKJrnl, 28 April and 24 November 1863.
30. MKJrnl, 28 April 1863, 25 January 1861.

31. *Gravesend Reporter*, 9 and 16 April 1864.
32. F.Barry Smith, "Sexuality in Britain," p. 182.
33. MKJrnl, 23 October 1876.
34. *Dover Express*, 1 August 1863; *Tonbridge Telegraph*, 29 June 1878.
35. Quoted by Bullough, *Sexual Variance*, p. 566.
36. MKJrnl, 10 December 1859, 17 July 1876.
37. MKJrnl, 26 July 1875, 28 October 1878.
38. Harvey, "Prosecutions for Sodomy," pp. 939–48.
39. PRO, ASSI 35, Indictments, Box 299 (Case of John Farrance).
40. *Kentish Express*, 1 May 1880.
41. *Times*, 31 July 1975.
42. MKJrnl, 7 April 1860, 28 October 1880.
43. *Kentish Observer*, 26 September 1867; MKJrnl, 22 October 1870.
44. MKJrnl, 31 December 1859.
45. *Chatham Observer*, 6 and 13 June 1874.
46. MKJrnl, 21 October 1880, 13 April and 5 October 1868.
47. *Gravesend Reporter*, 27 February 1869.
48. Daphne Simon, "Master and Servant," in *Democracy*, ed. Saville, pp. 160–64.
49. MKJrnl, 22 November 1859.
50. MKJrnl, 5 April and 7 June 1859; *Gravesend Reporter*, 14 January 1865.
51. *Deal Telegraph*, 28 March 1860; MKJrnl, 26 February 1861; *Kentish Express*, 8 January 1859.
52. James Edward Davis, *Master and Servant Act*, p. 6.
53. MKJrnl, 31 August and 12 October 1867.
54. Fraser, *Trade Unions*, p. 195.
55. MKJrnl, 21 July 1877.
56. *Tonbridge Telegraph*, 7 July 1877, 16 February 1878.
57. *Times*, 13 June 1863, p. 13; MKJrnl, 8 March 1864.
58. Fraser, *Trade Unions*, p. 192.
59. CCC, vol. 77, December 1872.
60. *Kentish Express*, 22 January 1876.
61. MKJrnl, 17 July 1876; PRO, ASSI 35, Indictments, Box 316 (Case of James Bauld).
62. For accounts of these meetings see MKJrnl, 8 November 1859 and every November thereafter.
63. MKJrnl, 5 April 1864, 2 September and 11 November 1872, 16 June 1873. For a full treatment of the dispute see Arnold, "'Revolt of the Field'"; p. 74ff.
64. MKJrnl, 11 and 25 May 1874, 4 April and 20 May 1878.
65. *Kentish Express*, 26 October and 9 and 16 November 1878; MKJrnl, 25 November 1878; *Faversham Mercury*, 1 and 15 February 1879.
66. MKJrnl, 3 and 10 March 1879. The same reluctance to use the courts against workers was evident in Kent during the Swing riots of the 1830s (Jessup, *History of Kent*, p. 156).

67. Regarding these changes also see David Jones, "Rural Crime and Protest," in *The Victorian Countryside*, ed. Mingay, p. 570. Regarding traditional practices see Sharpe, "Enforcing the Law," in *Crime and the Law*, ed. Gatrell et al., p. 106. Also see Bushaway, *By Rite*, p. 207ff.
68. David H. Morgan, "The Place of Harvesters in Nineteenth Century Village-Life," in *Village Life and Labour*, ed. Samuel, pp. 56, 59, 60.
69. MKJrnl, 1 November 1859; 29 January 1861; *Faversham Mercury*, 29 January 1861.
70. F. M. L. Thompson, "Landowners and the Rural Community," in *The Victorian Countryside*, ed. Mingay, pp. 459, 460.
71. MKJrnl, 17 January 1860.
72. Jones, *Crime*, pp. 73, 75. The entire third chapter of Jones's book is a very useful and insightful discussion of the Victorian poacher.
73. *Hansard's*, vol. 167 (June 24, 1862), c. 976.
74. MKJrnl, 12 March 1861.
75. Martin, *Secret People*, p. 196. Also see Jones, *Crime*, pp. 79, 80.
76. MKJrnl, 17 January 1860, 11 September 1865; PRO, Criminal Registers, HO 27, vol. 140.
77. MKJrnl, 15 January 1880.
78. Jones, *Crime*, p. 70.

Conclusion

1. MKJrnl, 11 December 1860, 11 September 1865.
2. MKJrnl, 21 December 1868, 14 March 1875, 21 July 1879. On the psychological significance of the ceremonial aspects of the assize see Thompson, "Patrician Society."
3. CPC, pp. 41, 42.
4. This point is made and very well demonstrated as it applies to eighteenth century justice in King, "Decision-Makers." King has managed to bring great light to the heated debate between Douglas Hay ("Property, Authority and the Criminal Law," in Hay et al., *Albion's Fatal Tree*, pp. 17–63), and John Langbein ("Albion's Fatal Flaws," pp. 96–120).
5. *Times*, 5 November 1878.

Bibliography

Primary Sources

United Kingdom. Public Record Office.
Home Office, Criminal Registers, HO 27, vols. 122, 125, 128, 131, 134, 137, 140, 143, 149, 152, 155, 161, 164, 167, 170, 173, 176, 179, 182, 185.
Assize Records:
Minute Books, ASSI 32, vol. 16–25.
Indictments, ASSI 35, Box 299–320.
Depositions, ASSI 36, Box 9–24.

Central Criminal Court Sessions Papers. Vols. 49–93 (1859–1880). London: Butterworths, 1860–1881.

United Kingdom. Parliament. Parliamentary Papers (House of Commons)
Judicial and Criminal Statistics. 1859–1881.

1860, vol. 64. — 1872, vol. 65.
1861, vol. 60. — 1873, vol. 70.
1862, vol. 56. — 1874, vol. 71.
1863, vol. 65. — 1875, vol. 81.
1864, vol. 56. — 1876, vol. 79.
1865, vol. 52. — 1877, vol. 86.
1866, vol. 68. — 1878, vol. 79.
1867, vol. 66. — 1879, vol. 76.
1867–1868, vol. 67. — 1880, vol. 77.
1868–1869, vol. 58. — 1881, vol. 95.
1870, vol. 63. — 1882, vol. 75.
1871, vol. 64.

Reports of Police Inspectors
1859 (ses. 1), vol. 22.
1864, vol. 35.
1866, vol. 58.
1867, vol. 57.
1872, vol. 50.

Report on Roman Catholic Prisoners. 1862, vol. 5.
Report of the Prison Commission. 1862, vol. 25.
Report on the State of Discipline in Gaols. 1863, vol. 9.
Report of the Penal Servitude Act Commission. 1863, vol. 21.

Report of the Select Committee on the Police. 1863, vol. 35.
Abstract of the 1861 Census of England and Wales. 1863, vol. 53.
Report from the Select Committee of the House of Lords on the Present State of Discipline in Gaols and Houses of Correction. 1863, vol. 55.
Report of the Capital Punishment Commission. 1866, vol. 21.
Report on Capital Convicts Reprieved Since 1859. 1870, vol. 57.
Abstract of the 1871 Census of England and Wales. 1873, vol. 71.
Report of the Commission Inquiring Into the Workings of the Master and Servant Act. 1867, 1874, vol. 24.
Reports to the Secretary of State for the Home Department on the State of the Law Relating to Brutal Assault. 1875, vol. 61.
Report from Kent Annual General Sessions in Reply to Request from Home Secretary re: Treatment and Punishment of Juvenile Offenders. 1881, vol. 53.
Abstract of the 1881 Census of England and Wales. 1883, vol. 78–79.

Great Britain. Parliament. *Hansard's Parliamentary Debates*, 3d Series.
Vols. 158–59 (1860).
Vol. 163 (1861).
Vol. 166 (1862).
Vols. 171–72 (1863).
Vol. 181 (1866).
Vols. 194–96 (1869).
Vol. 209 (1872).
Vol. 216 (1873).
Vol. 218 (1874).
Vol. 222 (1875).
Vol. 227 (1876).
Vol. 236 (1877).
Vols. 237–38 (1878).

Newspapers

Canterbury Journal, 1863, 1864, 1878.
Chatham and Rochester News, 1874.
Chatham and Rochester Observer, 1872, 1874, 1875, 1878, 1879.
Deal, Walmer and Sandwich Telegram, 1860.
Dover Express and East Kent Intelligencer, 1863, 1873, 1880.
Dover Times, 1863.
East Kent Times (Ramsgate), 1859.
Faversham Mercury, 1860, 1861, 1865, 1878–1880.
Gravesend and Dartford Reporter, 1859–1880.
Gravesend Free Press, 1859.
Gravesend Journal, 1864.
Greenwich and Deptford Chronicle, 1879.
Kentish Express (Ashford), 1859, 1860, 1868–1880.
Kentish Independent (Greenwich), 1859, 1869.
Kentish and Surrey Mercury (Greenwich), 1862, 1867–1870.
Kentish Observer (Canterbury), 1861–1868, 1879, 1880.
Maidstone and Kentish Journal, 1859–1880.
Orr's Kentish Journal (Greenwich), 1861–1863.
Rochester, Chatham and Strood Gazette, 1859–1864.

Sheerness Guardian, 1870.
Sittingbourne, Faversham and Sheerness Gazette, 1859.
The Standard (London), 1869.
The Times (London), 1859–1880.
Tonbridge Telegraph, 1864–1880.

Contemporary Works

Baxter, Wynne E., ed. *The Domesday Book for the County of Kent.* Lewes: Sussex Express Office, 1877.
Blackstone, William. *Commentaries on the Laws of England.* Edited by J. F. Archbold. London: William Reed, 1811.
Bligh, E. V. *This Was A Man.* Stratford: By the author, n.d.
Davis, James Edward. *The Criminal Law Consolidation Statutes of the 24 & 25 of Victoria.* London: Butterworths, 1861.
———. *The Master and Servant Act.* London: Butterworths, 1868.
Debrett's House of Commons and Judicial Bench. London, c.1870.
Foss, Judi. *Biographia Juridicia.* London, 1867.
Jervis, John. *Archbold's Pleading and Evidence in Criminal Case*, 19th ed. London: H. Sweet, 1878.
Kent Directory and Gazette. London: Melville & Co., 1858.
Oke, George C. *Magisterial Synopsis*, 9th ed. London: Butterworths, 1866.
Roscoe's Digest of the Law of Evidence, 9th ed. London, 1878.
Saunders, T. W. *The Magisterial Formulist*, 5th ed. London: Butterworths, 1877.
———. *The Summary Jurisdiction Act, 1879.* London: Butterworths, 1879.
Stephen, Henry John. *Mr. Sergeant Stephen's New Commentaries on the Laws of England.* 4 vols. London: Butterworths, 1890.
Stephen, James Fitzjames. *A Digest of the Criminal Law.* London: MacMillan, 1877.
——— and Herbert Stephen. *A Digest of the Law of Criminal Procedure in Indictable Offences.* London: MacMillan, 1883.

Secondary Sources

Alvarez, A. *The Savage God.* New York: Random House, 1970.
Anderson, Nancy F. "The 'Marriage of a Deceased Wife's Sister Bill' Controversy: Incest Anxiety and the Defense of Family Purity in Victorian England." *Journal of British Studies* 21 (1982).
Anderson, Olive. "Did Suicide Increase with Industrialization in Victorian England?" *Past and Present* 86 (1980).
———. *Suicide in Victorian and Edwardian England.* New York: Oxford University Press, 1987.
Andrew, Donna. "The Code of Honour and Its Critics: The Opposition to Duelling in England 1700–1850." *Social History* 5 (1980).

Arnold, Rollo. "The 'Revolt of the Field' in Kent, 1872–1879." *Past and Present* 64 (1972).
Arnstein, Walter. "The Murphy Riots: A Victorian Dilemma." *Victorian Studies* 19 (1975).
———. "Victorian Prejudice Re-examined." *Victorian Studies* 12 (1968).
Ashbee, Andrew. *A History of the Parish Church of All Saints, Snodland.* Maidstone: the author, 1980.
Bailey, Peter. "'A Mingled Mass of Perfectly Legitimate Pleasures': The Victorian Middle-Class and the Problem of Leisure." *Victorian Studies* 21 (1977).
———. "'Will the Real Bill Banks Please Stand Up?' Towards a Role Analysis of Mid-Victorian Working-Class Respectability." *Journal of Social History* 12 (1979).
Bailey, Victor. *Policing and Punishment in Nineteenth Century Britain.* New Brunswick, NJ: Rutgers University Press, 1981.
Bauer, Carol, and Lawrence Ritt. *Free and Ennobled: Source Readings in the Development of Victorian Feminism.* Oxford: Pergamon Press, 1979.
Beattie, J. M. *Crime and the Courts in England, 1660–1800.* Princeton, NJ: Princeton University Press, 1986.
Behlmer, George K. *Child Abuse and Moral Reform in England 1870–1908.* Palo Alto: Stanford University Press, 1982.
Best, Geoffrey. *Mid-Victorian Britain 1851–1875.* London: Weidenfield & Nicolson, 1971.
Bianchi, Herman, ed. *Deviance and Control in Europe: Papers from the European Group for the Study of Deviance and Social Control.* London: John Wiley & Sons, 1975.
Bond, Brian. "Recruiting the Victorian Army, 1870–92." *Victorian Studies* 5 (1961).
Branca, Patricia. *Silent Sisterhood: Middle Class Women in the Victorian Home.* London: Croom-Helm, 1975.
Brewer, John, and John Styles. *An Ungovernable People: The English and Their Law in the Seventeenth and Eighteenth Century.* New Brunswick, NJ: Rutgers University Press, 1980.
Bristow, Edward J. *Vice and Vigilance: Purity Movements in Britain Since 1700.* Dublin: Gill & McMillan, 1977.
Brown, Peter. "Society and the Separated." *Daedalus* 104 (1975).
Bullough, Vern L. *Sexual Variance in Society and History.* Chicago: University of Chicago Press, 1976.
Burman, Sandra. *Fit Work for Women.* New York: St. Martin's Press, 1979.
Bushaway, Bob. *By Rite: Custom, Ceremony and Community in England 1700–1880.* London: Junction Books, 1982.
Carter, John M. *Rape in Medieval England.* New York: University Press of America, 1985.
Chesney, Kellow. *The Anti-Society: An Account of the Victorian Underworld.* Boston: Gambit, 1970.

Clark, Anna. *Women's Silence, Men's Violence: Sexual Assault in England 1770–1845.* New York: Pandora, 1987.

Cobb, R. C. *The Police and the People.* New York: Oxford University Press, 1980.

Cohen, David, and Eric A. Johnson. "French Criminality: Urban-Rural Differences in the Nineteenth-Century." *Journal of Inter-Disciplinary History* 12 (1982).

Cole, G. D. H., and Raymond Postgate. *The British People 1746–1946.* London: Alfred Knopf, 1947.

Cominos, Peter T. "Late Victorian Social Respectability and the Social System." *International Review of Social History* 8 (1963).

Conley, Carolyn. "Rape and Justice in Victorian England." *Victorian Studies* 29 (1986).

Coppock, J. T. "The Changing Face of England: 1850–c.1900." In *A New Historical Geography of England After 1600*, edited by H. C. Darby. New York: Cambridge University Press, 1973.

Cornish, W. R., Jennifer Hart, A. H. Manchester, and J. Stevenson. *Crime and Law in Nineteenth Century Britain.* Dublin: Irish University Press, 1978.

Cott, Nancy. "Passionlessness: An Interpretation of Victorian Sexual Ideology, 1790–1850." *Signs* 4 (1979).

Critchley, T. A. *The Conquest of Violence: Order land Liberty in Britain.* London: Schocken, 1970.

Crossick, Geoffrey. *An Artisan Elite in Victorian Society: Kentish London 1840–1880.* London: Croom-Helm, 1978.

——— . "The Labour Aristocracy and Its Values: A Study of Mid-Victorian Kentish London." *Victorian Studies* 19 (1976).

Crow, Duncan. *The Victorian Woman.* New York: Stein & Day, 1972.

Crowther, M. A. "Family Responsibility and State Responsibility in Britain Before the Welfare State." *Historical Journal* 25 (1982).

Cunningham, Hugh. *Leisure in the Industrial Revolution, c.1780–1880.* New York: St. Martin's Press, 1980.

Curtis, L. P. *Anglo-Saxons and Celts: A Study of Anti-Irish Prejudice in Victorian England.* Bridgeport, CT: University of Bridgeport Press, 1968.

Danto, Bruce, John Brahms, and Austin H. Kutscher, eds. *The Human Side of Homicide.* New York: Columbia University Press, 1982.

Davey, B. J. *Lawless and Immoral: Policing a Country Town 1838–1857.* New York: St. Martin's Press, 1983.

Davidoff, Leonore. *The Best Circles: Women and Society in Victorian England.* New Jersey: Rowman & Littlefield, 1973.

——— . "Class and Gender in Victorian England: The Diaries of Arthur J. Munby and Hannah Cullwick." *Feminist Studies* 5 (1979).

——— . "Mastered for Life: Servant and Wife in Victorian and Edwardian England." *Journal of Social History* 7 (1974).

Davidson, Terry. *Conjugal Crime: Understanding and Changing the Wifebeating Pattern.* New York: Hawthorne Press, 1978.

Davis, Jennifer. "A Poor Man's System of Justice: The London Police Courts in the Second Half of the Nineteenth Century." *Historical Journal* 27 (1984).

Davis, Natalie. "The Reasons of Misrule: Youth Groups and Charivaris in Sixteenth Century France." *Past and Present* 50 (1971).

———. *Society and Culture in Early Modern France*. Palo Alto: Stanford University Press, 1975.

Demos, John. *Past, Present and Personal: The Family and the Life Course in American History*. New York: Oxford University Press, 1986.

Dewar, Diana. *Orphans of the Living: A Study of Bastardy*. London: Hutchinson, 1968.

Donovan, James M. "Justice Unblind: The Juries and the Criminal Classes in France, 1825–1914." *Journal of Social History* 15 (1981).

Dunae, Patrick. "Penny Dreadfuls: Late Nineteenth-Century Boys' Literature and Crime." *Victorian Studies* 22 (1978).

Dunbabin, J. P. D. *Rural Discontent in Nineteenth Century Britain*. London: Faber & Faber, 1974.

Dyos, H. J., and Michael Wolff, eds. *The Victorian City: Images and Realities*. London: Routledge and Kegan Paul, 1973.

Emsley, Clive. *Crime and Society in England 1750–1900*. New York: Longman, 1987.

———. "'The Thump of Wood on a Swede Turnip': Police Violence in Nineteenth Century England." *Criminal Justice History* 6 (1985).

Ensor, R. C. K. *England 1870–1914*. New York: Oxford University Press, 1936.

Finnegan, Frances. *Poverty and Prejudice: A Study of Irish Immigrants in York 1840–1875*. Cork: Cork University Press, 1982.

———. *Poverty and Prostitution: A Study of Victorian Prostitutes in York*. New York: Cambridge University Press, 1979.

Fletcher, Ronald. *The Family and Marriage in Britain*. London: Penguin Books, 1966.

Fraser, W. Hamish. *Trade Unions and Society: The Struggle for Acceptance, 1850–1880*. London: Rowman & Littlefield, 1974.

Fried, Albert, and Richard Elman, eds. *Charles Booth's London*. London: Pantheon, 1968.

Gash, Norman. *Aristocracy and the People: Britain 1815–1865*. Cambridge, MA: Harvard University Press, 1979.

Gatrell, V. A. C., Bruce Lenman, and Geoffrey Parker, eds. *Crime and the Law: The Social History of Crime in Western Europe since 1500*. London: Europa Publications, 1980.

Gay, Peter. *The Bourgeois Experience: Victoria to Freud*. New York: Oxford University Press, 1984.

Gibbs, Jack P. *Suicide*. London: Harper & Row, 1968.

Gibson, Ian. *The English Vice: Beating, Sex and Shame in Victorian England and After*. London: Duckworth, 1979.

Gillis, John R. "The Evolution of Juvenile Delinquency in England, 1890–1914." *Past and Present* 67 (1975).

———. "Servants, Sexual Relations and the Risks of Illegitimacy in London, 1801–1900." *Feminist Studies* 5 (1979).

———. *Youth and History.* London: Academic Press, 1974.

Given, James B. *Society and Homicide in Thirteenth-Century England.* Palo Alto: Stanford University Press, 1977.

Gorham, Deborah. "The 'Maiden Tribute of Modern Babylon' Re-Examined: Child Prostitution and the Idea of Childhood in Late-Victorian England." *Victorian Studies* 21 (1977).

———. *The Victorian Girl and The Feminine Ideal.* Bloomington: Indiana University Press, 1982.

Green, F. E. *A History of the English Agricultural Labourer, 1870–1920.* London: P. S. King & Son, 1920.

Green, Thomas Andrew. *Verdict According to Conscience: Perspectives on the English Criminal Trial Jury 1200–1800.* Chicago: University of Chicago Press, 1985.

Greenwood, M., W. J. Martin, and W. J. Russell. "Deaths by Violence 1837–1937." *Royal Statistical Society Journal* 104 (1941).

Gurr, Ted Robert. *Rogues, Rebels and Reformers: A Political History of Urban Crime and Conflict.* Beverly Hills: Sage Publications, 1976.

Halevy, Elie. *A History of the English People in the Nineteenth Century.* London: Ernest Benn, 1949.

Hall, Jerome. *Theft, Law and Society.* Boston: Little, Brown & Co., 1935.

Hammond, J. L., and Barbara Hammond. *The Skilled Labourer 1760–1832.* London: Longman, 1935.

———. *The Town Labourer 1760–1832: The New Civilization.* London: Longmans, Green & Co., 1925.

———. *The Village Labourer 1760–1832.* London: Longmans, Green & Co., 1912.

Hanawalt, Barbara. *Crime and Conflict in English Communities 1300–1348.* Cambridge, MA: Harvard University Press, 1979.

Harrison, Brian. "Animals and the State in Nineteenth Century England." *English Historical Review* 88 (1973).

———. *Drink and the Victorians: The Temperance Question in England 1815–1872.* Pittsburgh: University of Pittsburgh Press, 1971.

———. *Peaceable Kingdom: Stability and Change in Modern Britain.* New York: Oxford University Press, 1982.

———. *Separate Spheres: The Opposition to Women's Suffrage in Britain.* New York: Holmes & Meir, 1978.

———. "State Intervention and Moral Reform." In *Pressure From Without in Early Victorian England,* edited by Patricia Hollis. New York: St. Martin's Press, 1974.

Hartman, Mary. "Crime and the Respectable Woman: Toward a Pattern of

Middle-Class Female Criminality in the Nineteenth-century France and England." *Feminist Studies* 2 (1975).

———, and Lois Banner, eds. *Clio's Consciousness Raised: New Perspectives on the History of Women.* New York: Octagon Books, 1976.

Harvey, A. D. "Prosecutions for Sodomy in England at the Beginning of the Nineteenth Century." *Historical Journal* 21 (1978).

Hay, Douglas, Peter Linebaugh, John G. Rule, E. P. Thompson, and Cal Winslow. *Albion's Fatal Tree: Crime and Society in Eighteenth-Century England.* New York: Pantheon, 1975.

Hay, Douglas. "War, Dearth and Theft in the Eighteenth Century: The Record of the English Courts." *Past and Present* 95 (1982).

Heath, Francis George. *British Rural Life and Labour.* London: P. S. King & Co., 1911.

Henriques, Ursula. "Bastardy and the New Poor Law." *Past and Present* 37 (1967).

———. *Before the Welfare State: Social Administration in Early Industrial Britain.* London: Longman, 1979.

Herrup, Cynthia. *The Common Peace: Participation and the Criminal Law in Seventeenth Century England.* New York: Cambridge University Press, 1987.

———. "Law and Morality in Seventeenth-Century England." *Past and Present* 106 (1985).

Higginbotham, Ann R. "'The Sin of the Age': Infanticide and Illegitimacy in Victorian London." *Victorian Studies* 32 (1989).

Hobsbawm, Eric. *Bandits.* London: Delacorte Press, 1969.

Hoffer, Peter, and N. E. H. Hull. *Murdering Mothers: Infanticide in England and New England 1558–1803.* New York: New York University Press, 1981.

Hollis, Patricia, ed. *Pressure From Without.* New York: St. Martin's Press, 1974.

Horn, Pamela. *The Victorian Country Child.* London: Roundwood Press, 1974.

Humphries, Stephen. *Hooligans or Rebels?: An Oral History of Working-Class Childhood and Youth 1889–1939.* New York: Blackwell, 1983.

Ignatieff, Michael. *A Just Measure of Pain: The Penitentiary in the Industrial Revolution 1750–1850.* London: Pantheon, 1978.

Inglis, K. S. *Churches and the Working Classes in Victorian England.* London: Routledge & Kegan Paul, 1963.

Inglis, Ruth. *Sins of the Fathers: A Study of the Physical and Emotional Abuse of Children.* New York: St. Martin's Press, 1978.

Ingram, Martin. "Ridings, Rough Music and the 'Reform of Popular Culture' in Early Modern England." *Past and Present* 105 (1984).

Jessup, Frank W. *A History of Kent With Maps and Pictures.* London: Darwen Finlayson, 1958.

Jones, David. *Crime, Protest, Community and Police in Nineteenth Century Britain.* London: Routledge & Kegan Paul, 1982.

King, Peter. "Decision-Makers and Decision-Making in the English Criminal Law, 1750–1800." *Historical Journal* 27 (1984).

Lambert, Royston. "Central and Local Relations in Mid-Victorian England: The Local Government Act Office, 1858–71." *Victorian Studies* 6 (1962).

Landau, Norma. *The Justices of the Peace, 1679–1760.* Berkeley: University of California Press, 1984.

Lane, Roger. "Crime and the Industrial Revolution: British and American Views." *Journall of Social History* 7 (1973).

Langbein, John H. "Albion's Fatal Flaws." *Past and Present* 98 (1983).

Laqueur, Thomas Walter. *Religion and Respectability: Sunday Schools and Working Class Culture 1780–1850.* New Haven: Yale University Press, 1976.

Lees, Lynn Hollen. *Exiles of Erin: Irish Migrants in Victorian London.* Ithaca, NY: Cornell University Press, 1979.

Lieck, Albert. *Justice and Police in England.* London: Butterworths, 1929.

Lindemann, Barbara S. "'To Ravish and Carnally Know': Rape in Eighteenth Century Massachusetts." *Signs* 10 (1984).

MacDonald, Michael. "The Secularization of Suicide in England, 1660–1800." *Past and Present* 111 (1986).

McHugh, Paul. *Prostitution and Victorian Social Reform.* New York: St. Martin's Press, 1980.

McNay, Michael. *Portrait of a Kentish Village: East Malling 1827–1978.* Maidstone: the author, 1980.

Magarey, Susan. "The Invention of Juvenile Delinquency in Early Nineteenth Century England." *Labour History* 34 (1978).

Mapp, Alf. *The Golden Dragon: Alfred the Great and His Times.* Lasalle, IL: Open Court Publishing, 1975.

Marcus, Steven. *The Other Victorians: A Study of Sexuality and Pornography in Mid-Nineteenth Century England.* New York: Basic Books, 1966.

Marsh, David. *The Changing Social Structure of England and Wales 1871–1951.* London: Routledge & Kegan Paul, 1958.

Martin, E. W. *The Secret People: English Village Life After 1750.* London: Phoenix, 1954.

———. *Where London Ends: English Provincial Life After 1750.* London: Phoenix, 1958.

May, Margaret. "Innocence and Experience: The Evolution of Juvenile Delinquency in the Mid-Nineteenth Century." *Victorian Studies* 17 (1973).

Mays, J. B. *Crime and its Treatment.* London: Longman, 1970.

Meacham, Standish. *A Life Apart: The English Working Class 1890–1914.* Cambridge, MA: Harvard University Press, 1977.

Melling, Elizabeth, ed. *Kentish Sources: Crime and Punishment.* Maidstone: Kent Council & Co., 1969.

Miller, Wilbur R. *Cops and Bobbies: Police Authority in New York and London 1830–1870.* Chicago: University of Chicago Press, 1973.

Mingay, G. E., ed. *The Victorian Countryside.* Boston: Routledge & Kegan Paul, 1981.

Mintz, Stephen. *A Prison of Expectations: The Family in Victorian Culture.* New York: New York University Press, 1983.

Mitchell, Sally. "Sentiment and Suffering: Women's Recreational Reading in the 1860s." *Victorian Studies* 21 (1977).

Monkkonen, Eric H. "The Organized Response to Crime in Nineteenth and Twentieth Century America." *Journal of Interdisciplinary History* 14 (1983).

Osborne, John W. *The Silent Revolution: The Industrial Revolution in England as a Source of Cultural Change.* New York: Charles Scribner's Sons, 1970.

Page, William. *Victoria County History of Kent*, Vol. 3. London: St. Catherine's Press, 1932.

Perkin, Harold. *The Origins of Modern English Society 1780–1880.* London: Routledge & Kegan Paul, 1969.

———. *The Structured Crowd: Essays In English Social History.* Totowa, NJ: Barnes & Noble, 1981.

Peterson, M. Jeanne. "Dr. Acton's Enemy: Medicine, Sex and Society in Victorian England." *Victorian Studies* 29 (1986).

Philips, David. *Crime and Authority in Victorian England: The Black Country 1835–1860.* London: Croom-Helm, 1977.

Pinchbeck, Ivy, and Margaret Hewitt. *Children in English Society.* 2 vols. London: Routledge & Kegan Paul, 1973.

Pollock, Linda. *Forgotten Children: Parent-Child Relations from 1500–1900.* New York: Cambridge University Press, 1983.

Price, Richard. "The Working Men's Club Movement and Victorian Social Reform Ideology." *Victorian Studies* 15 (1971).

Prothero, I. J. *Artisans and Politics in Early Nineteenth-Century London: John Gast and His Times.* Baton Rouge: Louisiana State University Press, 1979.

Quinault, R., and J. Stevenson. *Popular Protest and Public Order.* London: George Allen & Unwin, 1974.

Radzinowicz, Leon. *A History of English Criminal Law and Its Administration from 1750.* 5 vols. London: Stevens & Sons, 1948–1986.

Reid, Douglas. "The Decline of St. Monday, 1766–1876." *Past and Present*, 71 (1976).

Rennie, Ysabel. *The Search for Criminal Man.* Lexington, MA: D. C. Heath, 1978.

Richter, Donald. "The Role of Mob Riot in Victorian Elections, 1865–1885." *Victorian Studies* 15 (1971).

Rose, Lionel. *The Massacre of the Innocents: Infanticide in Britain 1800–1939.* Boston: Routledge & Kegan Paul, 1986.

Rose, Michael E. *The English Poor Law 1780–1930.* Newton Abbot, England: David & Charles, 1971.

Ross, Ellen. "'Fierce Questions and Taunts': Married Life in Working-Class London, 1870–1914." *Feminist Studies* 8 (1982).

Rude, George. *Criminal and Victim: Crime and Society in Early Nineteenth-Century England.* New York: Oxford University Press, 1985.

——— . *The Crowd in History: A Study of Popular Disturbances in France and England 1730–1848.* New York: John Wiley & Sons, 1964.

Russell, Conrad. *The Crisis of Parliaments.* London: Oxford University Press, 1971.

Samuel, Raphael, ed. *Village Life and Labour.* London: Routledge & Kegan Paul, 1975.

Sanders, Wiley, ed. *Juvenile Offenders for a Thousand Years.* Chapel Hill: University of North Carolina Press, 1970.

Saville, John, ed. *Democracy and the Labour Movement.* London: Lawrence & Wishart, 1954.

Seccombe, Wally. "Patriarchy Stabilized: The Construction of the Male Breadwinner Wage Norm in Nineteenth Century Britain." *Social History* 11 (1986).

Sharpe, J. A. *Crime in Early Modern England 1550–1750.* London: Longman, 1984.

——— . "Domestic Homicide in Early Modern England." *Historical Journal* 24 (1981).

——— and Lawrence Stone. "Debate: The History of Violence in England: Some Observations." *Past and Present* 108 (1985).

Shurkin, Joel N. *The Invisible Fire: The Story of Mankind's Victory over the Ancient Scourge of Smallpox.* New York: G. P. Putnam's Sons, 1979.

Simon, Daphne. "Master and Servant." *Democracy and the Labour Movement*, edited by John Saville. London: Lawrence & Wishart, 1954.

Sindall, Rob. "The Criminal Statistics of Nineteenth Century Cities: A New Approach." *Urban History Yearbook* (1986).

——— . "Middle-Class Crime in Nineteenth Century England." *Criminal Justice History* 4 (1983).

Skelley, Alan Ramsey. *The Victorian Army at Home: The Recruitment and Terms and Conditions of the British Regular 1859–1899.* London: Croom-Helm, 1977.

Smith, F. B. "Mayhew's Convict." *Victorian Studies* 22 (1978/1979).

Smith, Philip Thurmond. *Policing Victorian London: Political Policing, Public Order and the London Metropolitan Police.* Westport, CT: Greenwood Press, 1985.

Stead, Philip John. *The Police of Britain.* New York: Macmillan, 1985.

Stearns, Peter N. *Be a Man! Males in Modern Society.* New York: Holmes & Meir, 1979.

Steedman, Carolyn. *Policing the Victorian Community: The Formation of English Provincial Police Forces 1856–1880.* Boston: Routledge & Kegan Paul, 1984.

Stevenson, S. J. "The Habitual Criminal in Nineteenth Century England: Some Observations on the Figures." *Urban History Yearbook* (1986).

Stone, Lawrence. "Interpersonal Violence in English Society." *Past and Present* 101 (1983).

———. "Rejoinder." *Past and Present* 108 (1985).

Storch, Robert D. "The Plague of Blue Locusts: Police Reform and Popular Resistance in Northern England, 1840–57." *International Review of Social History* 20 (1975).

———. "The Policeman as Domestic Missionary: Urban Discipline and Popular Culture in Northern England, 1850–1880." *Journal of Social History* 9 (1976).

———. *Popular Culture and Custom in Nineteenth Century England.* New York: St. Martin's Press, 1982.

Straus, Murray, Richard Gelles, and Suzanne Steinmetz. *Behind Closed Doors: Violence in the American Family.* New York: Anchor Books, 1980.

Swift, Roger. "The Outcast Irish in the British Victorian City: Problems and Perspectives." *Irish Historical Studies* 25 (May 1987).

———, and Sheridan Gilley, eds. *The Irish in the Victorian City.* London: Croom-Helm, 1985.

Taylor, William. *Drinking, Homicide and Rebellion in Colonial Mexican Villages.* Palo Alto: Stanford University Press, 1979.

Tholfsen, Trygve. *Working Class Radicalism in Mid-Victorian England.* New York: Columbia University Press, 1977.

Thompson, E. P. "Eighteenth Century English Society: Class Struggle Without Class?" *Social History* 3 (1978).

———. "Patrician Society, Plebian Culture." *Journal of Social History* 7 (1974).

———. "'Rough Music': Le Charivari Anglais." *Annales Economies Societas Civilisations* 27 (1972).

———. *Whigs and Hunters: The Origins of the Black Act.* New York: Pantheon, 1975.

Tobias, J. J. *Crime and Industrial Society in the Nineteenth Century.* New York: Schocken, 1967.

Tomes, Nancy. "'A Torrent of Abuse': Crimes of Violence Between Working Class Men and Women in London, 1840–1873." *Journal of Social History* 11 (1978).

Vicinus, Martha, ed. *A Widening Sphere: Changing Roles of Victorian Women.* Bloomington: Indiana University Press, 1977.

———, ed. *Suffer and be Still: Women in the Victorian Age.* Bloomington: Indiana University Press, 1972.

Vorspan, Rachel. "Vagrancy and the New Poor Law in Late Victorian and Edwardian England." *English Historical Review* 92 (1977).

Walker, Nigel. *The Historical Perspective.* Vol. I of *Crime and Insanity in England.* Edinburgh: Edinburgh University Press, 1968.

Walker, Samuel. *Popular Justice: A History of American Criminal Justice.* New York: Oxford University Press, 1980.

Walkowitz, Judith R. "Jack the Ripper and the Myth of Male Violence." *Feminist Studies* 8 (1982).

——— . "Notes on the History of Victorian Prostitution." *Feminist Studies* 1 (1974).

——— . *Prostitution and Victorian Society: Women, Class and the State.* Cambridge University Press, 1980.

Weeks, Jeffrey. *Sex, Politics and Society: The Regulation of Sexuality Since 1800.* London: Longman, 1981.

Weisser, Michael R. *Crime and Punishment in Early Modern Europe.* Atlantic Highlands, NJ: Humanities Press, 1979.

West Kent Federation of Women's Institutes. *Old Days in the Kent Hop Gardens.* Maidstone: West Kent Federation of Women's Institutes, 1962.

Winstanley, Michael. *Life in Kent at the Turn of the Century.* Folkestone: Davidson & Son, 1978.

Wolfgang, Marvin E. *Patterns in Criminal Homicide.* Philadelphia: University of Pennsylvania, 1958.

——— . *The Subculture of Violence.* London: Tavistock, 1967.

Wohl, Anthony S., ed. *The Victorian Family: Structure and Stresses.* New York: St. Martin's Press, 1978.

Wrigley, E. A., ed. *Nineteenth Century Society.* New York: Cambridge University Press, 1972.

Yeo, Eileen, and Stephen Yeo, eds. *Popular Culture and Class Conflict 1590–1914: Explorations in the History of Labour and Leisure.* Atlantic Highlands, NJ: Humanities Press, 1981.

Young, G. M. *Victorian England: Portrait of an Age*, 2nd ed. New York: Oxford University Press, 1953.

Zehr, Howard. *Crime and the Development of Modern Society: Patterns of Criminality in Nineteenth Century Germany and France.* Totowa, NJ: Rowman & Littlefield, 1976.

Index